Information and Network Security

Dr.C.S. Pillai

B.S. Shakunthala

Published by

BONFRING®
Intellectual Integrity

Information and Network Security

9 789386 176608 >

ISBN 978-93-86176-60-8

Author

Dr.C.S. Pillai

B.S. Shakunthala

Bonfring

309, 2nd Floor, 5th Street Extension, Gandhipuram,

Coimbatore-641 012.

Tamilnadu, India.

E-mail: info@bonfring.org

Website: www.bonfring.org

Phone: 0422 4213231

Preface

The importance of **Information and Network Security** is well known in various engineering fields. The book uses plain, lucid language to explain fundamental of this subject .This book provides logical method of explaining various complicated concepts and stepwise methods to explain the important topics.

Each chapter is well supported with necessary illustrations, practical examples and solved problems.

All care has been take care to make students comfortable in understanding the basic concepts of the subject.

We wish to express our thanks to all those who helped in making this book a reality.

We wish to thank the publisher and the entire team who have taken immense pain to get this book in time with quality printing.

Dr.C.S. Pillai
B.S. Shakunthala

Acknowledgement

INFORMATION AND NETWORK SECURITY

PART – A

Unit - 1

PLANNING FOR SECURITY: Introduction; Information Security Policy, Standards, and Practices; The Information Security Blue Print; Contingency plan and a model for contingency plan. **6 Hours**

Unit - 2

SECURITY TECHNOLOGY-1: Introduction; Physical design; Firewalls; Protecting Remote Connections. **6 Hours**

Unit - 3

SECURITY TECHNOLOGY – 2: Introduction; Intrusion Detection Systems (IDS); Honey Pots, Honey Nets, and Padded cell systems; Scanning and Analysis Tools. **6 Hours**

Unit - 4

CRYPTOGRAPHY: Introduction; A short History of Cryptography; Principles of Cryptography; Cryptography Tools; Attacks on Cryptosystems. **8 Hours**

PART – B

Unit - 5

INTRODUCTION TO NETWORK SECURITY, AUTHENTICATION

APPLICATIONS: Attacks , services, and Mechanisms; Security Attacks; Security Services; A model for Internetwork Security; Internet Standards and RFCs. Kerberos, X.509 Directory Authentication Service. **8 Hours**

Unit - 6

ELECTRONIC MAIL SECURITY: Pretty Good Privacy (PGP); S/MIME. **6 Hours**

Unit - 7

IP SECURITY: IP Security Overview; IP Security Architecture; Authentication Header; Encapsulating Security Payload; Combining Security Associations; Key Management. **6 Hours**

Unit - 8

WEB SECURITY: Web security requirements; Secure Socket layer (SSL) and Transport layer Security (TLS); Secure Electronic Transaction (SET). **6 Hours**

Text Books

1. **Principles of Information Security** - Michael E. Whitman and Herbert J. Mattord, 2nd Edition, Thompson, 2005.
2. **Network Security Essentials Applications and Standards** - William Stallings, Person Education, 2000.

Reference Book

1. **Cryptography and Network Security** - Behrouz A. Forouzan, Tata McGraw-Hill, 2007.

Unit	Contents	Page No

Part A

Part B

UNIT-1

PLANNING FOR SECURITY

Learning Objectives

Upon completion of this chapter you should be able to:

1) Understand management's responsibilities and role in the development, maintenance, and enforcement of information security policy, standards, practices, procedures, and guidelines.
2) Understand the differences between the organization's general information security policy and the requirements and objectives of the various issue-specific and system-specific policies.
3) Know what an information security blueprint is and what its major components are.
4) Understand how an organization institutionalizes its policies, standards, and practices using education, training, and awareness programs.
5) Become familiar with what viable information security architecture is, what it includes, and how it is used.
6) Explain what contingency planning is and how incident response planning, disaster recovery planning, and business continuity plans are related to contingency planning.

1.1. Introduction

1) The creation of an information security program begins with the creation and/or review of the organization's information security policies, standards, and practices.
2) Then, the selection or creation of information security architecture and the development and use of a detailed information security blueprint will create the plan for future success.
3) This blueprint for the organization's information security efforts can be realized only if it operates in conjunction with the organization's information security policy.
4) Without policy, blueprints, and planning, the organization will be unable to meet the information security needs of the various communities of interest.
5) The organizations should undertake at least some planning: strategic planning to manage the allocation of resources, and contingency planning to prepare for the uncertainties of the business environment.

1.2. Information Security Policy, Standards, and Practices

1) Management from all communities of interest must consider policies as the basis for all information security efforts like planning, design and deployment.
2) Policies direct how issues should be addressed and technologies used.
3) Policies do not specify the proper operation of equipments or software-this information should be placed in the standards, procedures and practices of user's manuals and systems documentation.
4) Security policies are the least expensive control to execute, but the most difficult to implement properly.
5) Shaping policy is difficult because:
   - Never conflict with laws.
   - Stand up in court, if challenged.
   - Be properly administered through dissemination and documented acceptance.

Definitions

- A policy is a plan or course of action, as of a government, political party, or business, intended to influence and determine decisions, actions, and other matters. A policy is a plan or course of action used by an organization to convey instructions from its senior-most management to those who make decisions, take actions, and perform other duties on behalf of the organization.
- Policies are organizational laws. Policies must define what is right, what is wrong, what the penalties for violating policy, and what the appeal process is..
- Standards, on the other hand, are more detailed statements of what must be done to comply with policy.
- Standards may be published, scrutinized, and ratified by a group, as in formal or de jury standards.
- Practices, procedures, and guidelines effectively explain how to comply with policy.
- For a policy to be effective it must be properly disseminated, read, understood and agreed to by all members of the organization
- Finally, practices, procedures, and guidelines effectively explain how to comply with policy.
- Fig shows policies as the force that drives standards, which in turn drive practices, procedures, and guidelines.

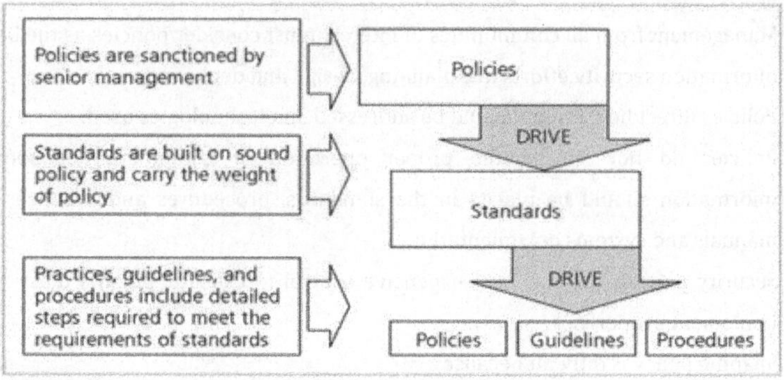

FIGURE **Policies, Standards, and Practices**

- Policies are written to support the mission, vision and strategic planning of an organization.
- The MISSION of an organization is a written statement of an organization's purpose.
- The VISION of an organization is a written statement about the organization's goals- where will the organization be in five years? In ten?
- Strategic planning is the process of moving the organization towards its vision.
- A policy must be disseminated by all means possible, including printed personal manuals, organization intranets, and periodic supplements.
- All members of the organization must read, understand, and agree to the policies.
- Policies should be considered as the living documents.
- Government agencies discuss policy in terms of national security and national policies to deal with foreign states.
- A security policy can also represent a credit card agency's policy for processing credit card numbers.
- In general, a security policy is a set of rules that protect an organization's assets.
- An information security policy provides rules for the protection of the information assets of the organization.
- The task of information security professionals is to protect the confidentiality, integrity and availability of information and information systems whether in the state of transmission, storage, or processing.
- This is accomplished by applying policy, education and training programs, and technology.

Types of Policy

Management must define three types of security policy according to the National Institute of Standards and Technology's special publication 800-14.

1) General or security program policies.
2) Issue-specific security policies.
3) Systems-specific security policies.

General or Security Program Policy Enterprise Information Security Policy (EISP)

A security program policy (SPP) or EISP is also known as

1) A general security policy.
2) IT security policy.
3) Information security policy.

EISP

1) The EISP is based on and directly supports the mission, vision, and direction of the organization and Sets the strategic direction, scope, and tone for all security efforts within the organization
2) The EISP is an executive-level document, usually drafted by or with, the Chief Information Officer (CIO) of the organization and is usually 2 to 10 pages long.
3) The EISP does not usually require continuous modification, unless there is a change in the strategic direction of the organization.
4) The EISP guides the development, implementation, and management of the security program. It contains the requirements to be met by the information security blueprint or framework.
5) It defines then purpose, scope, constraints, and applicability of the security program in the organization.
6) It also assigns responsibilities for the various areas of security, including systems administration, maintenance of the information security policies, and the practices and responsibilities of the users.
7) Finally, it addresses legal compliance.
8) According to NIST, the EISP typically addresses compliance in two areas:
    - General compliance to ensure meeting the requirements to establish a program and the responsibilities assigned therein to various organizational components and
    - The use of specified penalties and disciplinary action.

Issue-Specific Security Policy (ISSP)

- As various technologies and processes are implemented, certain guidelines are needed to use them properly
- The ISSP:
  - Addresses specific areas of technology like.
    1) Electronic mail.
    2) Use of the Internet.
    3) Specific minimum configurations of computers to defend against worms and viruses.
    4) Prohibitions against hacking or testing organization security controls.
    5) Home use of company-owned computer equipment.
    6) Use of personal equipment on company networks.
    7) Use of telecommunications technologies (FAX and Phone).
    8) Use of photocopy equipment.

    Requires frequent updates contains an issue statement on the organization's position on an issue.
- There are a number of approaches to take when creating and managing ISSPs within an organization.
- Three approaches:
  - Independent ISSP documents, each tailored to a specific issue. A single comprehensive ISSP document covering all issues.
  - A modular ISSP document that unifies policy creation and administration, while maintaining each specific issues requirements.
- The independent document approach to take when creating and managing ISSPs typically has a scattershot effect.
- Each department responsible for a particular application of technology creates a policy governing its use, management, and control.
- This approach to creating ISSPs may fail to cover all of the necessary issues, and can lead to poor policy distribution, management, and enforcement.
- The single comprehensive policy approach is centrally managed and controlled.
- With formal procedures for the management of ISSPs in place, the comprehensive policy approach establishes guidelines for overall coverage of necessary issues and clearly identifies processes for the dissemination, enforcement, and review of these guidelines.

- Usually, these policies are developed by those responsible for managing the information technology resources.
- The optimal balance between the independent and comprehensive ISSP approaches is the modular approach.
- It is also certainly managed and controlled but tailored to the individual technology issues.
- The modular approach provides a balance between issue orientation and policy management.
- The policies created with this approach comprise individual modules, each created and updated by individuals responsible for the issues addressed.
- These individuals report to a central policy administration group that incorporates specific issues into an overall comprehensive policy.

Example ISSP Structure

- Statement of Policy.
- Authorized Access and Usage of Equipment.
- Prohibited Usage of Equipment.
- Systems Management.
- Violations of Policy.
- Policy Review and Modification.
- Limitations of Liability.

Statement of Policy

1) The policy should begin with a clear statement of purpose.
2) Consider a policy that covers the issue of fair and responsible use of WWW and the Internet.
3) The introductory section of this policy should outline these topics:
   - What is the scope of this policy?
   - Who is responsible and accountable for policy implementation?
   - What technologies and issues does it address?

Authorized Access and Usage of Equipment

1) This section of the policy addresses who can use the technology governed by the policy, and what it can be used for.
2) Remember that an organization's information systems are the exclusive property of the

organization, and users have no particular right of use.

3) Each technology and process is provided for business operations.

4) Use for any other purpose constitutes misuse of equipment.

5) This section defines —fair and responsible use|| of equipment and other organizational assets, and should also address key legal issues such as protection of personal information and privacy.

Prohibited Usage of Equipment

1) While the policy section details what the issue or technology can be used for, this section outlines what it cannot be used for.

2) Unless a particular use is clearly prohibited, the organization cannot penalize its employees for misuse.

3) The following can be prohibited: Personal Use, Disruptive use or misuse, criminal use, offensive or harassing materials, and infringement of copyrighted, licensed, or other intellectual property.

Systems Management

1) There may be some overlap between an ISSP and a systems-specific policy, but the systems management section of the ISSP policy statement focuses on the user's relationship to systems management.

2) Specific rules from management include regulating the use of e-mail, the storage of materials, authorized monitoring of employees, and the physical and electronic scrutiny of e-mail and other electronic documents.

3) It is important that all such responsibilities are designated as belonging to either the systems administrator or the users; otherwise both parties may infer that the responsibility belongs to the other party.

Violations of Policy

1) Once guidelines on equipment use have been outlined and responsibilities have been assigned, the individuals to whom the policy applies must understand the penalties and repercussions of violating the policy.

2) Violations of policy should carry appropriate, not draconian, penalties.

3) This section of the policy statement should contain not only the specifics of the penalties for each category of violation but also instructions on how individuals in the organization can report observed or suspected violations.

4) Many individuals feel that powerful individuals in the organization can discriminate,

single out, or otherwise retaliate against someone who reports violations.

5) Allowing anonymous submissions is often the only way to convince individual users to report the unauthorized activities of other, more influential employees.

Policy Review and Modification

1) Because any document is only as good as its frequency of review, each policy should contain procedures and a timetable for periodic review.
2) As the needs and technologies change in the organization, so must the policies that govern their use.
3) This section should contain a specific methodology for the review and modification of the policy, to ensure that users do not begin circumventing it as it grows obsolete.

Limitations of Liability

1) The final consideration is a general statement of liability or set of disclaimers
2) If an individual employee is caught conducting illegal activities with organizational equipment or assets, management does not want the organization held liable.
3) So the policy should state that if employees violate a company policy or any law using company technologies, the company will not protect them, and the company is not liable for its actions.
4) It is inferred that such a violation would be without knowledge or authorization by the organization.

Systems-Specific Policy (SysSP)

While issue-specific policies are formalized as written documents, distributed to users, and agreed to in writing, Sys SPs are frequently codified as standards and procedures to be used When configuring or maintaining systems. Systems-specific policies fall into two groups:

1) Access control lists (ACLs) consist of the access control lists, matrices, and capability tables governing the rights and privileges of a particular user to a particular system.
   - An ACL is a list of access rights used by file storage systems, object brokers, or other network communications devices to determine which individuals or groups may access an object that it controls.(Object Brokers are system components that handle message requests between the software components of a system)
2) A similar list, which is also associated with users and groups, is called a Capability Table. This specifies which subjects and objects a user or group can access. Capability tables are frequently complex matrices, rather than simple lists or tables.

3) Configuration rules: comprise the specific configuration codes entered into security systems to guide the execution of the system when information is passing through it.

ACL Policies

1) ACL's allow configuration to restrict access from anyone and anywhere. Restrictions can be set for a particular user, computer, time, duration-even a particular file.
2) ACL's regulate:
   - Who can use the system.
   - What authorized users can access.
   - When authorized users can access the system.
   - Where authorized users can access the system from.
   - How authorized users can access the system.
3) The WHO of ACL access may be determined by an individual person's identity or that person's membership in a group of people with the same access privileges.
4) Determining WHAT users are permitted to access can include restrictions on the various attributes of the system resources, such as the type of resources (printers, files, communication devices, or applications), name of the resource, or the location of the resource.
5) Access is controlled by adjusting the resource privileges for the person or group to one of Read, Write, Create, Modify, Delete, Compare, or Copy for the specific resource.
6) To control WHEN access is allowed, some organizations choose to implement time-of-day and / or day-of-week restrictions for some network or system resources.
7) For the control of WHERE resources can be accessed from, many network-connected assets have restrictions placed on them to block remote usage and also have some levels of access that are restricted to locally connected users.
8) When these various ACL options are applied cumulatively, the organization has the ability to describe fully how its resources can be used.
9) In some systems, these lists of ACL rules are known as Capability tables, user profiles, or user policies. They specify what the user can and cannot do on the resources within that system.

Rule Policies

1) Rule policies are more specific to the operation of a system than ACL's.
2) Many security systems require specific configuration scripts telling the systems what actions to perform on each set of information they process.

3) Examples of these systems include firewalls, intrusion detection systems, and proxy servers.
4) Fig shows how network security policy has been implemented by Check Point in a firewall rule set.

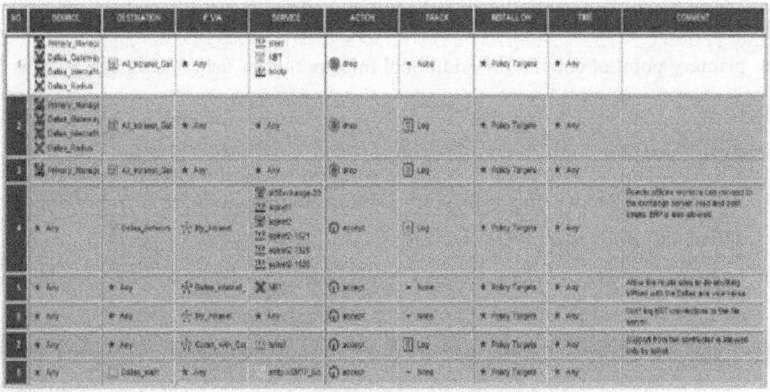

VPN-1/Firewall-1 Policy Editor courtesy of Check Point Software Technologies Ltd.

Checkpoint VPN-1/Firewall-1 Policy Editor

Policy Management

1) Policies are living documents that must be managed and nurtured, and are constantly changing and growing.
2) Documents must be properly disseminated (Distributed, read, understood, and agreed to) and managed.
3) Special considerations should be made for organizations undergoing mergers, takeovers, and partnerships.
4) In order to remain viable, policies must have:
   - An individual responsible for reviews.
   - A schedule of reviews.
   - A method for making recommendations for reviews.
   - A specific effective and revision date.

Responsible Individual

1) The policy champion and manager is called the policy administrator.
2) Policy administrator is a mid-level staff member and is responsible for the creation, revision, distribution, and storage of the policy.

3) It is good practice to actively solicit input both from the technically adept information security experts and from the business-focused managers in each community of interest when making revisions to security policies.
4) This individual should also notify all affected members of the organization when the policy is modified.
5) The policy administrator must be clearly identified on the policy document as the primary point of contact for additional information or for revision suggestions to the policy.

Schedule of Reviews

1) Policies are effective only if they are periodically reviewed for currency and accuracy and modified to reflect these changes.
2) Policies that are not kept current can become liabilities for the organization, as outdated rules are enforced or not, and new requirements are ignored.
3) Organization must demonstrate with due diligence, that it is actively trying to meet the requirements of the market in which it operates.
4) A properly organized schedule of reviews should be defined (at least annually) and published as part of the document.

Review Procedures and Practices

1) To facilitate policy reviews, the policy manager should implement a mechanism by which individuals can comfortably make recommendations for revisions.
2) Recommendation methods can involve e-mail, office mail, and an anonymous drop box.
3) Once the policy Hs come up for review, all comments should be examined. Management –approved improvements should be implemented.
4) Most policies are drafted by a single, responsible individual and are then reviewed by a higher-level manager.
5) But even this method should not preclude the collection and review of employee input.

Policy and Revision Date

1) When policies are drafted and published without a date, confusion can arise when users of the policy are unaware of the policy's age or status.
2) If policies are not reviewed and kept current, or if members of the organization are following undated versions, disastrous results and legal headaches can ensue.
3) It is therefore, important that the policy contain the date of origin, along with the date(s) of any revisions.

4) Some policies may also need a SUNSET clause indicating their expiration date.
5) Automation can streamline the repetitive steps of writing policy, tracking the workflow of policy approvals, publishing policy once it is written and approved, and tracking when individuals have read the policy.
6) Using techniques from computer based training and testing, organizations can train staff members and also improve the organization's awareness program.
7) NetIQ corporation quotes that:

- SOFTWARE THAT PUTS YOU IN CONTROL OF SECURITY POLICY CREATION, DISTRIBUTION, EDUCATION, AND TRACKING FOR COMPLIANCE
- VigilEnt Policy Center makes it possible to manage security policy dynamically so that you can create, distribute, educate, and track understanding of information security policies for all employees in the organization.
- It enables to keep policies up-to-date, change them quickly as needed, and ensure that they are being understood properly, all through a new automated, interactive, web-based software application.

Information Classification

1) The classification of information is an important aspect of policy.
2) The same protection scheme created to prevent production data from accidental release to the wrong party should be applied to policies in order to keep them freely available, but only within the organization.
3) In today's open office environments, it may be beneficial to implement a clean desk policy.
4) A clean desk policy stipulates that at the end of the business day, all classified information must be properly stored and secured.

Systems Design

1) At this point in the Security SDLC, the analysis phase is complete and the design phase begins–many work products have been created.
2) Designing a plan for security begins by creating or validating a security blueprint.
3) Then use the blueprint to plan the tasks to be accomplished and the order in which to proceed.
4) Setting priorities can follow the recommendations of published sources, or from published standards provided by government agencies, or private consultants.

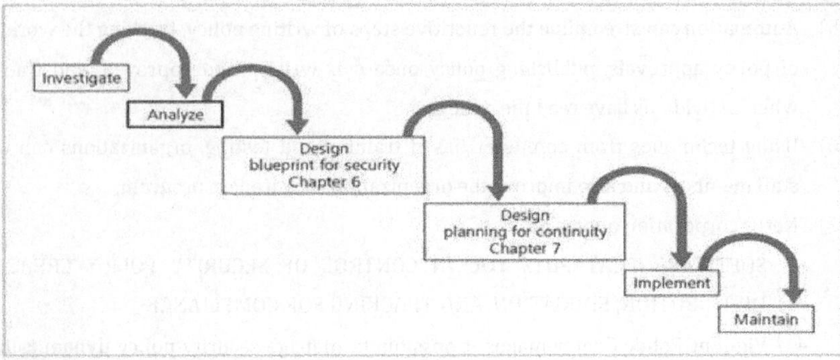

FIGURE SecSDLC Methodology

1.3. Information Security Blueprints

1) One approach is to adapt or adopt a published model or framework for information security
2) A framework is the basic skeletal structure within which additional detailed planning of the blueprint can be placed as it is developed of refined
3) Experience teaches us that what works well for one organization may not precisely fit another
4) This **security blueprint** is the basis for the design, selection, and implementation of all security policies, education and training programs, and technological controls.
5) The security blueprint is a more detailed version of the **security framework**, which is an outline of the overall information security strategy for the organization and the roadmap for planned changes to the information security environment of the organization.
6) The blueprint should specify the tasks to be accomplished and the order in which they are to be realized and serve as a scalable, upgradeable, and comprehensive plan for the information security needs for coming years.
7) One approach to selecting a methodology by which to develop an information security blueprint is to adapt or adopt a published model or framework for information security.
8) This framework can be an outline of steps involved in designing and later implementing information security in the organization.
9) There is a number of published information security frameworks, including those from government sources presented later in this chapter.

10) Because each information security environment is unique, the security team may need to modify or adapt pieces from several frameworks.
11) Experience teaches you that what works well for one organization may not precisely fit another.
12) Therefore, each implementation may need modification or even redesign before it suits the needs of a particular asset-threat problem.

ISO 17799/BS 7799

1) One of the most widely referenced and often discussed security models is the Information Technology–Code of Practice for Information Security Management, which was originally published as British Standard BS 7799.
2) This Code of Practice was adopted as an international standard by the International Organization for Standardization (ISO) and the International Electro technical Commission (IEC) as ISO/IEC 17799 in 2000 as a framework for information security.

Content Outline

The Sections of ISO/IEC 17799

1) Organizational Security Policy.
2) Organizational Security Infrastructure.
3) Asset Classification and Control.
4) Personnel Security.
5) Physical and Environmental Security.
6) Communications and Operations Management.
7) System Access Control.
8) System Development and Maintenance.
9) Business Continuity Planning.
10) Compliance.

1) The stated purpose of ISO/IEC 17799 is to –give recommendations for information security management for use by those who are responsible for initiating, implementing, or maintaining security in their organization.
2) It is intended to provide a common basis for developing organizational security standards and effective security management practice and to provide confidence in inter-organizational dealings.
3) This International Standard is actually drawn from only the first volume of the two-volume British Standard 7799.

4) Volume 2 of BS7799 picks up where ISO/IEC 17799 leaves off.
5) Where Volume 1 of BS7799 and ISO/IEC 17799 are focused on a broad overview of the various areas of security, providing information on 127 controls over ten broad areas.
6) Volume 2 of BS7799 provides information on how to implement Volume 1 and ISO/IEC 17799 and how to set up an information security management system (ISMS).

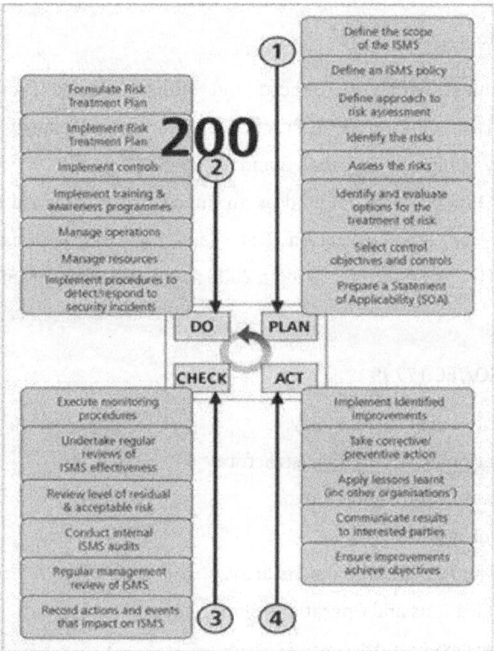

Courtesy of Gamma Secure Systems

FIGURE **BS7799:2 Major Process Steps**[10]

7) Several countries have not adopted 17799 claiming there are fundamental problems:
   - The global information security community has not defined any justification for a code of practice as identified in the ISO/IEC 17799.
   - 17799 lacks—the necessary measurement precision of a technical standard.
   - There is no reason to believe that 17799 is more useful than any other approach currently available.
   - 17799 is not as complete as other frameworks available.
   - 17799 is perceived to have been hurriedly prepared given the tremendous impact its adoption could have on industry information security control.

8) Organizational Security Policy is needed to provide management direction and support.

Objectives

1) Organizational Security Policy.
2) Organizational Security Infrastructure.
3) Asset Classification and Control.
4) Personnel Security.
5) Physical and Environmental Security.
6) Communications and Operations Management.
7) System Access Control.
8) System Development and Maintenance.
9) Business Continuity Planning.
10) Compliance.

NIST Security Models

1) Another approach available is described in the many documents available from the Computer Security Resource Center of the National Institute for Standards and Technology (csrc.nist.gov) – Including:
   - NIST SP 800-12 – An Introduction to Computer Security: The NIST Handbook.
   - NIST SP 800-14 - Generally Accepted Security Principles and Practices for Securing Information Technology System.
   - NIST SP 800-18 - The Guide for Developing Security Plans for IT Systems.
   - SP 800-26: Security Self Assessment Guide for Information Technology Systems.
   - SP 800-30: Risk Management for Information Technology Systems.
2) They have been broadly reviewed by government and industry professionals, and are among the references cited by the federal government when it decided not to select the ISO/IEC 17799 standards.

Table of Contents

1. Introduction 1.1
   - 1.1. Principles
   - 1.2. Practices
   - 1.3. Relationship of Principles and Practices
   - 1.4. Background
   - 1.5. Audience

3.6.2. Identify Resources

3.6.3. Develop Scenarios

3.6.4. Develop Strategies

3.6.5. Test and Revise Plan

3.7. Computer Security Incident Handling

3.7.1. Uses of a Capability

3.7.2. Characteristics

3.8. Awareness and Training

3.9. Security Considerations in Computer Support and Operations

3.10. Physical and Environmental Security

3.11. Identification and Authentication

3.11.1. Identification

3.11.2. Authentication

3.11.3. Passwords

3.11.4. Advanced Authentication

3.12. Logical Access Control 3.12.1 Access Criteria

3.12.2 Access Control Mechanisms

3.13. Audit Trails

3.13.1. Contents of Audit Trail Records

3.13.2. Audit Trail Security

3.13.3. Audit Trail Reviews

3.13.4. Keystroke Monitoring

3.14. Cryptography

NIST SP 800-14

1) Security Supports the Mission of the Organization.
2) Security is an Integral Element of Sound Management.
3) Security Should Be Cost-Effective.
4) Systems Owners Have Security Responsibilities Outside Their Own Organizations.
5) Security Responsibilities and Accountability Should Be Made Explicit.
6) Security Requires a Comprehensive and Integrated Approach.
7) Security Should Be Periodically Reassessed.
8) Security is Constrained by Societal Factors.
9) 33 Principles enumerated.

Security Supports the Mission of the Organization

1) Failure to develop an information security system based on the organization's mission, vision and culture guarantees the failure of the information security program.

Security is an Integral Element of Sound Management

1) Effective management includes planning, organizing, leading, and controlling.
2) Security enhances these areas by supporting the planning function when information security policies provide input into the organization initiatives.
3) Information security specifically supports the controlling function, as security controls.
4) Support sound management by means of the enforcement of both managerial and security policies.

Security should be Cost-effective

1) The costs of information security should be considered part of the cost of doing business, much like the cost of computers, networks, and voice communications systems.
2) These are not profit-generating areas of the organization and may not lead to competitive advantages.
3) Information security should justify its own costs.
4) Security measures that do not justify cost benefit levels must have a strong business case (such as a legal requirement) to warrant their use.

Systems Owners have Security Responsibilities Outside their Own Organizations

1) Whenever systems store and use information from customers, patients, clients, partners, and others, the security of this information becomes a serious responsibility for the owner of the systems.

Security Responsibilities and Accountability Should Be Made Explicit

1) Policy documents should clearly identify the security responsibilities of users, administrators, and managers.
2) To be legally binding, this information must be documented, disseminated, read, understood, and agreed to.
3) Ignorance of law is no excuse, but ignorance of policy is.
4) Regarding the law, the organization should also detail the relevance of laws to issue-specific security policies.
5) These details should be distributed to users, administrators, and managers to assist them in complying with their responsibilities.

Security Requires a Comprehensive and Integrated Approach

1) Security personnel alone cannot effectively implement security.
2) Security is every ones responsibility.
3) The THREE communities of interest (information technology management and professionals, information security management and professionals, as well as the users, managers, administrators, and other stakeholders of the broader organization) should participate in the process of developing a comprehensive information security program.

Security should be Periodically Re-Assessed

1) Information security that is implemented and then ignored is considered negligent, the organization having not demonstrated due diligence.
2) Security is an ongoing process.
3) It cannot be implemented and then expected to function independently without constant maintenance and change.
4) To be effective against a constantly shifting set of threats and constantly changing user base, the security process must be periodically repeated.
5) Continuous analysis of threats, assets, and controls must be conducted and new blueprint developed.
6) Only through preparation, design, implementation, eternal vigilance, and ongoing maintenance can secure the organization's information assets.

Security is Constrained by Societal Factors

1) There are a number of factors that influence the implementation and maintenance of security.
2) Legal demands, shareholder requirements, even business practices affect the implementation of security controls and safeguards.
3) For example, security professionals generally prefer to isolate information assets from the Internet, which is the leading avenue of threats to the assets, but the business requirements of the organization may preclude this control measure.

Principles for securing Information Technology Systems.

- NIST SP 800-14 Generally Accepted principles and Practices for securing Information Technology System.
- Principles for securing Information Technology Systems NIST SP 800-14 Generally Accepted principles and Practices for securing Information Technology Systems.

Principle 1	Establish a sound security policy as the foundation for design.
Principle 2	Treat security as an integral part of the overall system design.
Principle 3	Clearly delineate the physical and logical security boundaries geverned by associated security policies.
Principle 4	Reduce risk to an acceptable level.
Principle 5	Assume that Principles for securing. Information Technology Systems NIST SP 800-14 Generally Accepted principles and Practices for securing Information Technology Systems external systems are insecure.
Principle 6	Identify potential trade-offs between reducing risk and increased costs and decrease in other aspects of operational effectiveness.
Principle 7	Implement layered security (ensure no single point of vulnerability).
Principle 8	Implement tailored system security measures to meet organizational security goals.
Principle 9	Strive for simplicity.
Principle 10	Design and operate an IT system to limit vulnerability and to be resilient in response.
Principle 11	Minimize the system elements to be trusted.
Principle 12	Implement security through a combination of measures distributed physically and logically.
Principle 13	Provide assurance that the system is, and continues to be , resilient in the face of expected threats.
Principle 14	Limit or contain vulnerabilities.
Principle 15	Formulate security measures to address multiple. overlapping information domains.
Principle 16	Isolate public access systems from mission critical. resources (data, processes etc..)
Principle 17	Use boundary mechanisms to separate computing systems and network infrastructures.
Principle 18	Where possible, base security on open standards for portability and interoperability.
Principle 19	Use common language in developing security requirements.
Principle 20	Design and implement audit mechanism to detect unauthorized use and to support incident investigations.
Principle 21	Design security to allow for regular adoption of new technology, including a secure and logical technology upgrade process.
Principle 22	Authenticate users and process to ensure appropriate access control decisions both within and across domains.
Principle 23	Use unique identities to ensure accountability.
Principle 24	Implement least privilege.
Principle 25	Do not implement unnecessary security mechanisms.
Principle 26	Protect information while being processed, in transit, and in storage.
Principle 27	Strive for operational ease of use.
Principle 28	Develop and exercise contingency or disaster recovery procedures to ensure appropriate availability.
Principle 29	Consider custom products to achieve adequate security.
Principle 30	Ensure proper security in the shutdown or disposal of a system.
Principle 31	Protect against all likely classes of —attacks.
Principle 32	Identify and prevent common errors and vulnerabilities.
Principle 33	Ensure that developers are trained in how to develop secure software.

IETF Security Architecture

1) The Security Area Working Group acts as an advisory board for the protocols and areas developed and promoted through the Internet Society and the Internet Engineering Task Force (IETF).
2) RFC 2196: Site Security Handbook provides an overview of five basic areas of security.
3) There are also chapters on important Topics like:
   - Security policies.
   - Security technical architecture.

- Security services.
- Security incident handling.

RFC 2196: Site Security handbook

Table of Contents

6. Ongoing Activities
7. Tools and Locations
8. Mailing Lists and Other Resources
9. References

VISA International Security Model

1) VISA International promotes strong security measures and has security guidelines.
2) Developed two important documents that improve and regulate its information systems.
   - Security Assessment Process.
   - Agreed Upon Procedures.
3) Both documents provide specific instructions on the use of the VISA cardholder Information Security Program
4) The-Security Assessment Process.
   - Document is a series of recommendations for the detailed examination of an organization's systems with the eventual goal of integration into the VISA system
5) The-Agreed Upon procedures.
   - Document outlines the policies and technologies required for security systems that carry the sensitive cardholder information to and from VISA systems
6) Using the two documents, a security team can develop a sound strategy for the design of good security architecture
7) The only down side to this approach is the very specific focus on systems that can or do integrate with VISA's systems.

Baselining and Best Practices

1) Baselining and best practices are solid methods for collecting security practices, but they can have the drawback of providing less detail than would a complete methodology.
2) It is possible to gain information by baselining and using best practices and thus work backwards to an effective design.
3) The Federal Agency Security Practices Site (fasp.csrc.nist.gov) is designed to provide best practices for public agencies, but these policies can be adapted easily to private institutions.
4) The documents found in this site include specific examples of key policies and planning documents, implementation strategies for key technologies and position descriptions

for key security personnel.

5) of particular value is the section on program management, which include the following:
    - A summary guide: public law, executive orders, and policy documents.
    - Position description for computer system security officer.
    - Position description for information security officer.
    - Position description for computer specialist.
    - Sample of an information technology (IT) security staffing plan for a large service application (LSA).
    - Sample of information technology (IT) security program policy.
    - Security handbook and standard operating procedures.
    - Telecommuting and mobile computer security policy.

References

1) Internet Security Task Force (www.ca.com/ISTF).
2) Computer Emergency Response Team (CERT) at Carnegie Mellon University (www.cert.org).
3) The Technology manager's forum (www.techforum.com).
4) The Information Security Forum (www.isfsecuritystandard.com).
5) The Information Systems Audit and Control association (www.isaca.com).
6) The International Association of Professional Security Consultants (www.iapsc.org).
7) Global Grid Forum (www.gridforum.org)
8) SearchSecurity.com and NIST's Computer Resources Center

1.4. Planning for Security-Hybrid Framework

This section presents a Hybrid framework or a general outline of a methodology that organizations can use to create a security system blueprint as they fill in the implementation details to address the components of a solid information security plan

Hybrid Framework for a Blue Print of an Information Security

System

The NIST SP 800-26 framework of security includes philosophical components of the Human Firewall Project, which maintains that people, not technology, are the primary defenders of information assets in an information security program, and are uniquely responsible for their protection.

NIST SP 800-26

NIST SP 800-26 Security Self–Assessment Guide for Information Technology systems.

Management Controls

1) Risk Management.
2) Review of Security Controls.
3) Life Cycle Maintenance.
4) Authorization of Processing (Certification and Accreditation).
5) System Security Plan.

Operational Controls

1) Personnel Security.
2) Physical Security.
3) Production, Input/Output Controls.
4) Contingency Planning.
5) Hardware and Systems Software.
6) Data Integrity.
7) Documentation.
8) Security Awareness, Training, and Education.
9) Incident Response Capability.

Technical Controls

1) Identification and Authentication.
2) Logical Access Controls.
3) Audit Trails.

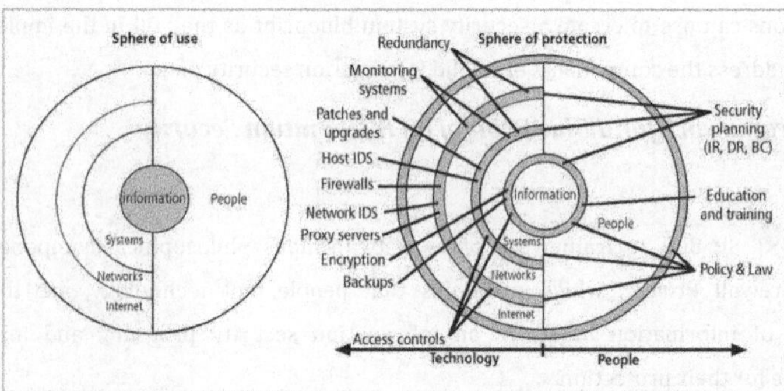

The Sphere of Security

1) The sphere of security (Fig above) is the foundations of the security framework.
2) The spheres of security illustrate how information is under attack from a variety of sources.
3) The sphere of use illustrates the ways in which people access information; for example, people read hard copies of documents and can also access information through systems.
4) Information, as the most important asset in the model is at the center of the sphere.
5) Information is always at risk from attacks through the people and computer systems that have access to the information.
6) Networks and Internet represent indirect threats, as exemplified by the fact that a person attempting to access information from the Internet must first go through the local networks and then access systems that contain the information.

Sphere of Use

1) Generally speaking, the concept of the sphere is to represent the 360 degrees of security necessary to protect information at all times.
2) The first component is the –sphere of use.
3) Information, at the core of the sphere, is available for access by members of the organization and other computer-based systems:
   - To gain access to the computer systems, one must either directly access the computer systems or go through a network connection.
   - To gain access to the network, one must either directly access the network or go through an Internet connection.

The Sphere of Protection

1)	Fig illustrates that between each layer of the sphere of use there must exist a layer of protection to prevent access to the inner layer from the outer layer.
2)	Each shaded band is a layer of protection and control.
3)	For example, the items labeled – Policy & law|| and –Education & Training|| are located between people and the information.
4)	Controls are also implemented between systems and the information, between networks and the computer systems, and between the Internet and Internal networks.
5)	This Reinforces the Concept of –DEFENCE IN DEPTH||
6)	As illustrated in the sphere of protection, a variety of controls can be used to protect the information.
	The items of control shown in the figure are not intended to be comprehensive but rather illustrate individual safeguards that can protect the various systems that are located closer to the center of the sphere.
7)	However, because people can directly access ring as well as the information at the core of the

	model, the side of the sphere of protection that attempts to control access by relying on people requires a different approach to security than the side that uses technology.
8)	The ―sphere of protection‖ overlays each of the levels of the ―sphere of use‖ with a layer of security, protecting that layer from direct or indirect use through the next layer
9)	The people must become a layer of security, a ―**human firewall**‖ that protects the information from unauthorized access and use.
10)	The members of the organization must become a safeguard, which is effectively trained, implemented and maintained or else they too will represent a threat to the information.
11)	Information security is therefore designed and implemented in three layers. • Policies. • People (education, training, and awareness programs). • Technology.
12)	While the design and implementation of the people layer and the technology layer overlap, both must follow the sound management policies.
13)	Each of the layers constitutes controls and safeguards that are put into place to protect the information and information system assets that the organization values.
14)	The order of the controls within the layers follows prioritization scheme.
15)	But before any controls and safeguards are put into place, the policies defining the management philosophies that guide the security process must already be in place.

Three Levels of Control

1) Safeguards provide THREE levels of control.
    - Managerial Controls.
    - Operational Controls.
    - Technical Controls.

Managerial Controls

1) Managerial controls cover security processes that are designed by the strategic planners and performed by security administration of the organization.
    - Management Controls address the design and implementation of the security planning process and security program management.
    - They also address risk management and security control reviews.
    - Management controls further describe the necessity and scope of legal compliance and the maintenance of the entire security life cycle.

Operational Controls

1) Operational controls deal with the operational functionality of security in the organization.
    - They include management functions and lower-level planning, such as disaster recovery and incident response planning.
2) Operational controls also address personnel security, physical security, and the protection of production inputs and outputs.
    - In addition, operational controls guide the development of education, training,

and awareness programs for users, administrators and management.

- Finally, they address hardware and software systems maintenance and the integrity of data.

Technical Controls

1) Technical controls address those tactical and technical issues related to designing and implementing security in the organization as well as issues related to examining and selecting the technologies appropriate to protecting information.
2) While operational controls address the specifics of technology selection and acquisition of certain technical components.
3) They also include logical access controls, such as identification, authentication, authorization, and accountability.
4) Technical controls also address the development and implementation of audit trails for accountability.
5) In addition, these controls cover cryptography to protect information in storage and transit.
6) Finally they include the classification of assets and users, to facilitate the authorization levels needed.

Summary

Using the three sets of controls just described, the organization should be able to specify controls to cover the entire spectrum of safeguards, from strategic to tactical, and from managerial to technical.

The Framework

Management Controls

1) Program Management.
2) System Security Plan.
3) Life Cycle Maintenance.
4) Risk Management.
5) Review of Security Controls
6) Legal Compliance

Operational Controls

1) Contingency Planning.
2) Security ETA.

3) Personnel Security.
4) Physical Security.
5) Production Inputs and Outputs.
6) Hardware & Software Systems Maintenance.
7) Data Integrity.

Technical Controls

1) Logical Access Controls.
2) Identification, Authentication, Authorization, and Accountability.
3) Audit Trails.
4) Asset Classification and Control.
5) Cryptography.

Design of Security Architecture

1) To inform the discussion of information security program architecture and to illustrate industry best practices, the following sections outline a few key security architectural components.
2) Many of these components are examined in an overview.
3) An overview is provided because being able to assess whether a framework and/or blueprint are on target to meet an organization's needs requires a working knowledge of these security architecture components.

Defense in Depth

1) One of the basic tenets of security architectures is the implementation of security in layers.
2) This layered approach is called Defense in Depth.
3) Defense in depth requires that the organization establishes sufficient security controls and safeguards so that an intruder faces multiple layers of control.
4) These layers of control can be organized into policy, training, and education and technology as per the NSTISSC model.
5) While policy itself may not prevent attacks, it certainly prepares the organization to handle them.
6) Coupled with other layers, policy can deter attacks.
7) Training and education are similar.
8) Technology is also implemented in layers, with detection equipment working in tandem with reaction technology, all operating behind access control mechanisms.

9) Implementing multiple types of technology and thereby preventing the failure of one system from compromising the security of the information is referred to as redundancy.

10) Redundancy can be implemented at a number of points through the security architecture such as firewalls, proxy servers, and access controls.

11) Fig illustrates the concept of building controls in multiple, sometimes redundant layers.

12) The Fig shows the use of firewalls and intrusion detection systems(IDS) that use both packet -level rules (shown as the header in the diagram) and the data content analysis (shown as 0100101000 in the diagram).

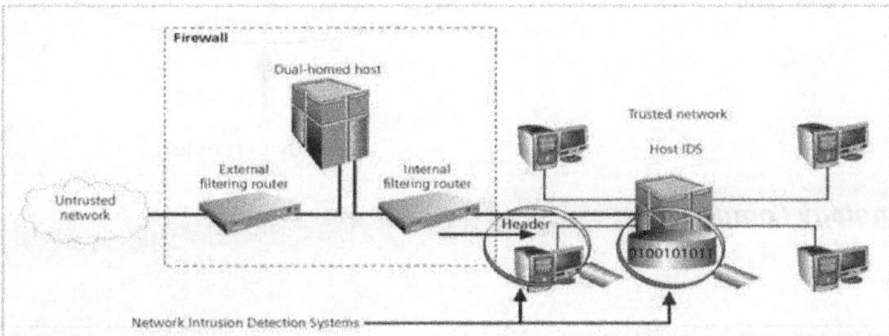

FIGURE **Defense in Depth**

Security Perimeter

1) .	A perimeter is the boundary of an area. A security perimeter defines the edge between the outer limit of an organizations security and the beginning of the outside world.
2)	A security perimeter is the first level of security that protects all internal systems from outside threats , as pictured in Fig below.
3)	Unfortunately, the perimeter does not protect against internal attacks from employee threats or on-site physical threats.
4)	There can be both an electronic security perimeter, usually at the organization's exterior network or internet connection, and a physical security perimeter, usually at the gate to the organization's offices.
5)	Both require perimeter security.
6)	Security perimeters can effectively be implemented as multiple technologies that safeguard the protected information from those who would attack it.
7)	Within security perimeters the organization can establish security domains, or areas of trust within which users can freely communicate.
8)	The assumption is that if individuals have access to all systems within that particular domain
9)	The presence and nature of the security perimeter is an essential element of the overall security framework, and the details of implementing the perimeter make up a great deal of the particulars of the completed security blueprint.
10)	The key components used for planning the perimeter are with respect to firewalls, DMZs, Proxy servers, and intrusion detection systems.

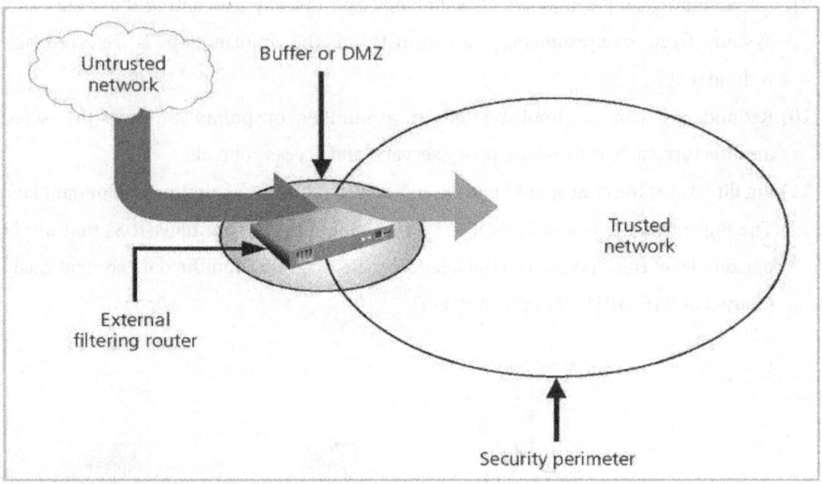

Key Technology Components

Firewalls

A Firewall is a device that selectively discriminates against information following into or out of the organization
A Firewall is usually a computing device, or a specially configured computer that allows or prevents information from entering or exiting the defined area based on a set of predefined rules.
Firewalls are usually placed on the security perimeter, just behind or as part of a gateway router.
While the gateway router is primarily designed to connect the organization's systems to the outside world, it too can be used as the front-line defense against attacks as it can be configured to allow only a few types of protocols to enter.
There are a number of types of firewalls, which are usually classified by the level of information they can filter.
Firewalls can be packet filtering, stateful packet filtering, proxy or application level.
A firewall can be a single device or a firewall subnet, which consists of multiple firewalls creating a buffer between the outside and inside networks.
Thus, firewalls can be used to create to security perimeters like the one shown in Fig.
A buffer against outside attacks is frequently referred to as a Demilitarized Zone (DMZ).
The DMZ is a no-mans land between the inside and outside networks; it is also where some organizations place web servers.

DMZs

A buffer against outside attacks is frequently referred to as a Demilitarized Zone (DMZ).
The DMZ is a no-mans land between the inside and outside networks; it is also where some organizations place web servers.
A buffer against outside attacks is frequently referred to as a Demilitarized Zone (DMZ).
These servers provide access to organizational web pages, without allowing web requests to enter the interior networks.

Proxy Servers

An alternative approach to the strategies of using a firewall subnet or a DMZ is to use a proxy server, or proxy firewall.
A proxy server performs actions on behalf of another system
When deployed, a proxy server is configured to look like a web server and is assigned the domain name that users would be expecting to find for the system and its services.
When an outside client requests a particular web page, the proxy server receives the requests as if it were the subject of the request, then asks for the same information from the true web server (acting as a proxy for the requestor), and then responds tot eh request as a proxy for the true web server.
This gives requestors the response they need without allowing them to gain direct access to the internal and more sensitive server.
The proxy server may be hardened and become a bastion host placed in the public area of the network or it might be placed within the firewall subnet or the DMZ for added protection.
For more frequently accessed web pages, proxy servers can cache or temporarily store the page, and thus are sometimes called cache servers.
Fig below shows a representative example of a configuration using a proxy

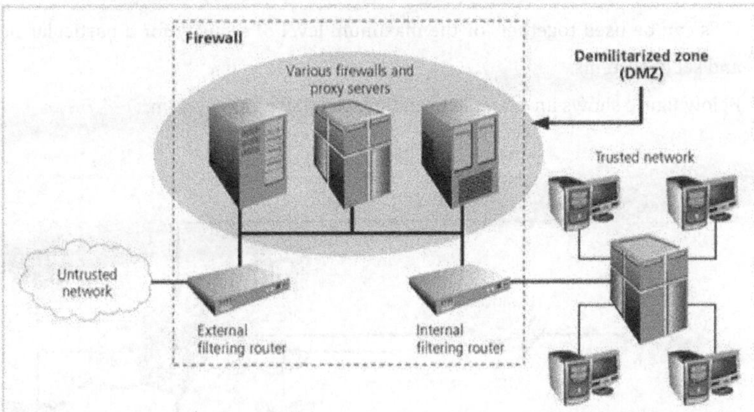

Intrusion Detection Systems (IDSs)

1) In an effort to detect unauthorized activity within the inner network or individual machines, an organization may wish to implement Intrusion Detection Systems (IDSs).
2) IDSs come in TWO versions, with Hybrids possible.

Host Based IDS

1) Host based IDSs are usually installed on the machines they protect to monitor the status of various files stored on those machines.
2) The IDS learns the configuration of the system, assigns priorities to various files depending on their value, and can then alert the administrator of suspicious activity.

Network Based IDS

1) Network based IDSs look at patterns of network traffic and attempt to detect unusual activity based on previous baselines.
2) This could include packets coming into the organization's networks with addresses from machines already within the organization (IP Spoofing).
3) It could also include high volumes of traffic going to outside addresses(As in a Denial of Service Attack)
4) Both Host and Network based IDSs require a database of previous activity.
5) In the case of host based IDSs, the system can create a database of file attributes, as well as maintain a catalog of common attack signatures.
6) Network-based IDSs can use a similar catalog of common attack signatures and develop databases of – normal–activity for comparison with future activity.
7) IDSs can be used together for the maximum level of security for a particular network and set of systems.
8) Below figure shows an example of an Intrusion Detection System.

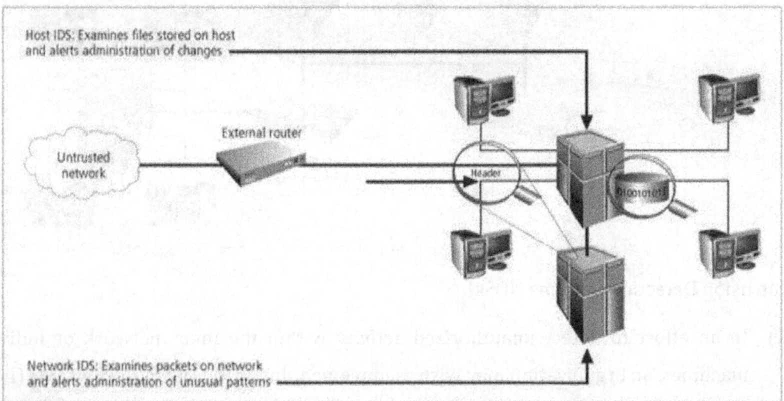

FIGURE **Intrusion Detection Systems**

Summary

1) This cursory overview of Technology components is meant to provide sufficient understanding to allow a decision maker to determine what should be implemented and when to bring in additional expertise to better craft the security design.

2) After your organization has selected a model, created a framework, and flashed it out into a blue print for implementation, you should make sure your planning includes the steps needed to create a training and awareness program that increases information security knowledge and visibility and enables people across the organization to work in secure ways that enhance the safety of the organization's information assets.

1.5. Contingency Planning

Learning Objectives

Upon completion of this part you should be able to:

- Understand the steps involved in incident reaction and incident recovery.
- Define the disaster recovery plan and its parts.
- Define the business continuity plan and its parts.
- Grasp the reasons for and against involving law enforcement officials in incident responses and when it is required.

1) A key role for all managers is planning.
2) Unfortunately for managers, however, the probability that some form of attack will occur, whether from inside or outside, intentional or accidental, human or nonhuman, annoying or catastrophic factors, is very high.
3) Thus, managers from each community of interest within the organization must be ready to act when a successful attack occurs.

Continuity Strategy

1) Managers must provide strategic planning to assure continuous information systems availability ready to use when an attack occurs.
2) Plans for events of this type are referred to in a number of ways:
   - Business Continuity Plans (BCPs)
   - Disaster Recovery Plans (DRPs)
   - Incident Response Plans (IRPs)
   - Contingency Plans

Contingency Planning (CP)

1) Incident Response Planning (IRP)
2) Disaster Recovery Planning (DRP)
3) Business Continuity Planning (BCP)

The primary functions of these three planning types:

1) IRP focuses on immediate response, but if the attack escalates or is disastrous the process changes to disaster recovery and BCP.
2) DRP typically focuses on restoring systems after disasters occur, and as such is closely associated with BCP.
3) BCP occurs concurrently with DRP when the damage is major or long term, requiring more than simple restoration of information and information resources.

Components of CP

1) An incident is any clearly identified attack on the organization's information assets that would threaten the asset's confidentiality, integrity, or availability.
2) An Incidence Response Plan (IRP) deals with the identification, classification, response, and recovery from an incident.
3) A Disaster Recovery Plan (DRP) deals with the preparation for and recovery from a disaster, whether natural or man-made.
4) A Business Continuity Plan (BCP) ensures that critical business functions continue.

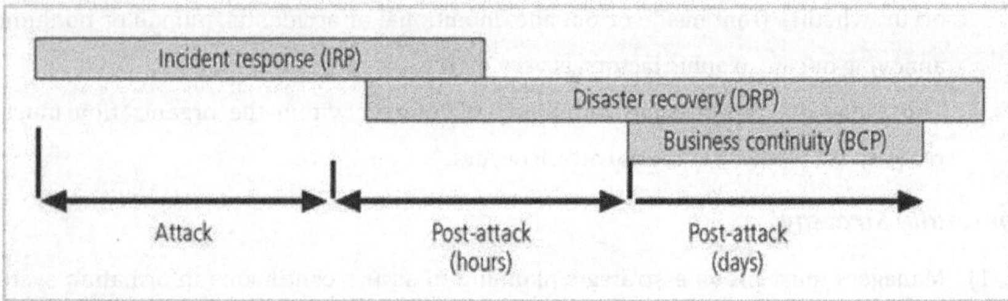

FIGURE Contingency Planning Timeline

Contingency Planning Team

1) Champion: The CP project must have a high level manager to support, promote , and endorse the findings of the project.
2) Project Manager: A champion provides the strategic vision and the linkage to the power structure of the organization.
3) Team members: The team members for this project should be the managers or their representatives from the various communities of interest: Business, Information technology, and information security.

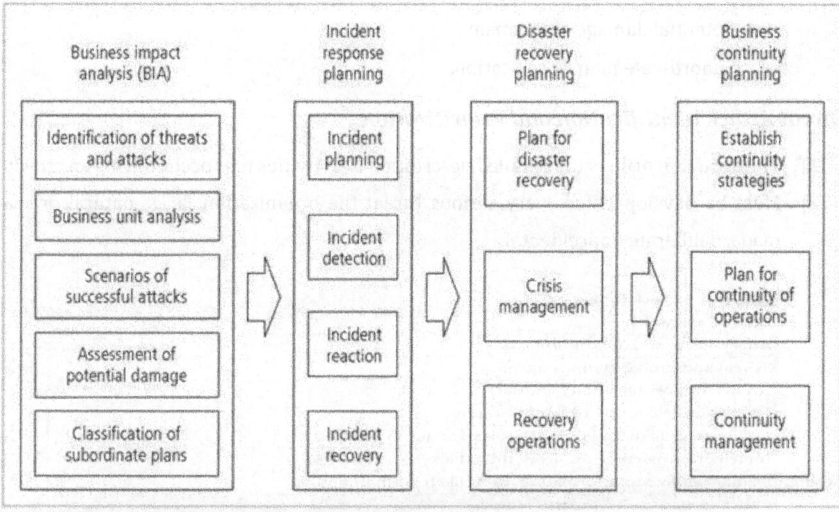

Major Steps in Contingency Planning

Business Impact Analysis

1) The first phase in the development of the CP process is the Business Impact Analysis.
2) A BIA is an investigation and assessment of the impact that various attacks can have on the organization.
3) It begins with the prioritized list of threats and vulnerabilities identified in the risk management.
4) The BIA therefore adds insight into what the organization must do to respond to attack, minimize the damage from the attack, recover from the effects, and return to normal operations.
5) Begin with Business Impact Analysis (BIA).

   If the attack succeeds, what do we do then?

   Obviously the organization's security team does everything In its power to stop these attacks, but some attacks, such as natural disasters, deviations from service providers, acts of human failure or error, and deliberate acts of sabotage and vandalism, may be unstoppable.

6) The CP team conducts the BIA in the following stages:

- Threat attack identification.
- Business unit analysis.

- Attack success scenarios.
- Potential damage assessment.
- Subordinate plan classification.

Threat Attack Identification and Prioritization

1) The **attack profile** is the detailed description of activities that occur during an attack.
2) Must be developed for every serious threat the organization faces, natural or man-made, deliberate or accidental.

TABLE Attack Profile

Date of analysis	
Attack name and description	
Threat and probable threat agent	
Known or possible vulnerabilities	
Likely precursor activities or indicators	
Likely attack activities or indicators of attack in progress	
Information assets at risk from this attack	
Damage or loss to information assets likely from this attack	
Other assets at risk from this attack	
Damage or loss to other assets likely from this attack	

Business Unit Analysis

1) The second major task within the BIA is the analysis and prioritization of business functions within the organization.
2) This series of tasks serves to identify and prioritize the functions within the organization's units (departments, sections, divisions, groups, or other such units) to determine which are most vital to the continued operations of the organization.

Attack Success Scenario Development

1) Next create a series of scenarios depicting the impact a successful attack from each threat could have on each prioritized functional area with:
   - Details on the method of attack.
   - The indicators of attack.
   - The broad consequences.

Potential Damage Assessment

1) From the attack success scenarios developed, the BIA planning team must estimate the cost of the best, worst, and most likely cases.
2) Costs include actions of the response team.
3) This final result is referred to as an attack scenario end case.

Subordinate Plan Classification

Once potential damage has been assessed, a subordinate plan must be developed or identified.
Subordinate plans will take into account the identification of, reaction to, and recovery from each attack scenario.
An attack scenario end case is categorized as disastrous or not.

Incident Response Planning

1) Incident response planning covers the identification of, classification of, and response to an incident.
2) What is incident? What is incident Response?
3) An incident is an attack against an information asset that poses a clear threat to the confidentiality, integrity, or availability of information resources.
4) If an action that threatens information occurs and is completed, the action is classified as an incident. An incident.
5) Attacks are only classified as incidents if they have the following characteristics:

They are directed against information assets.
They have a realistic chance of success.
They could threaten the confidentiality, integrity, or availability of information resources.

Incident Response-IR

IR is therefore the set of activities taken to plan for, detect, and correct the impact of an incident on information assets.

1) IR is more reactive than proactive.
2) IR consists of the following FOUR phases:
   - Planning
   - Detection
   - Reaction
   - Recovery

Incident Planning

1) Planning for incidents is the first step in the overall process of incident response planning.
2) Planning for an the BIA.
3) With this information in hand, the planning team can develop a series of predefined responses that guide the organizations incident response (IR) team and information

security staff.

4) This assumes TWO things:
   - The organization has an IR team and
   - The organization can detect the incident.
5) The IR team consists of those individuals who must be present to handle the systems and functional areas that can minimize the impact of an incident as it takes place.
6) IR team verifies the threat, determines the appropriate response, ands co-ordinates the actions necessary to deal with the situation.

#Format and Content

1) The IR plan must be organized in such a way to support, rather than impede, quick and easy access to require information, such as to create a directory of incidents with tabbed sections for each incident.
2) To respond to an incident, the responder simply opens the binder, flips to the appropriate section, and follows the clearly outlined procedures for an assigned role.

Storage

1) Where is the IR plan stored?
2) Note that the information in the IR plan should be protected as sensitive information.
3) If attackers gain knowledge of how a company responds to a particular incident, they can improve their chances of success in the attacks.
4) The document could be stored adjacent to the administrator's workstation, or in a book case in the server room.

Testing

A plan untested is not a useful plan

1) Train as you fight, and fight as you train.
2) Even if an organization has what appears on paper to be an effective IR plan, the procedures that come from the plan has been practiced and tested.
3) Testing can be done by the following FIVE strategies:
   1. Check list: copies of the IR plan are distributed to each individual with a role to play during an actual incident. These individuals each review the plan and create a checklist of correct and incorrect components.
   2. Structured walkthrough: in a walkthrough, each involved individual practices the steps he/she will take during an actual event.

3. This can consist of an —on the ground|| walkthrough, in which everyone discusses hi/her actions at each particular location and juncture or it can be more of a —talk through|| in which all involved individuals sit around a conference table and discuss in turn how they would act as the incident unfolded.
4. Simulation: Simulation of an incident where each involved individual works individually rather than in conference, simulating the performance of each task required to react to and recover from a simulated incident.
5. Parallel: This test is larger in scope and intensity. In the parallel test, individuals act as if an actual incident occurred, performing the required tasks and executing the necessary procedures.
6. Full interruption: It is the final; most comprehensive and realistic test is to react to an incident as if it were real.

In a full interruption, the individuals follow each and every procedure, including the interruption of service, restoration of data from backups, and notification of appropriate individuals.

Best Sayings

The more you sweat in training, the less you bleed in combat.

1. Training and preparation hurt.
2. Lead from the front, not the rear.
3. You don't have to like it, just do it.
4. Keep it simple.
5. Never assume
6. You are paid for your results, not your methods.

Incident Detection

1. Individuals sometimes notify system administrator, security administrator, or their managers of an unusual occurrence.
2. This is most often a complaint to the help desk from one or more users about a technology service.
3. These complaints are often collected by the help desk and can include reports such as —the system is acting unusual||, — programs are slow||, — my computer is acting weird||, — data is not available||.

 # Incident Indicators

There are a number of occurrences that could signal the presence of an incident candidate. Donald Pipkin, an IT security expert identifies THREE categories of incident indicators:

1) POSSIBLE.
2) PROBABLE.
3) DEFINITE.

Possible Indicators

Presence of unfamiliar files: If users report discovering files in their home directories or on their office computers , or administrators find files that do not seem to have been placed in a logical location or that were not created by an authorized user, the presence of these files may signal the occurrence of an incident.

Possible Indicators

Presence or execution of unknown program or process: If users or administrators detect unfamiliar programs running or processes executing on office machines or network servers, this could be an incident.

Probable Indicators

a) Activities at Unexpected Times

If traffic levels on the organization's network exceed the measured baseline values, there is a probability that an incident is underway.

If systems are accessing drives, such as floppies, and CD –ROMS, when the end user is not using them, is an incident.

b) Presence of New Accounts

Periodic review of user accounts can reveal an account that the administrator does not remember creating, or accounts that are not logged in the administrator's journal. Even one unlogged new account is a candidate incident.

c) Reported Attacks

If users of the system report a suspected attack, there is a high probability that an incident is underway or has already occurred.

d) *Notification from IDS*

If the organization has installed host-based or network based intrusion detection system and if they are correctly configures, the notification from the IDS could indicate a strong likelihood that an incident is in progress.

Definite Indicators

Definite indicators are the activities which clearly signal that an incident is in progress or has occurred.

1) Use of Dormant Accounts: Many network servers maintain default accounts that came with the systems from the manufacturer. Although industry best practices indicate that these accounts should be changed or removed; some organizations ignore these practices by making the default accounts inactive.
2) In addition, systems may have any number of accounts that are not actively used, such as those of previous employees, employees on extended vacation or sabbatical, or dummy accounts set up to support system testing.
3) If any of these dormant accounts suddenly become active without a change in status for the underlying user, this indicates incident occurred.

Change to Logs

The smart administrator backs up systems logs as well as systems data. As a part of a routine incident scan, these logs may be compared to the online version to determine if they have been modified. If they have been modified, and the systems administrator cannot determine explicitly that an authorized individual modified them, an incident has occurred.

Presence of Hacker Tools

A number of hacker tools can be used periodically to scan internal computers and networks to determine what the hacker can see.

They are also used to support research into attack profiles

Incident Reaction

1) Incident reaction consists of actions that guide the organization to stop the incident, mitigate the impact of the incident, and provide information for the recovery from the incident.
2) In reacting to the incident there are a number of actions that must occur quickly including:

- Notification of key personnel.
- Assignment of tasks.
- Documentation of the incident.

Notification of Key Personnel

1) Most organizations maintain alert rosters for emergencies. An alert roster contains contact information for the individuals to be notified in an incident.
2) Two ways to activate an alert roster:
   - A sequential roster is activated as a contact person calls each and every person on the roster.
   - A hierarchical roster is activated as the first person calls a few other people on the roster, who in turn call a few other people, and so on.

Documenting an Incident

1) Documenting the event is important:
   - It is important to ensure that the event is recorded for the organization's records, to know what happened, and how it happened, and what actions were taken. The documentation should record the who, what, when, where, why, and how of the event.

Incident Recovery

1) The first task is to identify the human resources needed and launch them into action.
2) The full extent of the damage must be assessed.
3) The organization repairs vulnerabilities, addresses any shortcomings in safeguards, and restores the data and services of the systems.

Damage Assessment

1) There are several sources of information:
   - Including system logs.
   - Intrusion detection logs.
   - Configuration logs and documents.
   - Documentation from the incident response.
   - Results of a detailed assessment of systems and data storage.
2) Computer evidence must be carefully collected, documented, and maintained to be acceptable in formal proceedings.
3) Recovery

In the recovery process:

- Identify the vulnerabilities that allowed the incident to occur and spread and resolve them.
- Address the safeguards that failed to stop or limit the incident, or were missing from the system in the first place. Install, replace or upgrade them.
- Evaluate monitoring capabilities. Improve their detection and reporting methods, or simply install new monitoring capabilities.
- Restore the data from backups.
- Restore the services and processes in use.
- Continuously monitor the system.
- Restore the confidence of the members of the organization's communities of interest.
- Conduct an after-action review.

Disaster Recovery Planning

1) Disaster recovery planning (DRP) is planning the preparation for and recovery from a disaster.
2) The contingency planning team must decide which actions constitute disasters and which constitute incidents.
3) When situations are classified as disasters plans change as to how to respond - take action to secure the most valuable assets to preserve value for the longer term even at the risk of more disruption.
4) DRP strives to reestablish operations at the primary site.

DRP Step

1) There must be a clear establishment of priorities.
2) There must be a clear delegation of roles and responsibilities.
3) Someone must initiate the alert roster and notify key personnel.
4) Someone must be tasked with the documentation of the disaster.

Crisis Management

1) Crisis management is actions taken during and after a disaster focusing on the people involved and addressing the viability of the business.
2) The crisis management team is responsible for managing the event from an enterprise perspective and covers:

- Supporting personnel and families during the crisis.
- Determining impact on normal business operations and, if necessary, making a disaster declaration.
- Keeping the public informed.
- Communicating with major customers, suppliers, partners, regulatory agencies, industry organizations, the media, and other interested parties.

Business Continuity Planning

1) Business continuity planning outlines reestablishment of critical business operations during a disaster that impacts operations.
2) If a disaster has rendered the business unusable for continued operations, there must be a plan to allow the business to continue to function.

Continuity Strategies

There are a number of strategies for planning for business continuity

1) In general there are three exclusive options:
   - Hot sites.
   - Warm sites.
   - Cold sites.
2) And three shared functions:
   - Timeshare.
   - Service bureaus.
   - Mutual agreements.

Off-Site Disaster Data Storage

To get these types of sites up and running quickly, the organization must have the ability to port data into the new site's systems like.

- Electronic vaulting - The bulk batch-transfer of data to an off-site facility.
- Remote Journaling - The transfer of live transactions to an off-site facility; only transactions are transferred not archived data, and the transfer is real-time.
- Database shadowing - Not only processing duplicate real-time data storage, but also duplicates the databases at the remote site to multiple servers.

The Planning Document

Establish responsibility for managing the document, typically the security administrator Appoint a secretary to document the activities and results of the planning session(s) Independent incident response and disaster recovery teams are formed, with a common planning committee Outline the roles and responsibilities for each team member Develop the alert roster and lists of critical agencies Identify and prioritize threats to the organization's information and information systems

The Planning Process

There are six steps in the Contingency Planning process:

1) Identifying the mission- or business-critical functions.
2) Identifying the resources that support the critical functions.
3) Anticipating potential contingencies or disasters.
4) Selecting contingency planning strategies.
5) Implementing the contingency strategies.
6) Testing and revising the strategy.

Using the Plan

1) During the incident.
2) After the incident.
3) Before the incident.

Contingency Plan Format

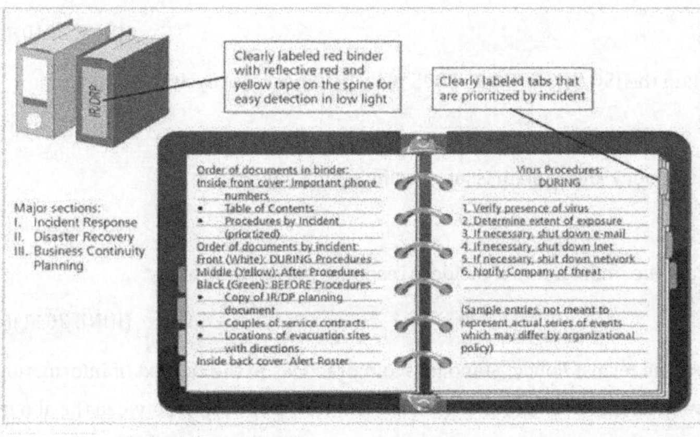

Contingency Plan Format

Law Enforcement Involvement

1) When the incident at hand constitutes a violation of law the organization may determine that involving law enforcement is necessary
2) There are several questions, which must then be answered:
   - When should the organization get law enforcement involved?
   - What level of law enforcement agency should be involved: local, state, or federal?
   - What will happen when the law enforcement agency is involved?

Question

1a).Discuss the system specific security policy .How managerial guidelines and technical specification can be used in SysSP?

(December 2010)(10 marks)

1b).Who is responsible for policy management? How a policy is managed. Explain? Responsible individual.

(December 2010)(10 marks)

1a).Explain issue-specific Security policy?

(Jun-2012)(10 marks)

1b).Draw a systematic diagram showing the major steps in contingency Planning. Explain in Detail. Business impact analysis.

(JUN-2012)(10 marks)

1a). Explain the Pipkin's three categories of incident indicators.

(JUNE 2010)(12 Marks)

1b). Explain the ISO/IEC 270 01 : 2005 plan-DO-Check-Act cycle.

(JUNE 2010)(8 Marks)

1a). Define policy and explain issue specific security policy.

(JUNE 2011)(10 Marks)

1b).Explain the importance of incident response planning strategy.

(JUNE 2011)(10 marks)

1a).Define the terms: Policy, Standards and practices in the context of information security. Draw a schematic diagram depicting the inter-relationship between the above.

(Dec 2011)(6Marks)

1b).What are the policies that must be defined by the management (of organizations) as per NIST SP 800-14 ? Describe briefly the specific areas covered by any two of these policies.

(Dec 2011)(7 Marks)

1c). What are the components of contingency planning? Describe briefly the important steps involved in the recovery process after the extent of damage caused by an incident has been assessed.

(Dec 2011)(7 Marks)

UNIT-2

SECURITY TECHNOLOGY-1

Firewalls and VPNs

Learning Objectives

Understand the role of physical design in the implementation of a comprehensive security program.

Understand firewall technology and the various approaches to firewall implementation.

Identify the various approaches to remote and dial-up access protection-that is, how these connection methods can be controlled to assure confidentiality of information, and the authentication and authorization of users.

Understand content filtering technology.

Describe the technology that enables the use of Virtual Private Networks.

2.1. Introduction

As one of the methods of control that go into a well-planned information security program, technical controls are essential in enforcing policy for many IT functions that do not involve direct human control. Networks and computer systems make millions of decisions every second and operate in ways and at speeds that people cannot control in real time. Technical control solutions, properly implemented, can improve an organization's ability to balance the often conflicting objectives of making information more readily and widely available against increasing the information's levels of confidentiality and integrity.

2.2. Physical Design

The physical design of an information security program is made up of two parts: Security Technologies and physical security.

Physical design extends the logical design of the information security program-which is found in the information security blueprint and the contingency planning elements-and make it ready for implementation.

Physical design encompasses the selection and implementation of technologies and processes that mitigate risk from threats to the information assets of organization assets of an organization.

The Physical Design Process

1) Selects specific technologies to support the information security blueprint identifies complete technical solutions based on these technologies, including deployment, operations, and maintenance elements, to improve the security of the environment.
2) Designs physical security measures to support the technical solution.
3) Prepares project plans for the implementation phase that follows.

Firewalls

A firewall in an information security program is similar to a building's firewall in that it prevents specific types of information from moving between the outside world, known as the untrusted network (eg., the Internet), and the inside world, known as the trusted network.

The firewall may be a separate computer system, a software service running on an existing router or server, or a separate network containing a number of supporting devices.

Firewall Categorization Methods

1) Firewalls can be categorized by processing mode, development era, or structure.
2) There are FIVE major processing–mode categories of firewalls: Packet filtering Firewalls, Application gateways, Circuit gateways, MAC layer firewalls and Hybrids. (Hybrid firewalls use a combination of other three methods, and in practice, most firewalls fall into this category).
3) Firewalls categorized by which level of technology they employ are identified by generation, with the later generations being more complex and more recently developed.
4) Firewalls categorized by intended structure are typically divided into categories. Including residential-or commercial-grade, hardware-based, software-based, or appliance-based devices.

Firewalls Categorized by Processing Mode

The Five Processing Modes are

1) Packet Filtering.
2) Application Gateways.
3) Circuit Gateways.
4) MAC layer firewalls.
5) Hybrids.

A. *Packet Filtering*

Packet filtering firewall or simply filtering firewall examine the header information of data packets that come into a network. A packet filtering firewall installed on a TCP/IP based network typically functions at the Ip level and determines whether to drop a packet (Deny) or forward it to the next network connection (Allow) based on the rules programmed into the firewall. Packet filtering firewalls examine evry incoming packet header and can selectively filter packets based on header information such as destination address, source address, packet types, and other key information. The below shows the structure of an IP packet

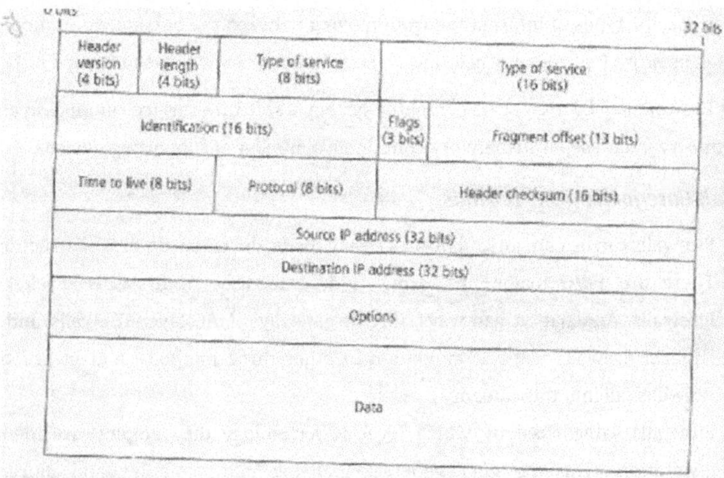

FIGURE **IP Packet Structure**

Packet Filtering firewalls san network data packets looking for compliance with or vilation of the rules of the firewalls database. Filtering firewalls inspect packets at the network layer, or Layer 3 of the OSI model. If the device finds a packet that matches a restriction, it stops the packet from travelling from one network to another. The restrictions most commonly implemented in packet filtering firewalls are based on a combination of the following:

1) IP source and destination address.
2) Direction (in bound or outbound).
3) Transmission Control Protocol (TCP) or User Datagram protocol (UDP) source and destination port requests.

A Packets content will vary in structure, depending on the nature of the packet. The two primary service types are TCP and UDP .Fig 6-2 and 6-3 show the structure of these two major elements of the combined protocol known as TCP/IP Simple firewall models examine TWO aspects of the packet header: the destination and source address. They enforce address restrictions, rules designed to prohibit packets with certain address or partial addresses from passing through the device. They accomplish this through access control lists(ACLs), which are created and modified by the firewall administrators. Fig shows how a packet filtering router can be used as a simple firewall to filter data packets from inbound connections and allow outbound connections unrestricted access the public network.

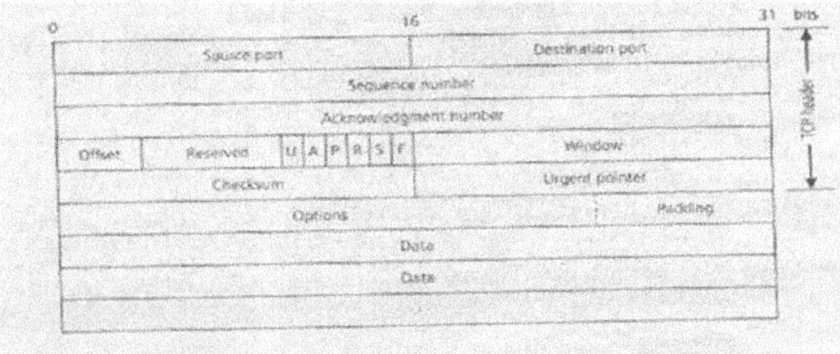

FIGURE TCP Packet Structure

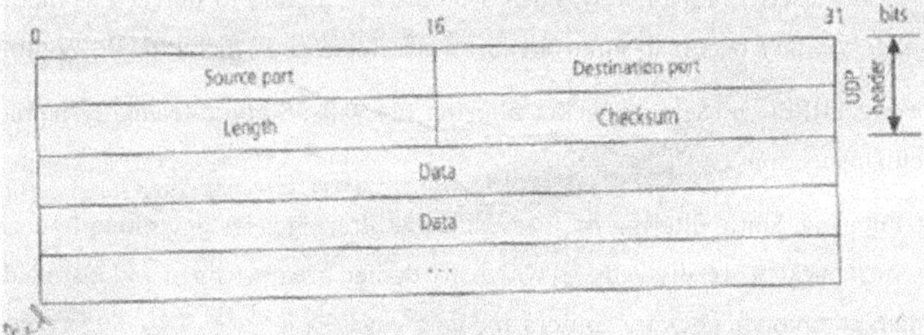

FIGURE UDP Datagram Structure

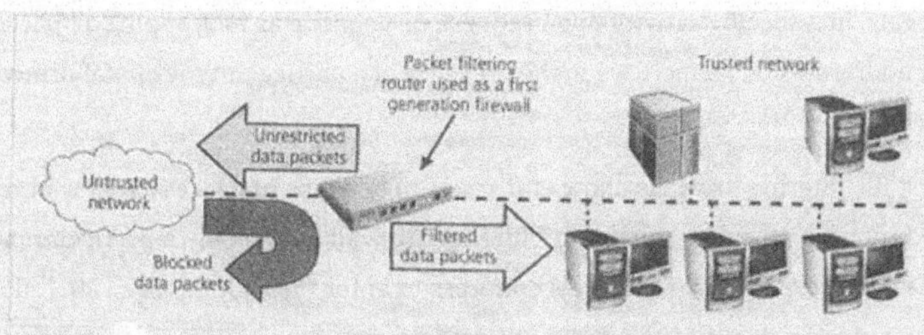

FIGURE Packet Filtering Router

For an example of an address restriction scheme, consider below Table. If an administrator were to configure a simple rule based on the content of the table, any attempt to connect that was made by an external computer or network device in the 192.168.*.* address range (192.168.0.0-192.168.255.255) would be allowed. The ability to restrict a specific service, rather than just a range of IP address, is available in a more advanced version of this first generation firewall.

Sample Firewall Rule and Format

Source Address	Destination Address	Service (HTTP, SMTP, FTP, Telnet)	Action (Allow or Deny)
172.16.x.x	10.10.x.x	Any	Deny
192.168.x.x	10.10.10.25	HTTP	Allow
192.168.0.1	10.10.10.10	FTP	Allow

The ability to restrict a specific service is now considered standard in most routers and is invisible to the user. Unfortunately, such systems are unable to detect the modification of packet headers, which occurs in some advanced attack methods, including IP spoofing attacks.

There are THREE subsets of packet filtering firewalls: Static filtering, Dynamic Filtering, and stateful inspection

Static Filtering: Static filtering requires that the filtering rules governing how the firewall decides which packets are allowed and which are denied are developed and installed. This type of filtering is common in network routers and gateways.

Dynamic Filtering: Dynamic Filtering allows to react to an emergent event and update or create rules to deal with the event. This reaction could be positive, as in allowing an internal user to engage in a specific activity upon request, or negative as in dropping all packets from a particular address when an increase in the presence of a particular type of malformed packet is detected.

While static filtering firewalls allow entire sets of one type of packet to enter in response to authorized requests, the dynamic packet filtering firewall allows only a particular packet with a particular source, destination, and port address to enter through the firewall. It does this by opening and closing doors in the firewall based on the information contained in the packet header, which makes dynamic packet filters an intermediate form, between traditional static packet filters and application proxies.

Stateful Inspection: Stateful Inspection firewalls, also called stateful firewalls, keep track of each network connection between internal and external systems using a state table.

A state table tracks the state and context of each packet in the conversation by recording which station sent what packet and when. Staeful inspection firewalls perform packet filtering like they can block incoming packets that are not responses to internal requests.

If the stateful firewall receives an incoming packet that it cannot match in its state table, it defaults to its ACL to determine whether to allow the packet to pass.

The primary disadvantage of this type of firewall is the additional processing required to manage and verify packets against the state table, which can leave the system vulnerable to a Dos or DDoS attack. In such an attack, the firewall system receives a large number of external packets, which slows the firewall because it attempts to compare all of the incoming packets first to the state table and then to the ACL.

On the positive side, these firewalls can track connectionless packet traffic, such as UDP and remote procedure calls (RPC) traffic.

Dynamic stateful filtering firewalls keep a dynamic state table to make changes within predefined limits tot eh filtering rules based on events as they happen. A state table looks similar to a firewall rule set but has additional information, as shown in table 6-2.

The state table contains the familiar source IP and port, and destination IP and port , but ads information on the protocol used (UDP or TCP), total time in seconds, and time remaining in seconds. Many state table implementations allow a connection to remain in place for up to 60 minutes without any activity before the state is deleted.

Below Table shows this in column labeled Total Time. The time remaining column shows a countdown of the time that is left until the entry is deleted.

State Table Entries

Source Address	Source Port	Destination Address	Destination Port	Time Remaining in Seconds	Total Time in Seconds	Protocol
192.168.2.5	1028	10.10.10.7	80	2725	3600	TCP

B. Application Gateways

The application gateway, also known as an application –level firewall or application firewall, is frequently installed on a dedicated computer, separate from the filtering router, but is commonly used in conjunction with a filtering router. The application firewall is also known as a proxy server, since it runs special software that acts as a proxy for a service request.

An organization that runs a Web server can avoid exposing thee server to direct traffic from users by installing a proxy server, configured with the registered domain's URL. This proxy server will then receives requests for Web pages, access the Web server on behalf of the external client, and return the requested pages to the users. These servers can store the most recently accessed pages in their requested pages to the users. These servers can store the most recently accessed pages in their internal cache, and are thus also called cache servers. The benefits from this type of implementation are significant.

One common example of an application–level firewall or proxy server is a firewall that blocks all requests for an responses to requests from Web pages and services from the internal computers of an organization, and instead makes all such requests and responses go to intermediate computers or proxies in the less protected areas of the organizations network. This technique of using proxy servers is still widely used to implement electronic commerce functions.

The primary disadvantage of application-level firewalls is that they are designd for specific protocol and cannot easily be reconfigured to protect against attacks on other protocols. Since application firewalls work at the application layer they are typically restricted to a single application (Eg, FTP, Telnet, HTTP, SMTP, SNMP). The processing time and resources necessary to read each packet down tot eh application layer diminishes the ability of these firewalls to handle multiple types of applications.

C. Circuit Gateways

The circuit firewall operates at the transport layer. Again connections are authorized based on addresses. Like filtering firewalls, circuit gateways firewalls do not usually look at data traffic flowing between one network and another, but they do prevent direct connections between one network and another. They accomplish this by creating tunnels connecting specific processes or systems on each side of the firewall, and then allow only authorized traffic, such as a specific type of TCP connection for only authorized users, in these tunnels. Writing for NIST in S 800-110, John Wack describes the operation of a circuit gateway as follows:—A circuit-level gateway replays TCP connections but does no extra processing or filtering of the protocol. For example, the use of a TELNET application server is a circuit –level gateway operation, since once the connection between the source and destination is established, the firewall simply passes bytes between the systems without further evaluation of the packet contents. Another Another example of a circuit –level gateway would be for NNTP, in which the NNTP server would connect to the firewall, and then internal systems NNTP clients would connect tot eh firewall. The firewall would again, simply pass bytes.

D. MAC layer Firewalls

MAC layer firewalls are designed to operate at the media access control layer of the OSI network mode. This gives these firewalls the ability to consider the specific host computer's identity in its filtering decisions. Using this approach, the MAC addresses the specific host computers are linked to ACL entries that identify the specific types of packets that can be sent to each host, and all other traffic is blocked.

Shows where in the OSI model each of the firewall processing modes inspects data.

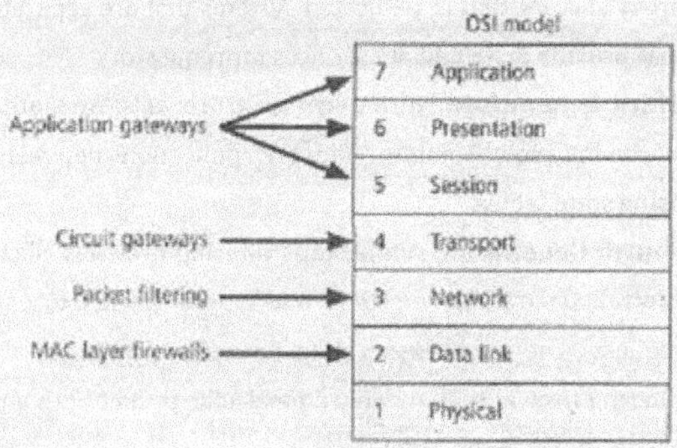

FIGURE **Firewall Types and the OSI Model**

E. Hybrid Firewalls

Hybrid Firewalls combine the elements of other types of firewalls-that is, the elements of packet filtering and proxy services, or of packet filtering and circuit gateways. Alternately, a hybrid firewall system may actually consist of two separate firewall devices: each is a separate firewall system, but they are connected so that they work in tandem. For example, a hybrid firewall system might include a packet filtering firewall that is set up to screen all acceptable requests then pass the requests to a proxy server, which in turn, requests services from a Web server deep inside the organization's networks. An added advantage to the hybrid firewall approach is that it enables an organization to make a security improvement without completely replacing its existing firewalls.

Firewalls Categorized by Development Generation

The first generation of firewall devices consists of routers that perform only simple packet filtering operations. More recent generations of firewalls offer increasingly complex capabilities, including the increased security and convenience of creating a DMZ-demilitarized zone. At present time, there are five generally recognized generations of firewalls, and these generations can be implemented in a wide variety of architectures.

1) **First Generation**: First generation firewalls are static packet filtering firewalls-that is, simple networking devices that filter packets according to their headers as the packets travel to and from the organization's networks.
2) **Second generation**: Second generation firewalls are application-level firewalls or proxy servers-that is, dedicated systems that are separate from the filtering router and that provide intermediate services for requestors.
3) **Third Generation**: Third generation firewalls are stateful inspection firewalls, which as you may recall, monitor network connections between internal and external systems using state tables.
4) **Fourth Generation**: While static filtering firewalls, such as first and third generation firewalls, allow entire sets of one type of packet to enter in response to authorized requests, the fourth generation firewalls, which are also known as dynamic packet filtering firewalls, allow only a particular packet with a particular source , destination, and port address to enter.
5) **Fifth Generation**: The fifth generation firewall is the kernel proxy, a specialized form that works under the Windows NT Executive, which is the kernel of Windows NT. This type of firewall evaluates packets at multiple layers of the protocol stack, by checking security in the kernel as data is passed up and down the stack. Cisco implements this technology in the security kernel of its Centri firewall. The Cisco security kernel contains three component technologies: The Interceptor/Packet analyser, the security analyser, the security verification engine (SVEN), and kernel Proxies. The interceptor captures packets arriving at the firewall server and passes them to the packet analyzer,

which reads the header information, extracts signature data, and passes both the data and the packet, map it to an existing session, or create a new session. If a current session exists, the SVEN passes the information through a custom-built protocol stack created specifically for that session. The temporary protocol stack uses a customized implementation of the approach widely known as Network Address Translation (NAT). The SVEN enforces the security policy that is configured into the Kernel Proxy as it inspects each packet.

Firewalls Categorized by Structure

Firewalls can also be categorized by the structure used to implement them; Most commercial grade firewalls are dedicated appliances. That is , they are stand –alone units running on fully customized computing platforms that provide both the physical network connection and firmware programming necessary to perform their function, whatever that function (static filtering, application proxy etc.,) may be. Some firewall applications use highly customized, sometimes proprietary hardware systems that are developed exclusively as firewall devices. Other commercial firewall systems are actually off-the-shelf general purpose computer systems. These computers then use custom application software running either over standard operating systems like Windows or Linux/Unix or on specialized variants of these operating systems. Most small office or residential-grade firewalls are either simplified dedicated appliances running on computing devices, or application software installed directly on the user's computer.

Commercial–Grade Firewall Appliances

Firewall appliances are stand-alone, self contained combinations of computing hardware and software. These devices frequently have many of the features of a general purpose computer with the addition of firmware based instructions that increase their reliability and performance and minimize the likelihood of being compromised. The customized software operating system that drives the device can be periodically upgraded, but can only be modified using a direct physical connection or after using extensive authentication and authorization protocols. The firewall rule sets are stored in non-volatile memory, and thus they can be changed by technical staff when necessary but are available each time the device is restarted.

Commercial Grade Firewall Systems: A commercial-grade firewall system consists of application software that is configured for the requirements of the firewall application and running on a general purpose computer. Organizations can install firewall software on an existing general purpose computer system, or they can purchase hardware that has been configured to the specifications that yield optimum performance for the firewall software. These systems exploit the fact that firewalls are essentially application software packages that use common general-purpose network connections to move data from one network to another.

Small Office/Home Office (SOHO) Firewall Applications: S more and more small business and residences obtain fast Internet connections with digital subscriber lines (DSL) or cable modem connections, they become more and more vulnerable to attacks. What many small business and work-from-home users don't realize that unlike dial-up connections, these high-speed services are always on and thus the computers connected to them are constantly connected. These computers are, therefore, much more likely to show up on the scanning actions performed by hackers than if they were only connected for the duration of a dial-up session. Coupled with the typically lax security capabilities of home computing operating systems like Windows 95, Windows 98 and even Windows Millenium Edition, most of these systems are wide open to outside intrusion. Even Windows XP Home Edition, a home computing operating system which can be securely configured, is often a soft target since few users bother to olearn how to congigure it securely. Just as organizations must protect their information, residential users must also implement some form of firewall to prevent loss, damage, or disclosure of personal information.

One of the most effective methods of improving computing security in the SOHO setting is through the implementation of a SOHO or residential grade firewall. These devices, also known as broadband gateways or DSL/Cable modem routers , connect the user's local area network or a specific computer system to the Internetworking device-in this case, the cable modem or DSL router provided by the Internet service provider (ISP). The SOHO firewall servers first as a stateful firewall to enable inside to outside access and can be configured to allow limited TP/IP port forwarding and /or screened subnet capabilities.

In recent years, the broadband router devices that can function as packet filtering firewalls have been enhanced to combine the features of wireless access points (WAPs) as well as small stackable LAN switches in a single device. These convenient combination devices give the residential/SOHO user the strong protection that comes from the use of Network Address Translation(NAT) services.NAT assigns non-routing loval address to the computer systems in the local area network and uses the single ISP assigned address to communicate with the Internet. Since the internal computers are not visible to the public network, they are very much less likely to be scanned or compromised. Many users implement these devices primarily to allow multiple internal users to share a single external Internet connection. Below figure shows a few examples of the SOHO firewall devices currently available on the market.

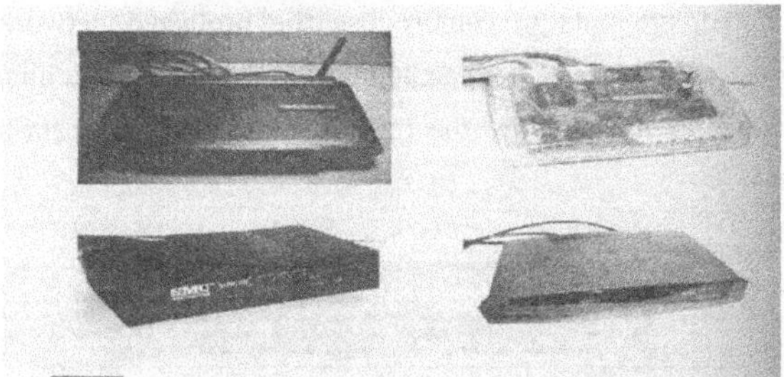

FIGURE SOHO Firewall Devices

Many of these firewalls provide more than simple NAT services. As illustrated in above Figure, some SOHO/residential firewalls include packet filtering, port filtering, and simple intrusion detection systems, and some can even restrict access to specific MAC addresses. Users may be able to configure port forwarding and enable outside users to access specific TCP or UDP ports on specific computers on the protected network.

Below Fig is an example of the set up screen from the SMC Barricade residential broadband router that can be used to identify which computers inside the trusted network may access the Internet.

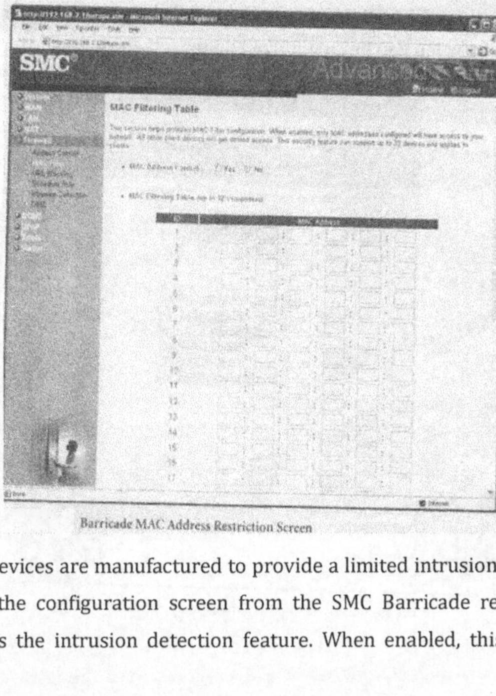

Barricade MAC Address Restriction Screen

Some firewall devices are manufactured to provide a limited intrusion detection capability. Below Fig shows the configuration screen from the SMC Barricade residential broadband router that enables the intrusion detection feature. When enabled, this feature will detect specific, albeit limited, attempts to compromise the protected network. In addition to recording intrusion attempts, the router can be made to use the contact information provided on this configuration screen to notify the firewall administrator of the occurrence of an intrusion attempt.

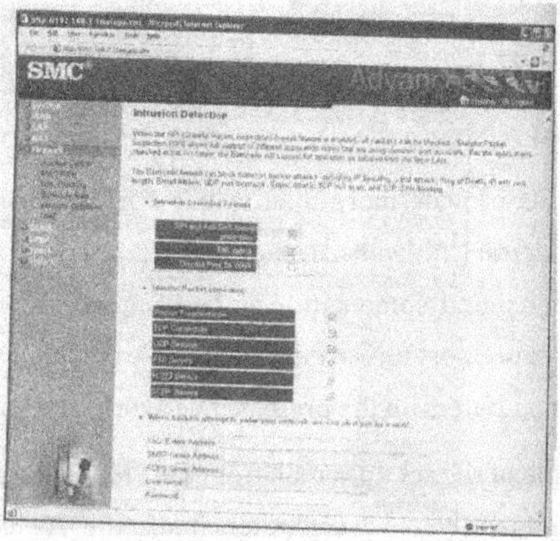

Below figure shows a continuation of the configuration screen for the intrusion detection feature. Note that the intrusion criteria are limited in number, but the actual threshold levels of the various activities detected can be customized by the administrator.

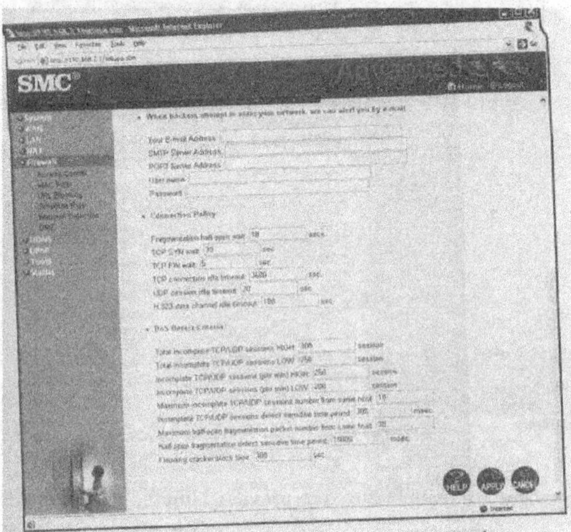

Barricade Intrusion Detection Configuration Screen Continued

Illustrates that even simple residential firewalls can be used to create a logical screened sub network (DMZ) that can provide Web services. This screen shows how barricade can be configured to allow Internet clients' access to servers inside the trusted network. The network administrator is expected to ensure that the exposed servers are sufficiently secured for this type of exposure.

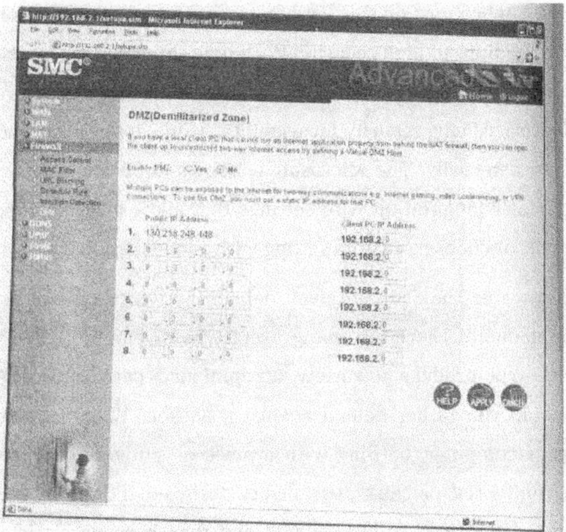

Barricade Demilitarized Zone Configuration Screen

Residential-Grade Firewall Software: Another method of protecting the residential user is to install a software firewall directly on the user's system. Many people have elected to implement these residential grade software based firewalls, but, unfortunately, they may not be as fully protected as they think. The majority of individuals who implement a software-based firewall use one of the products listed in Table 6-3.

Table 6-3 Common Software Firewalls
NetGuard and Esafe Desktop from Aladdin
Zone Labs ZoneAlarm
Kerio Personal Firewall
Agnitum Outpost Firewall
Sygate Personal Firewall
Deerfield Personal Firewall
Norton Personal Firewall
Black Ice Defender from NetworkICE
Tiny Personal Firewall

This list represents a selection of applications that claim to detect and prevent intrusion into the user's system, without affecting usability. The problem is that many of the applications on the list provide free versions of their software that are not fully functional , yet many users implement them thinking their systems are sufficiently protected. But the old adage of you get what you pay for certainly applies to software in this category. Thus, users who implement less-capable software often find that it delivers less complete protection. Some of these applications combine firewall services with other protections like antivirus, or intrusion detection.

There are limits to the level of configurability and protection that software firewalls can provide. Many of the applications on this list have very limited configuration options ranging from none to low to medium to high security. With only three or four levels of configuration, users may find that the application becomes increasingly difficult to use in everyday situations. They find themselves sacrificing security for usability, as the application, packet, or service to connect internally or externally. The Microsoft windows 2000 and XP versions of Internet explorer have a similar configuration with settings that allow users to choose from a list of preconfigured options, or choose a custom setting with a more detailed security configuration.

Software Vs. hardware: The SOHO firewall debate: So which type of firewall should the residential user implement? There are many users who swear by their software firewalls. Personal experience will produce a variety of opinioned perspectives. Ask yourself this question: where would you rather defend against a hacker? With the software option, the hacker is inside your computer, battling with a piece of software that may not have been correctly installed, configured, patched, upgraded or designed. If the software happens to have known vulnerability, the hacker could bypass it and then have unrestricted access to your system. With the hardware device, even if the hacker manages to crash the firewall system, your computer and information are still safely behind the now disabled connection, which is assigned a non routable IP address making it virtually impossible to reach from the outside.

Firewall Architectures

The configuration that works best for a particular organization depends on three factors: The objectives of the network, the organization's ability to develop and implement the architectures, and the budget available for the function. There are FOUR common architectural implementations of firewalls. These implementations are packet filtering routers, screened host firewalls, dual-homed firewalls, and screened subnet firewalls.

A. Packet Filtering Routers

Most organizations with a n Internet connections have some form of a router as the interface to the Internet at the perimeter between the organization's internal networks and the external service provider. Many of these routers can be configured to reject packets that the organization does not allow into the network. This is a simple but effective way to lower the organization's risk from external attack. The drawbacks to this type of system include a lack of auditing and strong authentication. Also, the complexity of the access control lists used to filter the packets can grow and degrade network performance. Fig 6-4 is an example of this type of architecture.

B. Screened Host Firewalls

This architecture combines the packet filtering router with a separate, dedicated firewall, such as an application proxy server. This approach allows the router to pre-screen packets to minimize the network traffic and loads on the internal proxy. The application proxy examines an application layer protocol, such as HTTP, and perform the proxy services. This separate host is often referred to as a bastion host; it can be a rich target for external attacks, and should be very thoroughly secured. Even though the bastion host/application proxy actually contains only cached copies of the internal Web documents, it can still present a promising target, because compromise of the bastion host can disclose the configuration of internal networks and possibly provide external sources with internal information. Since the bastion host stands as a slow defender on the network perimeter, it is also commonly referred to as the Sacrificial Host.

To its advantage, this configuration requires the external attack to compromise two separate systems, before the attack can access internal data. In this way, the bastion host protects the data more fully than the router alone. Below figure shows a typical configuration of a screened host architectural approach.

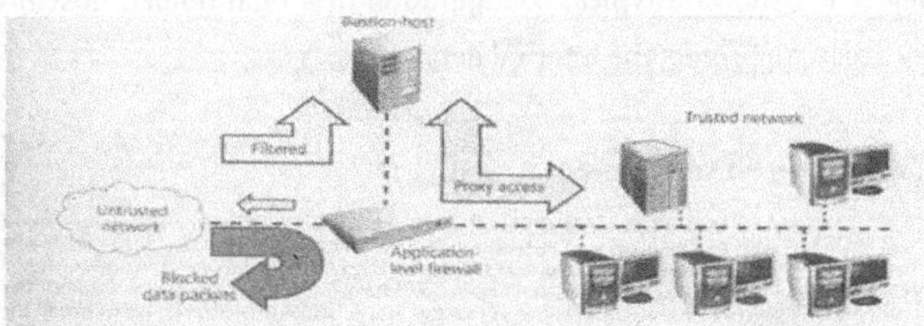

FIGURE Screened Host Firewall

C. Dual-Homed Host Firewalls

The next step up in firewall architectural complexity is the dual-homed host. When this architectural approach is used, the bastion host contains two NICs (Network Interface Cards) rather than one, as in the bastion host configuration. One NIC is connected to the external network, and one is connected to the internal network, providing an additional layer of protection. With TWO NICs, all traffic must physically go through the firewall to move between the internal and external networks.

Implementation of this architecture often makes use of NATs. NAT is a method of mapping real, valid, external IP addresses to special ranges of non-routable internal IP addresses, thereby creating yet another barrier to intrusion from external attackers.

The internal addresses used by NAT consist of three different ranges. Organizations that need Class A addresses can use the 10.x.x.x range, which has over 16.5 million usable addresses. Organization's that need Class B addresses can use the 192.168.x.x range, which has over 65,500 addresses. Finally, organiazations with smaller needs, such as those needing only a few Class C addresses, can use the c172.16.0.0 to 172.16.15.0 range, which has over 16 Class C addresses or about 4000 usable addresses.

See table 6-4 for a recap of the IP address ranges reseved fro non-public networks. Messages sent with internal addresses within these three internal use addresses is directly connected to the external network, and avoids the NAT server, its traffic cannot be routed on the public network. Taking advantage of this , NAT prevents external attacks from reaching internal machines with addresses in specified ranges. If the NAT server is a multi-homed bastion host, it translates between the true, external IP addresses assigned to the organization by public network naming authorities and the internally assigned, non-routable IP addresses. NAT translates by dynamically assigning addresses to internal communications and tracking the conversions with sessions to determine which incoming message is a response to which outgoing traffic. Below Fig shows a typical configuration of a dual homed host firewall that uses NAT and proxy access to protect the internal network.

Table 6-4 Reserved Non-Routable Address Ranges

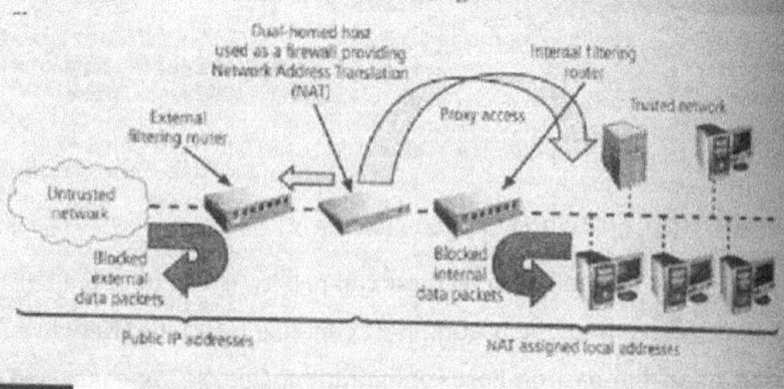

FIGURE Dual-Homed Host Firewall

Another benefit of a dual-homed host is its ability to translate between many different protocols at their respective data link layers, including Ethernet , Token Ring, Fiber Distributed Data interface (FDDI) , and Asynchronous Transfer Method (ATM). On the downside, if this dual-homed host is compromised, it can disable the connection to the external network, and as traffic volume increases, it can become over-loaded. Compared to more complex solutions, however, this architecture provides strong overall protection with minimal expense.

D. Screened Subnet Firewalls (with DMZ)

The dominant architecture used today is the screened subnet firewall. The architecture of a screened subnet firewall provides a DMZ. The DMZ can be a dedicated port on the firewall device linking a single bastion host, or it can be connected to a screened subnet, as shown in Fig. Until recently, servers providing services through an untrusted network were commonly placed in the DMZ. Examples of these include Web servers, file transfer protocol (FTP) servers, and certain database servers. More recent strategies using proxy servers have provided much more secure solutions.

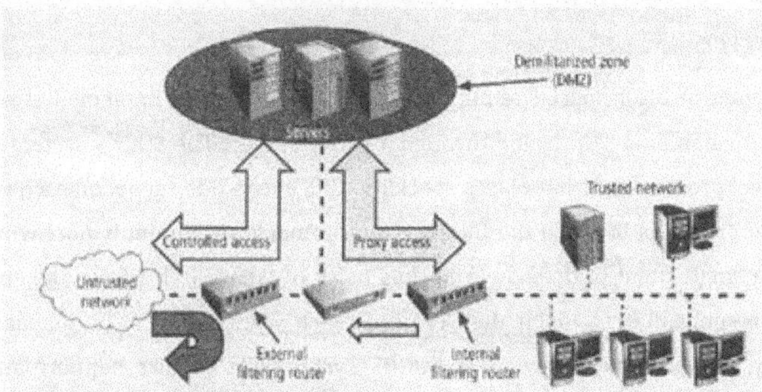

FIGURE Screened Subnet (DMZ)

A common arrangement finds the subnet firewall consisting of two or more internal bastion hosts behind a packet filtering router, with each host protecting the trusted network. There are many variants of the screened subnet architecture. The first general model consists of two filtering routers, with one or more dual-homed bastion hosts between them. In the second general model, as illustrated in Fig, the connections are routed as follows:

1) Connections from the outside or un trusted network are routed through an external filtering router.

2) Connections from the outside or un trusted network are routed into-and then out of – a routing firewall to the separate network segment known as the DMZ.

3) Connections into the trusted internal network are allowed only from the DMZ bastion host servers.

The screened subnet is an entire network segment that performs two functions: it protects the DMZs systems and information from outside threats by providing a network of intermediate security; and it protects the internal networks by limiting how external connections can gain access to internal systems. Although extremely secure, the screened subnet can be expensive to implement and complex to configure and manage. The value of the information it protects must justify the cost.

Another facet of the DMZ is the creation of an area of known as an extranet. AN extranet is a segment of the DMZ where additional authentication and authorization controls are put into place to provide services that are not available to the general public. An example would be an online retailer that allows anyone to browse the product catalog and place items into a shopping cart, but will require extra authentication and authorization when the customer is ready to check out and place an order.

Socks Server

Deserving of brief special attention is the SOCKS firewall implementation. SOCKS is the protocol for handling TCP traffic through a proxy server. The SOCKS system is a proprietary circuit level proxy server that places special SOCKS client-side agents on each workstation. The general approach is to place the filtering requirements on the individual workstation rather than on a single point of defense (and thus point of failure). This frees the entry router from filtering responsibilities, but it then requires each workstation to be managed as a firewall detection and protection device. A SOCKS system can require support and management resources beyond those usually encountered for traditional firewalls since it is used to configure and manage hundreds of individual clients as opposed to a single device or small set of devices.

Selecting the Right Firewall

When selecting the best firewall for an organization, you should consider a number of factors. The most important of these is the extent to which the firewall design provides the desired protection. When evaluating a firewall, questions should be created that cover the following topics:

1. What type of firewall technology offers the right balance between protection and cost for needs of the organization
2. What features are included in the base price? What features are available at extra cost? Are all cost factors known?
3. How easy is to set up and configure the firewall? How accessible are the staff technicians who can competently configure the firewall?
4. Can the candidate firewall adapt to the growing network in the target organization?

The second most important issue is the cost. Cost may keep a certain make, model or type out of reach for a particular security solution. As with all security decisions, certain compromises may be necessary in order to provide a viable solution under the budgetary constraints stipulated by management.

Configuring and Managing Firewalls

Once the firewall architecture and technology have been selected, the initial configuration and ongoing management of the firewalls needs to be considered. Good policy and practice dictates that each firewall device whether a filtering router, bastion host, or other firewall implementation, must have its own set of configuration rules that regulate its actions.

In theory packet filtering firewalls use a rule set made up of simple statements that regulate source and destination addresses identifying the type of requests and /or the ports to be used and that indicate whether to allow or deny the request.

In actuality, the configuration of firewall policies can be complex and difficult. IT professionals familiar with application programming can appreciate the problems associated with debugging both syntax errors and logic errors. Syntax errors in firewall policies are usually easy to identify, as the systems alert the administrator to incorrectly configured policies. However, logic errors, such as allowing instead of denying, specifying the wrong port or service type, and using the wrong switch, are another story.

These and a myriad of other simple mistakes can take a device designed to protect user's communications and turn it into one giant choke point. A choke point that restricts all communications or an incorrectly configured rule can cause other unexpected results. For example, novice firewall administrators often improperly configure a virus-screening e-mail gateway, which, instead of screening e-mail for malicious code, results in the blocking of all incoming e-mail and causes, understandably, a great deal of frustration among users.

Configuring firewall policies is as much an art as it si a science. Each configuration rule must be carefully crafted, debugged, tested, and placed into the access control list in the proper sequence. The process of writing good, correctly sequenced firewall rules ensures that the actions taken comply with the organization's policy. The process also makes sure that those rules that can be evaluated quickly and govern broad access are performed before those that may take longer to evaluate and affect fewer cases, which in turn, ensures that the analysis is completed as quickly as possible for the largest number of requests. When configuring firewalls , keep one thing in mind: when security rules conflict with the performance of business, security often loses. If users can't work because of a security restriction, the security administration is usually told, in no uncertain terms, to remove the safeguard. In other words, organizations are much more willing to live with potential risk than certain failure. The following sections describe the best practices most commonly used in firewalls and the best ways to configure the rules that support firewalls.

Best Practices for Firewalls

1. All traffic from the trusted network is allowed out. This allows members of the organization to access the services they need. Filtering and logging of outbound traffic is possible when indicated by specific organizational policies.
2. The firewall device is never directly accessible from the public network for configuration or management purposes. Almost all administrative access to teh firewall device is denied to internal users as well. Only authorized firewall administrators access the device through secure authentication mechanisms, with preference for a method that is based on cryptographically strong authentication and uses two-factor access control techniques.
3. Simple Mail Transport protocol (SMTP) data is allowed to pass through the firewall, but it should all be routed to a well-configured SMTP gateway to filter and route messaging traffic security.
4. All internet Control Message Protocol (ICMP) data should be denied. Known as the Ping service, ICMP is a common method for hacker reconnaissance and should be turned off to prevent snooping.
5. Telnet (Terminal Emulation) access to all internal servers from the public networks should be blocked. At the very least, telnet access to the organization's Domain Name Service (DNS) server should be blocked to prevent illegal zone transfers, and to prevent hackers from taking down the organization's entire network. If internal users need to come into an organization's network from outside the firewall, the organizations should enable them to use a Virtual Private Network (VPN) client, or other secure system that provides a reasonable level of authentication.
6. When web services are offered outside the firewall, HTTP traffic should be denied from reaching your internal networks through the use of some form of proxy access or DMZ architecture. That way, if any employees are running Web servers for internal use on their desktops, the services are invisible to the outside Internet.

If the Web server is behind the firewall, allow HTTP or HTTPS (also known as secure socket layer or SSL) through for the Internet at large to view it. The best solution is to place the Web servers containing critical data inside the network and use proxy services from a DMZ (screened network segment), and also to restrict Web traffic bound for internal network addresses in response to only those requests that originated from internal addresses. This restriction can be accomplished through NAT or other stateful inspection or proxy server firewall approaches. All other incoming HTTP traffic should be blocked. If the Web servers only contain advertising, they should be placed in the DMZ and rebuilt on a timed schedule or when -not if, but when-they are compromised.

Firewall Rules

Firewalls operate by examining a data packet and performing a comparison with some predetermined logical rules. The logic is based on a set of guidelines programmed in by a firewall administrator, or created dynamically and based on outgoing requests for information. This logical set is most commonly referred to as firewall rules, rule base, or firewall logic.

Most firewalls use packet header information to determine whether a specific packet should be allowed to pass through or should be dropped. In order to better understand more complex rules, it is important to be able to create simple rules and understand how they interact.

For the purpose of this discussion, assume a network configuration as illustrated in below Fig, with an internal and an external filtering firewall. In the exercise, the rules for both firewalls will be discussed, and a recap at the end of the exercise will show the complete rule sets for each filtering firewall.

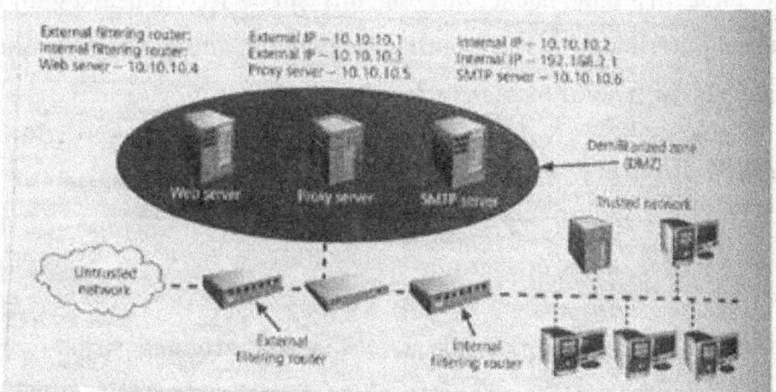

FIGURE Example Network Configuration

Some firewalls can filter packets by the name of a particular protocol as opposed to the protocol's usual port numbers. For instance, Telnet protocol packets usually go to TCP port 23, but can sometimes be directed to another much higher port number in an attempt to conceal the activity. The System or well-known ports are those from 0 through 1023, User or registered ports are those from 1024 through 49151, and Dynamic or Private Ports are those from 49152 through 65535.

The following example uses the port numbers associated with several well-known protocols to build a rule base. The port numbers to be used are listed in Table 6-5. Note that this is not an exhaustive list.

TABLE 6-5 Select Well-Known Port Numbers

Port Number	Protocol
7	Echo
20	File Transfer [Default Data] – (FTP)
21	File Transfer [Control] – (FTP)
23	Telnet
25	Simple Mail Transfer Protocol – (SMTP)
53	Domain Name Services – (DNS)
80	Hypertext Transfer Protocol – (HTTP)
110	Post Office Protocol version 3 – (POP3)
161	Simple Network Management Protocol – (SNMP)

Rule Set-1: Responses to internal requests are allowed. In most firewall implementations, it is desirable to allow a response to an internal request for information. In dynamic or stateful firewalls, this is most easily accomplished by matching the incoming traffic to an outgoing request in a state table. In simple packet filtering, this can be accomplished with the following rule for the External Filtering Router. (Note that the network address for the destination ends with .0; some firewalls use a notation of .X instead.)

TABLE 6-6 Rule Set 1

Source Address	Source Port	Destination Address	Destination Port	Action
Any	Any	10.10.10.0	>1023	Allow

From Table 6-6, you can see that this rule states that any incoming packet (with any source address and from any source port) that is destined for the internal network (whose destination address is 10.10.10.0) and for a destination port greater than 1023 (that is , any port out of the number range for the well-known ports) is allowed to enter. Why allow all such packets? While outgoing communications request information from a specific port (i.e a port 80 request for a Web page), the response is assigned a number outside the well-known port range. If multiple browser windows are open at the same time, each window can request a packet from a Web site, and the response is directed to a specific destination port, allowing the browser and Web server to keep each conversation separate. While this rule is sufficient for the external router (firewall), it is dangerous simply to allow any traffic in just because it is destined to a high port range. A better solution is to have the internal firewall router use state tables that track connections and prevent dangerous packets from entering this upper port range.

Rule set-2: The firewall device is never accessible directly from the public network. If hackers can directly access the firewall, they may be able to modify or delete rules and allow unwanted traffic through. For the same reason, the firewall itself should never be allowed to access other network devices directly. If hackers compromise the firewall and then use its permissions to access other servers or clients, they may cause additional damage or mischief. The rules shown in Table 6-7 prohibit anyone from directly accessing the firewall and the firewall from directly accessing any other devices. Note that this example is for the external filtering router/firewall only. Similar rules should be crafted for the internal router. Why are there separate rules for each IP addresses? The 10.10.10.1 address regulates external access to and by the firewall, while the 10.10.10.2 address regulates internal access. Not all hackers are outside the firewall!

TABLE 6-7 Rule Set 2

Source Address	Source Port	Destination Address	Destination Port	Action
Any	Any	10.10.10.1	Any	Deny
Any	Any	10.10.10.2	Any	Deny
10.10.10.1	Any	Any	Any	Deny
10.10.10.2	Any	Any	Any	Deny

Rule set-3: All traffic from the trusted network is allowed out. As a general rule it is wise not to restrict outgoing traffic, unless a separate router is configured to handle this traffic. Assuming most of the potentially dangerous traffic is inbound, screening outgoing traffic is just more work for the firewalls. This level of trust is fine for most organizations. If the organization wants control over outbound traffic, it should use a separate router. The rule shown in Table 6-8 allows internal communications out.

TABLE 6-8 Rule Set 3

Source Address	Source Port	Destination Address	Destination Port	Action
10.10.10.0	Any	Any	Any	Allow

Why should rule set-3 come after rule set-1 and 2? It makes sense to allow the rules that unambiguously impact the most traffic to be earlier in the list. The more rules a firewall must process to find one that applies to the current packet, the slower the firewall will run. Therefore, most widely applicable rules should come first since the first rule that applies to any given packet will be applied.

Rule set-4: The rule set for the Simple mail Transport Protocol (SMTP) data is shown in Table 6-9. As shown, the packets governed by this rule are allowed to pass through the firewall, but are all routed to a well-configured SMTP gateway. It is important that e-mail traffic reach your e-mail server, and only your e-mail server. Some hackers try to disguise dangerous packets as e-mail traffic to fool a firewall. If such packets can reach only the e-mail server, and the e-mail server has been properly configured, the rest of the network ought to be safe.

TABLE 6-9 Rule Set 4

Source Address	Source Port	Destination Address	Destination Port	Action
Any	Any	10.10.10.6	25	Allow

Rule set 5: All Internet Control Message Protocol (ICMP) data should be denied. Pings, formally known as ICMP echo requests, are used by internal systems administrators to ensure that clients and servers can reach and communicate. There is virtually no legitimate use for ICMP outside the network, except to test the perimeter routers. ICPM uses port 7 to request a response to a query (eg ―Are you there?‖) and can be the first indicator of a malicious attack. It's best to make all directly connected networking devices ―black holes‖ to external probes. Trace route uses a variation on the ICMP Echo requests, so restricting this one port provides protection against two types of probes. Allowing internal users to use ICMP requires configuring two rules, as shown in Table 6-10.

TABLE 6-10 Rule Set 5

Source Address	Source Port	Destination Address	Destination Port	Action
10.10.10.0	Any	Any	7	Allow
Any	Any	10.10.10.0	7	Deny

The first of these two rules allows internal administrators (and users) to use Ping. Note that this rule is unnecessary if internal permissions rules like those in rule set 2 is used. The second rule in Table 6-10 does not allow anyone else to use Ping. Remember that rules are processed in order. If an internal user needs to Ping an internal or external address, the firewall allows the packet and stops processing the rules. If the request does not come from an internal source, then it bypasses the first rule and moves to the second.

Rule set 6: Telnet (Terminal emulation) access to all internal servers from the public networks should be blocked. Though not used much in Windows environments, Telnet is still useful to systems administrators on Unix/Linux systems. But the presence of external requests for Telnet services can indicate a potential attack. Allowing internal use of Telnet requires the same type of initial permission rule you use with Ping. See Table 6-11. Note that this rule is unnecessary if internal permissions rules like those in rule set 2 are used.

TABLE 6-11 Rule Set 6

Source Address	Source Port	Destination Address	Destination Port	Action
10.10.10.0	Any	10.10.10.0	23	Allow
Any	Any	10.10.10.0	23	Deny

Rule set 7: when Web services are offered outside the firewall, HTTP traffic should be denied from reaching the internal networks through the use of some form of proxy access or DMZ architecture. With a Web server in the DMZ you simply allow HTTP to access the Web server, and use rule set 8, the Clean Up rule to prevent any other access. In order to keep the Web server inside the internal network, direct all HTTP requests to the proxy server, and configure the internal filtering router/firewall only to allow the proxy server to access the internal Web server. The rule shown in Table 6-12 illustrates the first example.

TABLE 6-12 Rule Set 7a

Source Address	Source Port	Destination Address	Destination Port	Action
Any	Any	10.10.10.4	80	Allow

This rule accomplishes two things: It allows HTTP traffic to reach the Web server, and it prevents non-HTTP traffic from reaching the Web server. It does the latter through the Clean Up rule (Rule 8). If someone tries to access the Web server with non-HTTP traffic (other than port 80), then the firewall skips this rule and goes to the next.

Proxy server rules allow an organization to restrict all access to a device. The external firewall would be configured as shown in Table 6-13.

TABLE 6-13 Rule Set 7b

Source Address	Source Port	Destination Address	Destination Port	Action
Any	Any	10.10.10.5	80	Allow

The effective use of as proxy server of course requires the DNS entries to be configured as if the proxy server were the Web server. The proxy server would then be configured to repackage any HTTP request packets into a new packet and retransmit to the Web server inside the firewall. Allowing for the retransmission of the repackaged request requires the rule shown in Table 6-14 to enable the proxy server at 10.10.10.5 to send to the internal router, presuming the IP address for the internal Web server is 192.168.2.4

TABLE 6-14 Rule Set 7c

Source Address	Source Port	Destination Address	Destination Port	Action
10.10.10.5	80	192.168.2.4	80	Allow

The restriction on the source address then prevents anyone else from accessing the Web server from outside the internal filtering router/firewall.

Rule set 8: The Clean up rule: As a general practice in firewall rule construction, if a request for a service is not explicitly allowed by policy, that request should be denied by a rule. The rule shown in Table 6-15 implements this practice and blocks any requests that aren't explicitly allowed by other rules.

TABLE 6-15 Rule Set 8

Source Address	Source Port	Destination Address	Destination Port	Action
Any	Any	Any	Any	Deny

Additional rules restricting access to specific servers or devices can be added, but they must be sequenced before the clean up rule. Order is extremely important, as misplacement of a particular rule can result in unforeseen results.

Tables 6-16 and 6-17 show the rule sets, in their proper sequences, for both external and internal firewalls.

TABLE 6-16 External Filtering Firewall Rule Set

Rule #	Source Address	Source Port	Destination Address	Destination Port	Action
1	Any	Any	10.10.10.0	>1023	Allow
2	Any	Any	10.10.10.1	Any	Deny
3	Any	Any	10.10.10.2	Any	Deny
4	10.10.10.1	Any	Any	Any	Deny
5	10.10.10.2	Any	Any	Any	Deny
6	10.10.10.0	Any	Any	Any	Allow
7	Any	Any	10.10.10.6	25	Allow
8	Any	Any	10.10.10.0	7	Deny
9	Any	Any	10.10.10.0	23	Deny
10	Any	Any	10.10.10.4	80	Allow
11	Any	Any	Any	Any	Deny

TABLE 6-17 Internal Filtering Firewall Rule Set

Rule #	Source Address	Source Port	Destination Address	Destination Port	Action
1	Any	Any	10.10.10.0	>1023	Allow
2	Any	Any	10.10.10.3	Any	Deny
3	Any	Any	192.168.2.1	Any	Deny
4	10.10.10.3	Any	Any	Any	Deny
5	192.168.2.1	Any	Any	Any	Deny
6	192.168.2.0	Any	Any	Any	Allow
7	10.10.10.5	Any	192.168.2.0	Any	Allow
8	Any	Any	Any	Any	Deny

Note that the rule allowing responses to internal communications comes first (appearing in Table 6-16 as Rule #1), followed by the four rules prohibiting direct communications to or from the firewall (Rules #2-5 in Table 6 16). After this comes the rule stating that all outgoing internal communications are allowed, followed by the rules governing access to the SMTP server, and denial of Ping, Telnet access, and access to the HTTP server. If heavy traffic to the HTTP server is expected, move the HTTP server rule closer to the top (For example, into the position of Rule #2), which would expedite rule processing for external communications. The final rule in Table 6-16 denies any other types of communications.

Note the similarities and differences in the two rule sets. The internal filtering router/firewall rule set, shown in Table 6-17, has to both protect against traffic to and allow traffic from the internal network (192.168.2.0). Most of the rules in Table 6-17 are similar to those in Table 6-16: allowing responses to internal communications (Rule #1); denying communications to/from the firewall itself (rule # 2-5); and allowing all outbound internal traffic (Rule #6). Note that there is no permissible traffic from the DMZ systems, except as in Rule #1.

Why isn't there a comparable rule for the 192.168.2.1 subnet? Because this is an unrouteable network, external communications are handled by the NAT server, which maps internal (192.168.2.0) addresses to external (10.10.10.0) addresses. This prevents a hacker from compromising one of the internal boxes and accessing the internal network with it. The exception is the proxy server (Rule #7 in Table 6-17), which should be very carefully configured. If the organization does not need the proxy server, as in cases where all externally accessible services are provided from machines in the DMZ, tehn rule #7 is not needed. Note that there are no Ping and Telnet rules in Table 6-17. This is because the external firewall filters these external requests out. The last rule, rule#8 provides cleanup.

Content Filters

Another utility that can contribute to the protection of the organization's systems from misuse and unintentional denial-of-service, and is often closely associated with firewalls, is the **content filter.**

A content filter is software filter-technically not a firewall –that allows administrators to restrict access to content from within a network. It is essentially a set of scripts or programs that restricts user access to certain networking protocols and internet locations, or restricts users from receiving general types or specific examples of Internet content. Some refer to content filters as reverse firewalls, as their primary focus is to restrict internal access to external material. In most common implementation models, the content filter has two components: rating and filtering. The rating is like a set of firewall rules for Web sites, and is common in residential content filters. The rating can be complex, with multiple access control settings for different levels of the organizations, or it can be simple, with a basic allow/deny scheme like that of a firewall. The filtering is a method used to restrict specific access requests to the identified resources, which may be Web sites, servers or whatever resources the content filter administrator configures. This is sort of a reverse control list (A capability table), in that whereas an access control list normally records a set of users that have access to resources, this control list records resources which the user cannot access.

The first types of content filters were systems designed to restrict access to specific Web sites, and were stand–alone software applications. These could be configured in either an exclusive manner. In an exclusive mode,, certain sites are specifically excluded. The problem with this approach is that there may be thousands of Web sites that an organization wants to exclude, and more might be added every hour. The inclusive mode works off a list of sites that are specifically permitted. In order to have a site added to the list, the user must submit a request to the content filter manager, which could be time-consuming and restrict business operations. Newer models of content filters are protocol–based, examining content as it is dynamically displayed and restricting or permitting Access based on a logical interpretation of content.

The most common content filters restrict users from accessing Web sites with obvious non-business related material, such as pornography, or deny incoming spam e-mail. Content filters can be small add-on software programs for the home or office, such as Net Nanny or surfControl, or corporate applications, such as the Novell Border manager. The benefit of implementing content filters is the assurance that employees are not distracted by non-business material and cannot waste organizational time and resources. The downside is that these systems require extensive configuration and on-going maintenance to keep the list of unacceptable destination or the source addresses for incoming restricted e-mail up-to-date. Some newer content filtering applications come with a service of downloadable files that update the database of restrictions. These applications work by matching either a list of disapproved or approved Web sites and by matching key content words, such as —nude|| and — sex||. Creators of restricted content have, of course, realized this and work to bypass the restrictions by suppressing these types of trip words, thus creating additional problems for networking and security professionals.

2.3. Protecting Remote Connections

The networks that organizations create are seldom used only by people at that location. When connections are made between one network and another, the connections are arranged and managed carefully. Installing such network connections requires using leased lines or other data channels provided by common carriers, and therefore these connections are usually permanent and secured under the requirements of a formal service agreement. But when individuals-whether they be employees from home, contract workers hired for specific assignments, or other workers who are travelling-seek to connect to an organization's network(s), a more flexible option must be provided. In the past, organization's provided these remote connections exclusively through dial-up services like Remote Authentication Service (RAS). Since the Internet has become more wide-spread in recent years, other options such as Virtual Private Networks (VPNs) have become more popular.

Dial-Up

Before the Internet emerged, organizations created private networks and allowed individuals and other organization's to connect to them using dail-up or leased line connections. The connections between company networks and the Internet use firewalls to safeguard that interface. Although connections via dial-up and leased lines are becoming less popular they are still quite common. And it si a widely held view that these unstructured, dial-up connection points represent a substantial exposure to attack. An attacker who suspects that an organization has dial-up lines can use a device called a war dialer to locate the connection points. A war-dialer is an automatic phone-dialling program that dials every number in a configured range (e.g., 555-1000 to 555-2000), and checks to see if a person , answering machine, or modem picks up. If a modem answers, the war dialer program makes a note of the number and then moves to the next target number. The attacker then attempts to hack into the network via the identified modem connection using a variety of techniques. Dial-up network connectivity is usually less sophisticated than that deployed with internet connections. For the most part, simple username and password schemes are the only means of authentication. However , some technologies such as RADIUS systems, TACAS, and CHAP password systems, have improved the authentication process, and there are even systems now that use strong encryption. Authenticating technologies such as RADIUS, TACAS, Kerberos, and SESAME are discussed below.

RADIUS and TACACS

RADIUS and TACACS are systems that authenticate the credentials of users who are trying to access an organization's network via a dial-up connection. Typical dial-up systems place the responsibility for the authentication of users on the system directly connected to the modems. If there are multiple points of entry into the dial-up system, this authentication system can become difficult to manage.

The RADIUS (Remote Authentication Dial-In User Service) System Centralizes

The management of user authentication by placing the responsibility for authenticating each user in the central RADIUS server. When a remote access server (RAS) receives a request for a network connection from a dial-up client, it passes the request along with the user's credentials to the RADIUS server. RADIUS then validates the credentials and passes the resulting decision (accept or deny) back to the accepting remote access server. Figure 6-15 shows the typical configuration of an RAS system. Similar in function to the RADIUS system is the Terminal Access Controller Access Control System (TACACS). TACACS is another remote access authorization system that is based on a client/server configuration. Like RADIUS, it contains a centralized database, and it validates the user's credentials at this TACACS server. There are three versions of TACACS: TACACS, Extended TACACS, and TACACS+. The original version combines authentication and authorization services. The extended version separates the steps needed to provide authentication of the individual or system attempting access from the steps needed to authorize that the authenticated individual or system is able to make this type of connection. The extended version then keeps records that show that the action of granting access has accountability and that the access attempt is linked to a specific individual or system. The plus version uses dynamic passwords and incorporates two-factor authentication.

Securing Authentication with Kerberos

Two authentication systems can be implemented to provide secure third-party authentication: Kerberos and Sesame. Kerberos-named after the three-headed dog of Greek mythology (spelled Cerberus in Latin), which guarded the gates to the underworld-uses symmetric key encryption to validate an individual user to various network resources.

Kerberos keeps a database containing the private keys of clients and servers-in the case of a client, this key is simply the client's encrypted password. Network services running on servers in the network register with Kerberos, as do the clients that use those services. The Kerberos system knows these private keys and can authenticate one network node (client or server) to another. For example, Kerberos can authenticate a user once-at the time the user logs in to a client computer-and then, at a later time during that session, it can authorize the user to have access to a printer without requiring the user to take any additional action. Kerberos also generates temporary session keys, which are private keys given to the two parties in a conversation. The session key is used to encrypt ali communications between these two parties. Typically a user logs into the network, is authenticated to the Kerberos system, and is then authenticated to other resources on the network by the Kerberos system itself. Kerberos consists of three interacting services, all of which use a database library:

1) Authentication server (AS), which is a Kerberos server that authenticates clients and servers.
2) Key Distribution Center (KDC), which generates and issues session keys.
3) Kerberos ticket granting service (TGS), which provides tickets to clients who request services. In Kerberos a ticket is an identification card for a particular client that verifies to the server that the client is requesting services and that the client is a valid member

of the Kerberos system and therefore authorized to receive service. The ticket consists of the client's and network address, a receive services. The ticket validation starting and ending time, and the session key, all, encrypted in the private key of the server from which the client is requesting services.

Kerberos is Based on the Following Principles

1) The KDC knows the secret keys of all clients and servers on the network.
2) The KDC initially exchanges information with the client and server by using these secret keys.
3) Kerberos authenticates a client to a requested service on a server through TGS and by issuing temporary session keys for communications between the client and KDC, the server and KDC, and the client and server.
4) Communications then take place between the client and server using these Temporary session keys.

Kerberos may be obtained free of charge from MIT at *http://web.mit.edu/is/help/*

Kerberos/, but if you use it, be aware of some fundamental problems. If the Kerberos servers are subjected to denial-of-service attacks, no client can request services. If the Kerberos servers, service providers, or clients' machines are compromised, their private key information may also be compromised.

Sesame

The Secure European System for Applications in a Multivendor Environment (SESAME) is the result of a European research and development project partly funded by the European Commission. SESAME is similar to Kerberos in that the user is first autherticated to an authentication server and receives a token. The token is then presented to a privilege attribute server (instead of a ticket granting service as in Kerberos) as proof of identity to gain a privilege attribute certificate(PAC).The PAC is like the ticketing in Kerberos; however, a PAC conforms to the standards of the European Computer Manufacturers Association (ECMA) and the International Organization for Standardization/International Telecommunications Union (ISO/ITU- T). The balances of the differences lie in the security protocols and distribution methods used. SESAME uses public key encryption to distribute secret keys.

SESAME also builds on the Kerberos model by adding additional and more sophisticated access control features, more scalable encryption systems, as well as improved manageability auditing features, and the delegation of responsibility for allowing access.

Virtual Private Network(VPNs)

Virtual Private Networks are implementations of cryptographic technology (which you learn about in Chapter 8 of this book). A Virtual Private Network (VPN) is a private and secure network connection between systems that uses the data communication capability of an unsecured and public network. The Virtual Private Network Consortium (VPN (www.vpnc.org*)* defines a VPN as "a private data network that makes use of the Public telecommunication infrastructure, maintaining privacy through the use of a tunneling protocol and security procedures. VPNs are commonly used to extend securely an organinization's internal network connections to remote locations beyond the trusted network.

The VPNC defines three VPN technologies: trusted VPNs, secure VPNs, and hybrid VPNs A trusted VPN, also known as legacy VPN, uses leased circuits from a service provider and conducts packet switching over these leased circuits. The organization must trust the service provider, who provides contractual assurance that no one else is allowed to use these circuits and that the circuits are properly maintained and protected-hence the name *trusted* VPN. Secure VPNs use security protocols and encrypt traffic transmitted across unsecured public networks like the internet. A hybrid VPN combines the two providing encrypted transmissions (as in secure VPN) over some or all of a trusted VPN network. A VPN that proposes to offer a secure and reliable capability while relying on public networks must accomplish the following, regardless of the specific technologies and protocols being used:

1) Encapsulating of incoming and outgoing data, wherein the native protocol of the client is embedded within the frames of a protocol that can be routed over the public network as well as be usable by the server network environment.

Encryption of incoming and outgoing data to keep the data contents private while in transit over the public network but usable by the client and server computers and/or the local networks on both ends of the VPN connection.
Authentication of the remote computer and, perhaps, the remote user as well.
Authentication and the subsequent authorization of the user to perform specific options are predicated on accurate and reliable identification of the remote system and/or user.

In the most common implementation, a VPN allows a user to turn the Internet in private network. As you know, the Internet is anything but private. However, using the tunneling approach an individual or organization can set up tunneling points across the Internet and send encrypted data back and forth, using the IP-packet-within-an-IP-packet method to transmit data safely and securely. VPNs are simple to set up and maintain usually require only that the tunneling points be dual-horned-that is, connecting a private network to the Internet or to another outside connection point. There is VPN support built into most Microsoft server software, including NT and 2000, as well as client support for VPN services built into XP. While true private network services connections can cost hundreds of thousands of dollars to lease, configure, and maintain, a VPN can cost next nothing. There are a number of ways to implement a VPN. IPSec, the dominant protocol used in VPNs, uses either transport mode or tunnel mode. IPSec can be used as a stand alone protocol, or coupled with the Layer 2 Tunneling Protocol (L2TP).

Transport Mode

In transport mode, the data within an IP packet is encrypted) but the header information is not. This allows the user to establish a secure link directly with the remote host, encrypting only the data contains of the packet. The downside to this implementation is that packet eavesdroppers can still determine the destination system. Once an attacker knows the destination, he or she may be able to compromise one of the end nodes and acquire the packet information from it. On the other hand, transport mode eliminates the need for special servers and tunneling software, and allows the end users to transmit traffic from anywhere. This is especially useful for traveling or telecommuting employees.

There are two popular uses for transport mode VPNs. The first is the end-to-end transport of encrypted data. In this model, two end users can communicate directly, encrypting and decrypting their communications as needed. Each machine acts as the end node VPN server and client In the second, a remote access worker or teleworker connects to an office network over the Internet by connecting to a VPN server on the perimeter. This allows the teleworker's system to work as if it were part of the local area network. The VPN server in this example acts as on intermediate node, encrypting traffic from the secure intranet and transmitting it to the remote client, and decrypting traffic from the remote client and transmitting it to its final destination. This model frequently allows the remote system to act as its own VPN server, which is a weakness, since most work-at-home employees are not provided with the same level of physical and logical security they would be if they worked in the office.

Offline

VPN vs. Dial-Up

Modern organizations can no longer afford to have their knowledge workers "chained|| to hardwired local networks and resources. The increase in broadband home services and public Wi-Fi networks has increased use of VPN technologies, enabling remote connections to the organization's network to be established from remote locations, as when, for example, employees work from home or are traveling on business trips. Road warriors can now access their corporate e-mail and local network resources from wherever they happen to be. Remote access falls into three broad categories:

1) Connections with full network access, where the remote computer acts as if it were a node on the organization's n work.
2) Feature-based connections, where users need access to specific, discrete network features like e-mail or file transfers.
3) Connections that allow remote control of a personal computer, usually in the worker's permanent office. It is the first category of connections that now use VPN instead of the traditional dial-up access based on dedicated inbound phone lines.

In the past, mobile workers used Remote Access Servers (RAS) over dial-up or ISDN leased lines to connect to company networks from remote locations (that is, when they were working from home or traveling). All things considered, RAS was probably more secure than the current practice of using a VPN, as the connection was made on a t private network. However, RAS is expensive because it depends on dedicated phone circuits specialized equipment, and aging infrastructure.

The alternative is VPN, which makes use of the public Internet. It is a solution that offers industrial-grade security. VPN today uses two different approaches to the technolgy-IPSec and Secure Sockets Layer (SSL). IPSec is more secure but is more expensive and requires more effort to administer. SSL is already available on most common Internet browsers and offers broader compatibility without requiring special software on the client computer. While SSL-based VPN has a certain attractiveness on account of its wide application cability and lower cost, it is not a perfect solution. The fact that it can be used nearly any where makes losses from user lapses and purposeful abuse more likely.

Tunnel Mode

In tunnel mode, the organization establishes two perimeter tunnel servers. These servers serve as the encryption points, encrypting all traffic that will traverse an unsecured network. In tunnel mode, the entire client packet is encrypted and added as the data of a packet addressed from one tunneling server and to another. The receiving ser decrypts the packet and sends it to the final address. The primary benefit to this model is that an intercepted packet reveals nothing about the true destination system. One example of a tunnel mode VPN is provided with Microsoft's Internet Security and Acceleration (ISA) Server. With ISA Server, an organization can establish a gateway-to-gateway tunnel, encapsulating data within the tunnel. ISA can use the Point to Point nneling Protocol (PPTP), Layer 2 Tunneling Protocol (L2TP), or Internet Securi1 Protocol (IPSec) technologies. Additional detail on these protocols is provided in Chapter 8. Figure 6-19 shows an example of tunnel mode VPN implementation. On the client end, a user with Windows 2000 or XP can establish a VPN by configuring his or her system connect to a VPN server. The process is straightforward. First, connect to the Internet through an ISP or direct network connection. Second, establish the link with the remote VPN server. Figure 6-20 shows the connection screens used to configure the VPN link. .

Questions

2a). Explain the major steps specified in BSS7799:2 document. How these steps help in security planning.

(December 2010) (10 marks)

2b). What is firewall? Show the working of screened host and dual homed firewall?

(December 2010) (10 marks)

2a). Explain the FIREWALL RULES.

(June-2012) (10 marks)

2b). What is VPN and explain the different techniques used to implement the VPN Virtual Private Network (VPNs)

(JUNE-2012) (10 marks)

2a). Explain the firewall rules.

(JUNE 2010) (10 marks)

2b). Explain the screened subnet firewall.

(JUNE 2010) (10 marks)

2a). What is firewall? Explain categories of firewalls based on processing mode.

(JUNE 2011) (10 Marks)

2b). What are virtual private networks? Explain different techniques to implement a VPN.

(JUNE 2011) (10 Marks)

2a). Explain the firewall rules.

(Dec 2011) (10 Marks)

2b). What is firewall? Show the working of screened host and dual homed firewall?

(December2011) (10 marks)

UNIT-3

SECURITY TECHNOLOGY-2

Intrusion Detection, Access Control, and Other Security Tools

Learning Objectives

Upon completion of this material, you should be able to:

1) Identify and describe the categories and operating models of intrusion detection Systems.
2) Identify and describe honey pots, honey nets, and padded cell systems.
3) List and define the major categories of scanning and analysis tools, and describe the Specific tools used within each of these categories.
4) Discuss various approaches to access control, including the use of biometric access Mechanisms.

3.1. Introduction

Chapter 6 began the discussion on the physical design of an information security program by covering firewalls, dial-up protection mechanisms, content filtering, and VPNs. This chapter builds on that discussion by describing some other technologies-namely, intrusion detection systems; honey pots, honey nets, and padded cell systems; scanning and analysis tools; and access control-that organizations can use to secure their information assets. The fact that information security is a discipline that relies on people in addition to technical controls to improve the protection of an organization's information assets cannot be overemphasized. Yet as noted in Chapter 6, technical solutions, properly implemented, can enhance the confidentiality, integrity, and availability of an organization's information assets.

In order to understand the technologies discussed in this chapter, especially intrusion detection systems, you must first understand the nature of the event they attempt to detect. An intrusion is a type of attack on information assets in which the Instigator attempts to gain entry into a system or disrupt the normal operations of a system with, almost always, the intent to do malicious harm. Even when such attacks are self propagating, as in the case of viruses and distributed denial of services, they were almost always instigated by an individual whose purpose is to, harm an organization. Often, the difference between types of intrusions lies with the attacker: some intruders don't care which organizations they harm and prefer to remain anonymous, while others, like Mafiaboy, crave the notoriety associated with breaking in.

Incident response is the identification of, classification of, response to, and recovery from an incident. The literature in the area of incident response discusses the subject in terms of prevention, detection, reaction, and correction. Intrusion prevention consists of activities that seek to deter an intrusion from occurring. Some important intrusion prevention activities are writing and implementing good enterprise information security policy, planning and performing effective information security programs, installing and testing technology-based information security countermeasures (such as firewalls and intrusion detection systems), and conducting and measuring the effectiveness of Employee training and awareness activities. (Intrusion detection consists of procedures and systems that are created and operated to detect system intrusion).

This includes the mechanisms an organization implements to limit the number of false positive alarms while ensuring the detection of true intrusion events. Intrusion reaction encompasses the actions an organization undertakes when an intrusion event is detected. These actions seek to limit the loss from an intrusion and initiate procedures for returning operations to a normal state as rapidly as possible. Intrusion correction activities finalize the restoration of operations to a normal state, and by seeking to identify the source and method of the intrusion in "order to ensure that the same type of attack cannot occur again, they return to intrusion prevention-thus closing the incident response loop.

In addition to intrusion detection systems, this chapter also covers honey pots and padded cell systems, scanning and analysis tools, and access control technologies. Honey pots and padded cell systems are mechanisms used to attempt to channel or redirect attackers whereas the intrusion detection systems record their actions and notify the system owner. In order to understand how attackers take advantage of network protocol and system weaknesses, you must learn about the specialized scanning and analysis tools they use to detect these weaknesses. The first line of defense against all attackers is an understanding of the basic access control technology built into information systems.

3.2. Intrusion Detection Systems (IDSs)

Information security intrusion detection systems (IDSs) were first commercially available in the late 1990s. An IDS works like a burglar alarm in that it detects a violation of its configuration (analogous to an opened or broken window) and activates an alarm. This alarm can be audible and/or visual (producing noise and lights, respectively), or it can be silent (taking the form of an e-mail message or pager alert).

With almost all IDSs, system administrators can choose the configuration of the various alerts and the associated alarm levels for each type of alert. Many IDSs enable administrators to configure the systems to notify them directly of trouble via e-mail or pagers. The systems can also be configured-again like a burglar alarm-to notify an external security service organization of a "break-in." The configurations that enable IDSs to provide such customized levels of detection and response are quite complex. A valuable source of information for more detailed study about IDS is National Institute of Standards and Technology (NIST) Special Publication 800-31, "Intrusion Detection Systems;' written by Rebecca Bace and Peter Mell and available through the NISI's Computer Security Resource Center at http://csrc.nist.gov.

IDS Terminology

In order to understand IDS operational behavior, you must first become familiar with some terminology that is unique to the field of IDSs. The following is a compilation of relevant IDS-related terms and definitions that were drawn from the marketing literature of a well-known information security company, TruSecure, but are representative across the industry:

Alert or Alarm: An indication that a system has just been attacked and/or continues to be under attack. IDSs create alerts of alarms to notify administrators that an attack is or was or occurring and may have been successful. Alerts and alarms may take the form of audible signals, e-mail messages, pager notifications, pop-up windows, or log entries (these are merely written, i.e., they do not involve taking any action).

False Attack Stimulus: An event that triggers alarms and causes a false positive when no actual attacks are in progress. Testing scenarios that evaluate the configuration of IDSs may use false attack stimuli to determine if the IDSs can distinguish between these stimuli and real attacks.

False Negative: The failure of an IDS system to react to an actual attack event. Of all failures, this is the most grievous, for the very purpose of an IDS is to detect attacks.

False Positive: An alarm or alert that indicates that an attack is in progress or that an attack has successfully occurred when in fact there was no such attack. A false positive alert can sometimes be produced when an IDS mistakes normal system operations/activity for an attack. False positives tend to make users insensitive to alarms, and will reduce their quickness and degree of reaction to actual intrusion events through the process of desensitization to alarms and alerts. This can make users less inclined, and therefore slow, to react when an actual intrusion occurs.

Noise: The ongoing activity from alarm events that are accurate and noteworthy but not necessarily significant as potentially successful attacks. Unsuccessful attacks are the most common source of noise in IDSs, and some of these may not even be attacks at all, but rather employees or the other users of the local network simply experimenting with scanning and enumeration tools without any intent to do harm. The issue faced regarding noise is that most of the intrusion events detected are not malicious and have no significant chance of causing a loss.

Site Policy: The rules and configuration guidelines governing the implementation and operation of IDSs within the organization.

Site Policy Awareness: An IDSs ability to dynamically modify its site policies in reaction or response to environmental activity. A so-called Smart ID can adapt its reaction activities based on both guidance learned over the time from the administrator and circumstances present in the local environment.

Using a device of this nature, the IDs administrator acquires logs of events that fit a specific profile instead of being alerted about minor changes, such as when a file is changed or a user login fails. Another advantage of using a Smart IDS is that the IDS knows when it does not need to alert the administrator-this would be the case when an attack using a known and documented exploit is made against systems that the IDS knows are patched against that specific kind of attack. When the IDS can accept multiple response profiles based on changing attack scenarios and environmental values, it can be made much more useful.

True Attack Stimulus: An event that triggers alarms and causes an IDS to react as if a real attack is in progress. The event may be an actual attack, in which an attacker is at work on a system compromise attempt, or it may be a drill, in which security personnel are using hacker tools to conduct tests of a network segment.

Confidence Value: A value associated with an IDS's ability to detect and identify an attack correctly. The confidence value an organization places in the IDS is based on experience and past performance measurements. The confidence value, which is a type of fuzzy logic, provides an additional piece of information to assist the administrator in determining whether an attack alert is indicating that an actual attack in progress, or whether the IDS is reacting to false attack stimuli and creating a false positive.

For example, if a system deemed capable of reporting a denial-of-service attack with 90% confidence sends an alert, there is a high probability that an actual attack is occurring.

Alarm Filtering: The process of classifying the attack alerts that an IDS produces in order to distinguish/sort false positives from actual attacks more efficiently. Once an \IDS has been installed and configured, the administrator can set up alarm filtering by first running the system for a while to track what types of false positives it generates and then adjusting the classification of certain alarms. For example, the administrator may set the IDS to discard certain alarms that he or she knows are produced by false attack stimuli or normal network operations. Alarm filters are similar to packet filters in that they can filter items by their source or destination IP addresses, but they have the additional capability of being able to filter by operating systems, confidence values, alarm type, or alarm severity.

Alarm Clustering: A consolidation of almost identical alarms into a single higher-level alarm. This consolidation will reduce the total number of alarms generated, thereby reducing administrative overhead, and will also indicate a relationship between the individual alarm elements.

Alarm Compaction: Alarm clustering that is based on frequency, similarity in attack signature, similarity in attack target, or other similarities. Like the previous form of alarm clustering, this will reduce the total number of alarms generated, thereby reducing administrative overhead, and will also indicate a relationship between the individual alarm elements when they have specific similar attributes.

Why Use an IDS?

According to the NIST's documentation on industry best practices, there are several compelling reasons to acquire and use an IDS:

1. To prevent problem behaviors by increasing the perceived risk of discovery and punishment for those who would attack or otherwise abuse the system.
    - To detect attacks and other security violations that are not prevented by other security measures.
    - To detect and deal with the preambles to attacks (commonly experienced as network probes and other 'doorknob rattling' activities).
    - To document the existing threat to an organization.
    - To act as quality control for security design and administration, especially of large and complex enterprises.
    - To provide useful information about intrusions that do take place, allowing improved diagnosis, recovery, and correction of causative factors.

One of the best reasons why organizations should install an IDS is that these systems can serve as straightforward deterrent measures, by increasing the fear of detection and discovery among would-be attackers. If internal and external users know that an organization has an intrusion detection system, they are less likely to probe or attempt to compromise it, just as criminals are much less likely to break into a house that has been clearly marked as having a burglar alarm.

The second reason for installing an 10S is to cover the organization when its network fails to protect itself against known vulnerabilities or is unable to respond to a rapidly changing threat environment There are many factors that can delay or undermine. An organization's ability to make its systems safe from attack and subsequent loss. For example, even though popular information security technologies such as scanning tools (to be discussed later in this chapter) allow security administrators to evaluate the readiness of their systems, they may still fail to detect or correct a known deficiency, or may perform the vulnerability-detection process too infrequently. In addition, even when vulnerability is detected in a timely manner, it cannot always be corrected quickly. Also, because such corrective measures usually involve the administrator installing patches and upgrades, they are subject to delays caused by fluctuation in the administrator's workload. To further complicate the matter, sometimes there are services that are known to be vulnerable, but they are so essential to ongoing operations that they cannot be disabled or otherwise protected in the short term. At such times-that is, when there is a known vulnerability or deficiency in the system-an IDS can be particularly effective, as it can be set up to detect attacks or attempts to exploit existing weaknesses. By, in effect, guarding these vulnerabilities, IDS can become an important part of the strategy of defense in depth.

The next reason why IDSs are useful is that they can help administrators detect the preambles to attacks. Most attacks begin with an organized and thorough probing of the organization's network environment and its defenses. This initial estimation of the defensive state of an organization's networks and systems is called doorknob rattling and is conducted first through activities collectively known as foot printing (which involves gathering information about the organization and its network activities and the subsequent process of identifying network assets), and then through another set of activities collectively known as fingerprinting (in which network locales are scanned for active systems, and then the network services offered by the host systems on that network are identified). When a system is capable of detecting the early warning signs of foot printing and fingerprinting, much as neighborhood watch volunteers might be capable of detecting potential burglars who ale casing their neighborhoods by skulking through and testing doors and windows, then the administrators may have time to prepare for a potential attack or to take actions to minimize potential losses from an attack.

A fourth reason for acquiring an IDS is documentation. In order to justify the expenses associated with implementing security technology like an IDS (and other controls such as firewalls), security professionals frequently have to make a business case. Since projects to deploy these technologies are often very expensive, almost all organizations require that project proponents document the threat from which the organization must be protected. The most frequent method used for doing this is to collect data on the attacks that are currently occurring in the organization and other similar organizations. While such data can be found in published reports or journal articles, first-hand measurements and analysis of the organization's own local network data are likely to be the most persuasive. As it happens, one means of collecting such data is by using IDS. Thus, IDSs are self-justifying systems-that is, they can serve to document the scope of the threat(s) an organization faces and thus produce data that can help administrators persuade management that additional expenditures in information security technologies (e.g., IDSs) are not only warranted, but critical for the ongoing protection of information assets. Measuring attack information with a freeware IDS tool (such as snort) may be a way to begin this process of documentation.

Another reason that supports the use of an IDS relates to the concepts of quality assurance and continuous improvement, which are both we!! known to most senior managers. In terms of quality control, IDSs support the concept of defense in depth, for they can consistently pick up information about attacks that have successfully compromised the outer layers of information security controls-that is, compromised controls such as a firewall.

This information can be used to identify and repair emergent or residual flaws in the security and network architectures, and thus help the organization expedite its incident response process and make other such continuous improvements.

A final reason for installing an IDS is that even if an IDS fails to prevent an intrusion, it can still assist in the after-attack review by helping a system administrator collect information on how the attack occurred, what the intruder accomplished, and which methods the attacker employed. This information can be used, as discussed in the preceding paragraph, to remedy deficiencies as well as trigger the improvement process to prepare the organization's network environment for future attacks. The IDS may also provide forensic information that may be useful as evidence, should the attacker be caught and criminal or civil legal proceedings pursued. In the case of handling forensic information, an organization should follow commonly accepted and legally mandated procedures for handling evidence. Foremost among these is that the information collected should be stored in a location and manner that precludes its subsequent modification. Other legal requirements and plans the organization has for the use of the data may warrant additional storage and handling constraints. As such, an organization may find it useful to consult with legal counsel when determining policy governing this situation.2

Types of IDSs and Detection Methods

IDSs operate as network-based, host-based, or application-based systems. A network-based !OS is focused on protecting network information assets. A host -based version is focused on protecting the server or host's information assets. Figure 7-1 shows an example that monitors both network connection activity and current information states on host servers. The application-based model works on one or more host systems that support a single application and is oriented to defend that specific application from special forms of attack. Regardless of whether they operate at the network, host, or application level, all IDSs use one of two detection methods: signature-based or statistical anomaly-based. Each of these approaches to intrusion detection is examined in detail in the following sections.

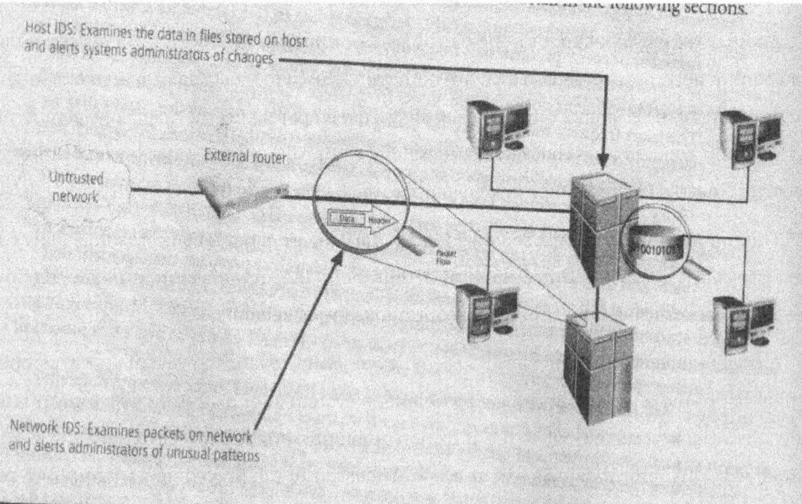

FIGURE 7-1 Intrusion Detection Systems

Network-Based IDS

A **network-based IDS (NIDS)** resides on a computer or appliance connected to a segment of an organization's network and monitors network traffic on that network segment, looking for indications of ongoing or successful attacks. When a situation occurs that the NIDS is programmed to recognize as an attack, it responds by sending notifications to administrators. When examining the packets "transmitted through an organization's networks, a NIDS looks for attack patterns within network traffic such as large collections of related items that are of a certain type, which could indicate that a denial-of service attack is underway, or the exchange of a series of related packets in a certain pattern, which could indicate that a port scan is in progress. A NIDS can detect many more types of attacks than a host-based IDS, but to do so, it requires a much more complex configuration and maintenance program.

A NIDS is installed at a specific place in the network (such as on the inside of an edge router) from where it is possible to watch the traffic going into and out of a particular network segment. The NIDS can be deployed to watch a specific grouping of host computers on a specific network segment, or it may be installed to monitor all traffic between the systems that make up an entire network. When placed next to a hub, switch, or other key networking device, the NIDS may use that device's monitoring port. The monitoring port, also known as a switched port analysis (SPAN) port or mirror port, is a specially configured connection on a network device that is capable of viewing all of the traffic that moves through the entire device. In the early '90s, before switches became the popular choice for connecting networks in a shared-collision domain, hubs were used. Hubs received traffic from one node, and retransmitted it to all other nodes. This configuration allowed any device connected to the hub to monitor all traffic passing through the hub. Unfortunately, it also represented a security risk, since anyone connected to the hub could monitor all the traffic that moved through that network segment. More recently, switches have been deployed on most networks, and they, unlike hubs, create dedicated point-to-point links between their ports. These links create a higher level of transmission security and privacy, and effectively prevent anyone from being able to capture, and thus eavesdrop on, the traffic passing through the switch. Unfortunately, however, this ability to capture the traffic is necessary for the use of an IDS. Thus, monitoring ports are required. These connections enable network administrators to collect traffic from across the network for analysis by the IDS as well as for occasional use in diagnosing network faults and measuring network performance.

Figure 7-2 shows a sample screen from Demark Pure Secure (see www.demarc.com) displaying events generated by the Snort Network IDS Engine (see www.snort.org).

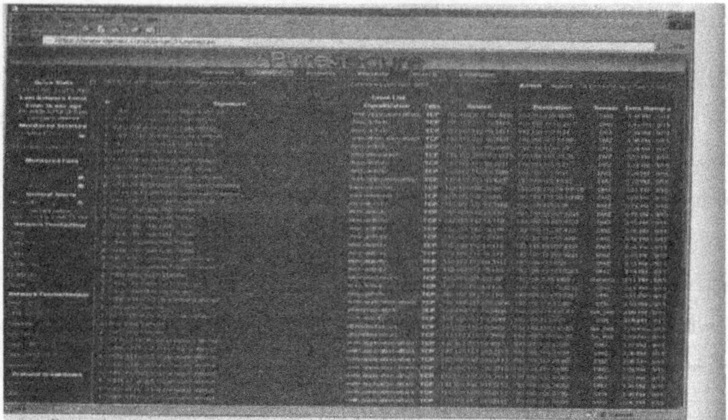

Courtesy Demarc Security, Inc.

FIGURE 7-2 Demarc Pure Secure Total Intrusion Detection

NIDS Signature Matching: To determine whether or not an attack has occurred or may be underway, NIDSs must look for attack patterns by comparing measured activity to known signatures in their knowledge base. This is accomplished by the comparison of cap turned network traffic using a special implementation of the TCP/IP stack that reassembles the packets and applies protocol stack verification, application protocol verification, and/or other verification and comparison techniques.

In the process of protocol stack verification, the NIDSs look for invalid data packets i.e., packets that are malformed under the rules of the TCPIIP protocol A data packet is verified when its configuration matches that defined by the various Internet protocols (e.g., TCP, UDP, IP). The elements of the protocols in use (IP, TCP, UDP, and application layers such as HTTP) are combined in a complete set called the protocol stack when the software is implemented in an operating system or application. Many types of intrusions, especially DoS and DDoS attacks, rely on the creation of improperly formed packets to take advantage of weaknesses in the protocol stack in certain operating systems or applications.

In application protocol verification, the higher-order protocols (e.g., HTTP, FTP, Telnet) are examined for unexpected packet behavior, or improper use. Sometimes an intrusion involves the arrival of valid protocol packets but in excessive quantities (in the case of the Tiny Fragment Packet attack, the packets are also excessively fragmented).

While the protocol stack verification looks for violations in the protocol packet structure, the application protocol verification looks for violations in the protocol packet use. One example of this kind of attack is DNS cache poisoning, in which valid packets exploit poorly configured DNS servers to inject false information to corrupt the servers' answers to routine

DNS queries from other systems on the network. Unfortunately, however, this higher-order examination of traffic can have the same effect on an IDS as it can on a firewall-that is, it slows the throughput of the system. As such, it may be necessary to have more than one NIDS installed, with one of them performing protocol stack verification and one performing application protocol verification.

Advantages and Disadvantages of NIDSs: The following is a summary, taken from Bace and Mell, of the advantages and disadvantages of NIDSs:

Advantages

1) Good network design and placement of NIDS devices can enable an organization to use a few devices to monitor a large network.
2) NIDSs are usually passive devices and can be deployed into existing networks with little or no disruption to normal network operations.
3) NIDSs are not usually susceptible to direct attack and, in fact, may not be detectable by attackers.

Disadvantages

1) A NIDS can become overwhelmed by network volume and fail to recognize attacks it might otherwise have detected. Some IDS vendors are accommodating the need for ever faster network performance by improving the processing of detection algorithms in dedicated hardware circuits to gain a performance advantage. Additional efforts to optimize rule set processing may also reduce overall effectiveness in detecting attacks.
2) NIDSs require access to all traffic to be monitored. The broad use of switched Ethernet networks has replaced the ubiquity of shared collision domain hubs. Since many switches have limited or no monitoring port capability, some networks are not capable of providing aggregate data for analysis by a NIDS. Even when switches do provide monitoring ports, they may not be able to mirror aJl activity with a consistent and reliable time sequence.
3) NIDSs cannot analyze encrypted packets, making some of the network traffic invisible to the process. The increasing use of encryption that hides the contents of some or all of the packet by some network services (such as SSL, SSH, and VPN) limits the effectiveness of NIDSs.
4) NIDSs cannot reliably ascertain if an attack was successful or not. This requires the network administrator to be engaged in an ongoing effort to evaluate the results of the lugs of suspicious network activity.

5) Some forms of attack are not easily discerned by NIDSs, specifically those involving fragmented packets. In fact, some NIDSs are particularly susceptible to malformed packets and may become unstable and stop functioning.4

Host-Based IDS

A host-based IDS (HIDS) works differently from a network-based version of IDS. While a network-based IDS resides on a network segment and monitors activities across that segment, a host-based IDS resides on a particular computer or server, known as the host, and monitors activity only on that system. HIDSs are also known as system integrity verifiers5 as they benchmark and monitor the status of key system files and detect when an intruder creates, modifies, or deletes monitored files. A HIDS is also capable of monitoring system configuration databases, such as Windows registries, in addition to stored configuration files like .ini, .cfg, and .dat files. Most HIDSs work on the principle of configuration or change management, which means they record the sizes, locations, and other attributes of system files. The HIDS then triggers an alert when one of the following changes occurs: file attributes change, new files are created, or existing files are deleted. A HIDS can also monitor systems logs for predefined events. The HIDS examines these files and logs to determine if an attack is Underway or has occurred, and if the attack is succeeding or was successful. The HIDS will maintain its own log file so that even when hackers successfully modify files on the target system to cover their tracks, the HIDS can provide an independent audit trail of the attack.

Once properly configured, a HIDS is very reliable. The only time a HIDS produces a false positive alert is when an authorized change occurs for a monitored file. This action can be quickly reviewed by an administrator and dismissed as acceptable. The administrator may choose then to disregard subsequent changes to the same set of files. If properly configured, a HIDS can also detect when an individual user attempts to modify or exceed his or her access authorization and give him or herself higher privileges.

A HIDS has an advantage over NIDS in that it can usually be installed in such a way that it can access information that is encrypted when traveling over the network. For this reason, a HIDS is able to use the content of otherwise encrypted communications to make decisions about possible or successful attacks.

Since the HIDS has a mission to detect intrusion activity on one computer system, all the traffic it needs to make that decision is coming to the system where the HIDS is running. The nature of the network packet delivery, whether switched or in a shared-collision domain, is not a factor.

A HIDS relies on the classification of files into various categories and then applies various notification actions, depending on the rules in the HIDS configuration. Most HIDSs provide only a few general levels of alert notification. For example, an administrator can configure a HIDS to treat the following types of changes as reportable security events: changes in a system folder (e.g., in C:\Windows or C:\WINNT); and changes within a security-related application (such as C:\TripWire). In other words, administrators can configure the system to alert on any changes within a critical data folder. The configuration rules may classify changes to a specific application folder (e.g., C:\Program Files\Office) as being normal, and hence unreportable. Administrators can configure the system to log all activity but to page them or e-mail them only if a reportable security event occurs. Although this change-based system seems simplistic, it seems to suit most administrators, who, in general, become concerned only if unauthorized changes occur in specific and sensitive areas of the host file system. Applications frequently modity their internal files, such as dictionaries and configuration templates, and users are constantly updating their data files. Unless a HIDS is very specifically configured, these actions can generate a large volume of false alarms.

Managed HIDSs can monitor multiple computers simultaneously. They do this by creating a configuration fiJe on each monitored host and by making each HIDS report back to a master console system, which is usually located on the system administrator's computer. This master console monitors the information provided from the managed hosts and notifies the administrator when it senseS recognizable attack conditions. Figure 7-3 provides a sample screen from Tripwire, a popular host-based IDS (see www.tripwire.com).

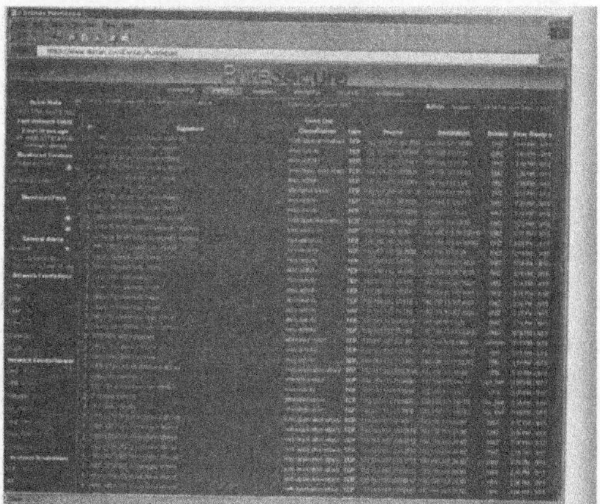

ourtesy Demarc Security, Inc.

IGURE 7-2 Demarc Pure Secure Total Intrusion Detection

In configuring a HIDS. the system administrator must begin by identifying and categorizing folders and files. One of the most common methods is to designate folders using a pattern of red, yellow, and green categories. Critical systems components are coded red, and usually include the system registry and any folders containing the OS kernel, and application software. Critically important data should also be included in the red category. Support components, such as device drivers and other relatively important files, are generally coded yellow; and user data is usually coded green. This is not to suggest that user data is unimportant, but in practical and strategic terms, monitoring changes to user data does have a lower priority. One reason for this is that users are often assigned storage space that they are expected to use routinely to maintain and back up their documents, files, and images; another reason is that user data files are expected to change frequently-that is, as users make modifications. Systems kernel files, on the other hand, should only change during upgrades or installations. Categorizing critical systems components at a different level from less important files will ensure that the level of response to change will be in proportion to the level of priority. Should the three-tier system be overly simplistic for an organization, there are systems that allow for an alternative scale of 0-100, with 100 being most mission-critical and zero being unimportant. It is not unusual, however, for these types of scales to be overly refined and result in confusion regarding, for example, the prioritization of responses to level 67 and 68 intrusions. Sometimes simpler is better.

Advantages and Disadvantages of HIDSs: The following is a summary, taken from Bace and Mell, of the advantages and disadvantages of HIDSs:

Advantages

1) A HIDS can detect local events on host systems and also detect attacks that may elude a network-based IDS.
2) A HIDS functions on the host system, where encrypted traffic will have been decrypted and is available for processing.
3) The use of switched network protocols does not affect a HIDS.
4) A HIDS can detect inconsistencies in how applications and systems programs were used by examining the records stored in audit logs. This can enable it to detect some types of attacks, including Trojan Horse programs.

Disadvantages

1) HIDSs pose more management issues since they are configured and managed on each monitored host. This means that it will require more management effort to install,

configure, and operate a HIDS than a comparably sized NIDS solution.

- A HIDS is vulnerable both to direct attacks and to attacks against the host operating system. Either circumstance can result in the compromise and/or loss of HIDS functionality.
- A HIDS is not optimized to detect multi-host scanning, nor is it able to detect the scanning of non-host network devices, such as routers or switches. Unless complex correlation analysis is provided, the HIDS will not be aware of attacks that span multiple devices in the network.
- A HIDS is susceptible to some denial-of-service attacks.
- A HIDS can use large amounts of disk space to retain the host as audit logs; and to function properly, it may require disk capacity to be added to the system.
- A HIDS can inflict a performance overhead on its host systems, and in some cases may reduce system performance below acceptable levels.7

Application-Based IDS

A refinement of the host-based IDS is the application-based IDS (App IDS). Whereas the HIDS examines a single system for file modification, the application-based IDS examines an application for abnormal events. It usually does this examination by looking at the. files created by the application and looking for anomalous occurrences such as users exceeding their authorization, invalid file executions, or other activities that would indicate that there is a problem in the normal interaction between the users, the application, and the data. By tracking the interaction between users and applications, the App IDS is able to trace specific activity back to individual users. One unique advantage of the App IDS is its ability to view encrypted data. Since the App IDS interfaces with data as it is processed by an application, and any encrypted data that enters an application is decrypted by the application itself, an App IDS does not need to become involved in the decryption process. This allows an App IDS to examine the encryption/decryption process and identity any potential anomalies in data handling or user access.

According to the Missouri State Information Infrastructure Protection Agency, "application-based IDS may be configured to intercept the following types of requests and use them in combinations and sequences to constitute an application's normal behavior:

File System (file read or write)

Network (packet events at the driver (NDIS) or transport (TDI) level) Configuration (read or write to the registry on Windows).

Execution Space (write to memory not owned by the requesting application; for example, attempts to inject a shared library DLL into another process) "8

Advantages and Disadvantages of App IDSs: The following is a summary, taken from Bace and Mell. of the advantages and disadvantages of App IDSs:

Advantages

1. An App IDS is aware of specific users and can observe the interaction between the Application and the user. This allows the App IDS to attribute unauthorized activities to specific and known users.
2. An App IDS is able to operate even when incoming data is encrypted since it is able to operate at the point in the process when the data has been decrypted by applications and has not been re-encrypted for storage.

Disadvantages

1) App IDSs may be more susceptible to attack than other IDS approaches, since applications are often less well protecte7:Ciha; network and first as components.
2) App IDSs are less capable of detecting software tampering and may be taken in by Trojan Horse code or other forms of spoofing, It is usually recommended that App IDS be used in combination with "HIDS and NIDS.9

Signature-Based IDS

The preceding sections described where the IDS system should be placed for the purpose of monitoring a network, a host, 0r an application Another important differentiation among IDSs is based on detection methods-in other words, on how the IDS should make decisions about intrusion activity. Two detection methods dominate: the signature-based approach and the statistical-anomaly approach. A signature-based IDS (sometimes called a knowledge-based IDS) examines data traffic in search of patterns that match known signatures-that is, preconfigured, predetermined attack patterns. Signature-based IDS technology is widely used because many attacks have clear and distinct signatures, for example: (I) foot printing and fingerprinting activities, described in detail earlier in this chapter, have an attack pattern that Includes the use of ICMP, DNS querying, and e-mail routing analysis; (2) exploits involve a specific attack sequence designed to take advantage of a vulnerability to gain access to a system; (3) denial-of-service (DoS) and distributed denial-of-service (DDoS) attacks, during which the attacker tries to prevent the normal usage of a system, entail overloading the system with requests so that the system's ability to process them efficiently is compromised/ disrupted and it begins denying services to authorized users.10

The problem with the signature-based approach is that as new attack strategies are identified the IDS's database of signatures must be continually updated. Failure to keep this database current can allow attacks that use new strategies to succeed. An IDS that uses signature-based methods works in ways much like most antivirus software. In fact, antivirus software is often classified as a form of signature-based IDS. This is why experts tell users that if they don't keep their antivirus software updated, it will nor work as effectively. Another weakness of the signature-based method is the time frame over which attacks occur. If attackers are purposefully slow and methodical, they may slip undetected through this type of IDS because their actions will not match those of their signatures, which often include the time allowed between steps in the attack. The only way for a signature-based IDS to resolve this vulnerability is for it to collect and analyze data over longer periods of time, a process that requires substantially larger data storage capability and additional processing capacity.

Statistical Anomaly-Based IDS

Another approach for detecting intrusions is based on the frequency with which certain network activities take place. The statistical anomaly-based IDS(stat-IDS) or behavior-based IDS collects statistical summaries by observing traffic that is known to be normal. This normal period of evaluation establishes a performance baseline. Once the baseline is established, the stat IDS will periodically sample network activity, and, using statistical methods, compare the sampled network activity to this baseline. When the measured activity is outside the baseline parameters, it is said to exceed the clipping level; at this point, the IDS will trigger an alert to notify the administrator. The data that is measured from the normal traffic used to prepare the baseline can include variables such as host memory or CPU usage, network packet types, and packet quantities. The measured activity is considered to be outside the baseline parameters (and thus will trigger an alert) when there is an anomaly, or inconsistency, in the comparison of these variables.

The advantage of the statistical anomaly-based approach is that the IDS can detect new types of attacks, for it is looking for abnormal activity of any type. Unfortunately, however, these systems require much more overhead and processing capacity than signature-based ones, as they must constantly compare patterns of activity against the baseline. Another drawback is that these systems may not detect minor changes to system variables and may generate many false positives. If the actions of the users or systems on a network vary widely, with periods of low activity interspersed with periods of frantic packet exchange, this type of IDS may not be suitable, because the dramatic swings from one level to another will almost certainly generate false alarms, Because of its complexity and impact on the overhead computing load of the host computer as well as the number of false positives it can generate, this type of IDS is less commonly used than the signature-based type.

Log File Monitors

A log file monitor (LFM) is an approach to IDS that is similar to the NIDS. Using LFM, the system reviews the log files generated by servers, network devices, and even other IDSs. These systems look for patterns and signature in the log files that may indicate that an attack or intrusion is in process or has already succeeded. While an individual host IDS is only able to look at the activity in one system, the LFM is able to look at multiple log files from a number of different systems, The patterns that signify an attack can be subtle and hard to distinguish when one system is examined in isolation, but they may be much easier to identify when the entire network and its systems are viewed holistically. Of course this holistic approach will require the allocation of considerable resources since it will involve the collection, movement, storage, and analysis of very large quantities of log data.

IDS Response Behavior

Each IDS will respond to external stimulation in different ways, depending on its configuration and function. Some may respond in active ways, collecting additional information about the intrusion, modifying the network environment, or even taking action against the intrusion. Others may respond in positive ways, setting off alarms or notifications, collecting passive data through SNMP traps, and the like.

Response Options for an IDS

Once an IDS detects an anomalous network situation, it has a number of options, depending on the policy and objectives of the organization that has configured it as well as the capabilities of the organization's system, In configuring an IDS's responses to alerts, the system administrator must exercise care to ensure that a response to an attack (or potential attack) does not compound the problem or create a situation that is more disastrous than that of a successful attack. For example, if a NIDS reacts to a suspected DoS attack by severing the network connection, the NIDS has just accomplished what the attacker had hoped. If the attacker discovers that this is the default response to a particular kind of attack, all he or she has to do is repeatedly attack the system at intervals in order to have the organization's own IDS response interrupt its normal business operations. An analogy to this approach would be the case of a potential car thief who walks up to a desirable target in the early hours of a morning, strikes the car's bumper with a rolled up newspaper, and then ducks into the bushes.

When the car alarm is triggered, the car owner wakes up, checks the car, determines there is no danger, resets the alarm, and goes back to bed. The thief then repeats the triggering actions every half hour or so until the owner gets so frustrated that he or she disables the alarm, believing it to be malfunctioning. The thief is now free to steal the car without worrying about triggering the alarm.

IDS responses can be classified as active or passive. An active response is one in which a definitive action is initiated when certain types of alerts are triggered. These automated responses include collecting additional information, changing or modifying the environment, and taking action against the intruders. In contrast, IDSs with passive response options simply report the information they have already collected and wait for the administrator to take actions. Generally, the administrator chooses a course of action after he or she has analyzed the collected data, and thus with passive-response IDSs, the administrator becomes the active component of the overall system. The latter is currently the most common implementation, although most systems allow some active options that are kept disabled by default.

The following list illustrates some of the responses an IDS can be configured to produce. Note that some of these are unique to a network-based or a host-based IDS, while others are applicable to both[11].

Audible/visual alarm: The IDS can trigger a .wav file, beep, whistle, siren, or other audible or visual notification to alert the administrator of an attack. The most common type of such notifications is the computer pop-up window. This display can be configured with color indicators and specific messages, and it can also contain specifics as to what type of attack is suspected, the tools used in the attack, the level of confidence the system has in its own determination, and the addresses and/or locations of the systems involved.

1) SNMP traps and Plug-ins: The Simple Network Management Protocol contains trap functions, which allow a device to send a message to the SNMP management console to indicate that a certain threshold has been crossed, either positively or negatively. The IDS can execute this trap, telling the SNMP console an event has occurred. Some of the advantages of this operation include the relatively standard implementation of SNMP in networking devices, the ability to configure the network system to use SNMP traps in this manner, the ability to use systems specifically to handle SNMP traffic, including IDS traps, and the ability to use standard communications networks.
2) E-mail message: The IDS can e-mail an individual to notify him or her of an event. Many administrators use personal digital assistants (PDAs) to check their e-mail frequently,

thus have access to immediate global notification. Organizations should use caution in relying on e-mail systems as the primary means of communication between the IDS and security personnel, for not only is e-mail inherently fraught with reliability issues, but an intruder may compromise the e-mail system and block the sending of any such notification messages.

3) Page or phone message: The IDS can be configured to dial a phone number, producing either an alphanumeric page or a modem noise on a phone call.
4) Log entry: The IDS can enter information about the event (e.g., addresses, time, systems involved, protocol information, etc.) into an IDS system log file, or operating system log file. These files can be stored on separate servers to prevent skilled attackers from deleting entries about their intrusions and thus hiding the details of their attack.
5) Evidentiary packet dump: Those organizations that have a need for legal uses of the IDS Data may choose to record all log data in a special way. This method will allow the organization to perform further analysis on the data and also submit the data as evidence in a future civil or criminal case. Once the data has been written using a cryptographic hashing algorithm (discussed in detail in Chapter 8), it becomes evidentiary documentation-that is, suitable for criminal or civil court use. This packet logging can, however, be resource-intensive, especially in denial-of-service attacks.

Take action against the intruder: It has become possible, although not advisable, to take action against an intruder. Known as trap and trace, hack-hacking, or traceback, this response option involves configuring intrusion detection systems to conduct a trace on the data leaving the attacked site and heading to the systems instigating the attacks. The idea here is that once these attacking systems are identified, some form of counterattack can be initiated. While this sounds tempting, it is ill advised and may not be legal. An organization only owns a network to its perimeter, and conducting traces or back-hacking to systems outside that perimeter may make the organization just as criminally liable as the individual(s) who began the attack. In addition, it is not uncommon for an attacker to compromise an intermediary system and use that system to conduct the attack. If an organization attempts a back-hack and winds up damaging or destroying data on the intermediary system, it has, in effect, attacked an innocent third party, and will therefore be regarded, in the eyes of that party, as an attacker. The matter can be further complicated if the hacker has used address spoofing, a means by which the attacker can freely change the address headers on the source fields in the IP headers and make the destination address recipients think the packets are coming from one location, when in reality they are coming from somewhere else. Any organization planning to configure any sort of retaliation effort into an automated intrusion detection system is strongly encouraged to seek legal counsel.

Launch program: An IDS can be configured to execute a specific program when it detects specific types of attacks. A number of vendors have specialized tracking, tracing, and response software that could be part of an organization's intrusion response strategy.

Reconfigure firewall: An IDS could send a command to the firewall to filter out suspected packets by IP address, port, or protocol. (It is, unfortunately, still possible for a skilled attacker to break in by simply spoofing a different address, shifting to a different port, or changing the protocols used in the attack.) While it may not be easy, an IDS can block or deter intrusions by one of the following methods:

1) Establishing a block for all traffic from the suspected attacker's IP address, or even from the entire source network from which the attacker appears to be operating. This blocking might be set for a specific period of time and be reset to normal rules after that period has expired.
2) Establishing a block for specific TCP or UDP port traffic from the suspected attacker's address or source network, blocking only the services that seem to be under attack.
3) Blocking all traffic to or from a network interface (such as the organization's Internet connection) if the severity of the suspected attack warrants that level of response. Terminate session: Terminating the session by using the TCP/IP protocol specified packet TCP close is a simple process. Some attacks would be deterred or blocked by session termination, but others would simply continue when the attacker issues a new session request. Terminate connection: The last resort for an IDS under attack would be to terminate the organization's internal or external connections. Smart switches can cut traffic to/from a specific port, should that connection be linked to a system that is malfunctioning or otherwise interfering protect information, as it may be the very goal of the attacker.

[The following sections are drawn from NIST SP 800-31 "Intrusion Detection Systems"]

Reporting and Archiving Capabilities

Many, if not all, commercial IDSs provide capabilities to generate routine reports and other detailed information documents. Some of these can output reports of system events and intrusions detected over a particular reporting period (for example, a week or a month). Some provide statistics or logs generated by the IDSs in formats suitable for inclusion in database systems or for use in report generating packages.

Failsafe Considerations for IDS Responses

Another factor for consideration when considering IDS architectures and products is the failsafe features included by the design and/or product. Failsafe features are those design features meant to protect the IDSs from being circumvented or defeated by an attacker. These represent a necessary difference between standard system management tools and security management tools. There are several areas that require failsafe measures. For instance, IDSs need to provide silent, reliable monitoring of attackers. Should the response function of an IDS break this silence by broadcasting alarms and alerts in plaintext over the monitored network, it would allow attackers to detect the-presence of the IDS. Worse yet, the attackers can directly target the IDS as part of the attack on the victim system. Encrypted tunnels or other cryptographic measures used to hide and authenticate IDS communications are excellent ways to secure and ensure the reliability of the IDS.

Electing IDS Approaches and Products

The wide array of intrusion detection products available today addresses a broad range of organizational security goals and considerations. Given that range of products and features, the process of selecting products that represent the best fit for any specific organization's needs is challenging. The following questions may be useful when preparing a specification for acquiring and deploying an intrusion detection product.

Technical and Policy Considerations

In order to determine which IDS would best meet the needs of a specific organization's environment, first consider that environment, in technical, physical, and political terms.

What Is Your Systems Environment? The first hurdle a potential IDS must clear is that of functioning in your systems environment. This is important, for if an IDS is not designed to accommodate the information sources that are available on your systems, it will not be able to see anything that goes on in your systems, whether that activity is an attack or it is normal

activity.

What are the technical specifications of your systems environment?

First, specify the technical attributes of your systems environment. Examples of information specified here would include network diagrams and maps specifying the number and locations of hosts; operating systems for each host; the number and types of network devices such as routers, bridges, and switches; number and types of terminal servers and dial-up connections; and descriptors of any network servers, including types, configurations, and application software and versions running on each. If you run an enterprise network management system, specify it here.

What are the Technical Specifications of Your Current Security Protections?

Once you have described the technical attributes of your systems environment, describe the security protections you already have in place. Specify numbers, types, and locations of network firewalls, identification and authentication servers, data and link encryptors, antivirus packages, access control products, specialized security hardware (such as crypto accelerator hardware for Web servers), Virtual Private Networks, and any other security mechanisms on your systems.

What are the Goals of Your Enterprise?

Some IDSs have been developed to accommodate the special needs of certain industries or market niches such as electronic commerce, health care, or financial markets. Define the functional goals of your enterprise (there can be several goals associated with a single organization) that are supported by your systems.

1) How formal is the system environment and management culture in your organization? Organizational styles vary, depending on the function of the organization and its traditional culture. For instance, military or other organizations that deal with national security issues tend to operate with a high degree of formality, especially when contrasted with university or other academic environments. Some IDSs offer features that support enforcement of formal use policies, with configuration screens that accept formal expressions of policy, and extensive reporting capabilities that do detailed reporting of policy violations.

What are Your Security Goals and Objectives?

Once you've specified the technical landscape of your organization's systems as well as the existing security mechanisms, it's time to articulate the goals and objectives you wish to attain by using an IDS.

1) Is the primary concern of your organization protecting from threats originating outside your organization?
2) Perhaps the easiest way to specify security goals is by categorizing your organization's threat concerns. Identify the concerns that your organization has regarding threats that originate outside the organization.

Is your organization concerned about insider attack?

Repeat the last step, this time addressing concerns about threats that originate from within your organization, encompassing not only the user who attacks the system from within (such as a shipping clerk who attempts to access and alter the payroll system) but also the authorized user who oversteps his privileges thereby violating organizational security policy or laws (a customer service agent who, driven by curiosity, accesses earnings and payroll records for public figures).

Does your organization want to use the output of your IDS to determine new needs?

System usage monitoring is sometimes provided as a generic system management tool to determine when system assets require upgrading or replacement. When such monitoring is performed by an IDS, the needs for upgrade can show up as anomalous levels of user activity.

Does your organization want to use an IDS to maintain managerial control (non-security related) over network usage?

In some organizations, there are system use policies that target user behaviors that may be classified as personnel management rather than system security issues. These might include accessing Web sites that provide content of questionable taste or value (such as pornography) or using organizational systems to send e-mail or other messages for the purpose of harassing individuals. Some IDSs provide features that accommodate detecting such violations of management controls.

What Is Your Existing Security Policy?

At this time, you should review your existing organization security policy. This will serve as the template against which features of your IDS will be configured. As such, you may find you need to augment the policy, or else derive the following items from it.

How is it structured?

It is helpful to articulate the goals outlined in the security policy in terms of the standard security goals (integrity, confidentiality, and availability) as well as more generic management goals (privacy, protection from liability, manageability).

What are the general job descriptions of your system users?

List the general job functions of system users (there are commonly several functions assigned to a single user) as well as the data and network accesses that each function requires.

Does the policy include reasonable use policies or other management provisions? As mentioned above, many organizations have system use policies included as part of security policies.

Has your Organization Defined Processes for Dealing with Specific Policy Violations?

It is helpful to have a clear idea of what the organization wishes to do when the IDS detects that a policy has been violated. If the organization doesn't intend to react to such violations, it may not make sense to configure the IDS to detect them. If, on the other hand, the organization wishes to actively respond to such violations, the IDS's operational staff should be informed of the organization's response policy so that they can deal with alarms in an appropriate manner.

Organizational Requirements and Constraints

Your organization's operational goals, constraints, and culture will affect the selection of the IDS and other security tools and technologies to protect your systems. Consider these organizational requirements and limitations.

What Are Requirements that Are Levied from Outside the Organization?

Is your organization subject to oversight or review by another organization? If so, does that oversight authority require IDSs or other specific system security resources?

Are there requirements for public access to information on your organization's systems? Do regulations or statutes require that information on your system be accessible by the public during certain hours of the day, or during certain date or time intervals?

Are there other security-specific requirements levied by law? Are there legal requirements for protection of personal information (such as earnings information or medical records) stored on your systems? Are there legal requirements for investigation of security violations that divulge or endanger that information?

Are there internal audit requirements for security best practices or due diligence? Do any of these audit requirements specify functions that the IDSs must provide or support?

Is the system subject to accreditation? If so, what is the accreditation authority's requirement for IDSs or other security protection?

Are there requirements for law enforcement investigation and resolution of security incidents? Do these specify any IDS functions, especially those having to do with collection and protection of IDS logs as evidence?

What Are Your Organization's Resource Constraints?

IDSs can protect 'the systems of an organization, but at a price. It makes little sense to incur additional expense for IDS features if your organization does not have sufficient systems or personnel to use them and take advantage of the alerts generated by the system.

What is the budget for acquisition and life cycle support of intrusion detection hardware, software, and infrastructure? Remember here that the acquisition of IDS software is not the only element that counts toward the total cost of ownership; you may also have to acquire a system on which to run the software, specialized assistance in installing and configuring the system, and training your personnel. Ongoing operations may also require additional staff or outside contractors.

Is there sufficient existing staff to monitor an intrusion detection system full time? Some lDSs are designed under the assumption that systems personnel will attend them around the clock. If you do not anticipate having such personnel available, you may wish to explore those systems that accommodate less than full-time attendance or else consider systems that are designed for unattended use.

Does your organization have authority to instigate changes based on the findings of an intrusion detection system? It is critical that you and your organization be clear about what you plan to do with the problems uncovered by an IDS. If you are not empowered to handle the incidents that arise as a result of the monitoring, you should consider coordinating your selection and configuration of the IDS with the party who is empowered.

lDSs Product Features and Quality

Is the Product Sufficiently Scalable for Your Environment? As mentioned before in this document, many IDSs are not able to scale to large or widely distributed enterprise network environments.

How Has the Product Been Tested?

Simply asserting that an IDS has certain capabilities is not sufficient to demonstrate that those capabilities are real. You should request additional demonstration of the suitability of a particular IDS to your environment and goals.

Has the product been tested against functional requirements? Ask the vendor about the assumptions made regarding the goals and constraints of customer environments. Has the product been tested against attack? Ask vendors for details of the security testing to which its products have been subjected. If the product includes network-based vulnerability assessment features, ask also whether test routines that produce system crashes or other denials of service have been identified and flagged in system documentation and interfaces.

What Is the User Level of Expertise Targeted by the Product?

Different IDS vendors target users with different levels of technical and security expertise. Ask the vendor what their assumptions are regarding the users of their products.

Is the Product Designed to Evolve as the Organization Grows?

One product design goal that will enhance its value to your organization over time is the ability to adapt to your needs over time.

Can the product adapt to growth in user expertise? Ask here whether the IDS's interface can be configured (with shortcut keys, customizable alarm features, and custom signatures) on the fly. Ask also whether these features are documented and supported. Can the product adapt to growth and change of the organization's systems infrastructure? This question has to do with the ability of the IDS to scale to an expanding and increasingly diverse network. Most vendors have experience in adapting their products as target networks grow. Ask also about commitments to support new protocol standards and platform types.

Can the product adapt to growth and change of the security threat environment? This question is especially critical given the current Internet threat environment, in which 30-40 new attacks are posted to the Web every month.

What Are the Support Provisions for the Product? Like other systems, IDSs require maintenance and support over time. These needs should be identified and prepared in a written report.

What are commitments for product installation and configuration support? Many vendors provide expert assistance to customers in installing and configuring IDSs; others expect that your own staff will handle these functions, and provide only telephone or e-mail help desk functions.

1) What are commitments for ongoing product support? In this area, ask about the vendor's commitment to supporting your use of their IDS product.
2) Are subscriptions to signature updates included? As most IDSs are misuse-detectors, the value of the product is only as good as the signature database against which events are analyzed. Most vendors provide subscriptions to signature updates for some period of time (a year is typical).
   - How often are subscriptions updated? In today's threat environment, in which 30-

40 new attacks are published every month, this is a critical question.

- How quickly after a new attack is made public will the vendor ship a new signature? If *you* are using IDSs to protect highly visible or heavily traveled Internet sites, it is especially critical that you receive the signatures for new attacks as soon as possible. Are software updates included? Most IDSs are software products and therefore subject to bugs and revisions. Ask the vendor about software update and bug patch support, and determine to what extent they are included in the product you purchase.
- How quickly will software updates and patches be issued after a problem is reported to the vendor? As software bugs in IDSs can allow attackers to nullify their protective effect, it is extremely important that problems be fixed, reliably and quickly.
- Are technical support services included? What is the cost? In this category, technical support services mean vendor assistance in tuning or adapting your IDS to accommodate special needs, be they monitoring a custom or legacy system within your enterprise, or reporting IDS results in a custom protocol or format
- What are the contact provisions for contacting technical support (e-mail, telephone, online chat, web-based reporting)? The contact provisions will *likely* tell you whether these technical support services arc accessible enough to support incident handling or other time-sensitive needs.
- Are there any guarantees associated with the IDS? As in other software products, IDSs traditionally have few guarantees associated with them; however, in an attempt to gain market share, some vendors are initiating guarantee programs.

3) What training resources does the vendor provide as part of the product? Once an IDS is selected, installed, and configured, it must still be operated by your personnel. In order for these people to make optimal use of the IDS, they should be trained in its use. Some vendors provide this training as part of the product package.

4) What additional training resources are available from the vendor and at what cost? In the case that the IDS's vendor does not provide training as part of the IDS package, you should budget appropriately to train your operational personnel.

Strengths and Limitations of IDSs

Although intrusion detection systems are a valuable addition to an organization's security infrastructure, there are things they do well, and other things they do not do well. As you plan the security strategy for your organization's systems, it is important for you to understand what IDSs should be trusted to do and what goals might be better served by other types of security mechanisms.

Strengths of Intrusion Detection Systems

Intrusion detection systems perform the following functions well:

- Monitoring and analysis of system events and user behaviors.
- Testing the security states of system configurations.

Baselining the security state of a system, then tracking any changes to that baseline.

Recognizing patterns of system events that correspond to known attacks.

Recognizing patterns of activity that statistically vary from normal activity.

Managing operating system audit and logging mechanisms and the data they generate.

Alerting appropriate staff by appropriate means when attacks are detected.

Measuring enforcement of security policies encoded in the analysis engine.

Providing default information security policies.

Allowing non-security experts to perform important security monitoring functions.

Limitations of Intrusion Detection Systems

Intrusion detection systems cannot perform the following functions:

1) Compensating for weak or missing security mechanisms in the protection infrastructure.

   Such mechanisms include firewalls, identification and authentication, link encryption, access control mechanisms, and virus detection and eradication.
2) Instantaneously detecting, reporting, and responding to an attack, when there is a heavy network or processing load.
3) Detecting newly published attacks or variants of existing attacks.
4) Effectively responding to attacks launched by sophisticated attackers.
5) Automatically investigating attacks without human intervention.
6) Resisting attacks that are intended to defeat or circumvent them.
7) Compensating for problems with the fidelity of information sources.
8) Dealing effectively with switched networks.

{The preceding sections were drawn from NIST SP 800-31 "Intrusion Detection Systems"]

Deployment and Implementation of an IDS

Deploying and implementing an IDS is not always a straightforward task. The strategy for deploying an IDS should consider a number of factors, the foremost being how the IDS will be managed and where it should be placed. These factors will determine the number of administrators needed to install, configure, and monitor the IDS, as well as the number of management workstations, the size of the storage needed for retention of the data generated by the systems, and the ability of the organization to detect and respond to remote threats.

IDS Control Strategies

An IDS can be implemented via one of three basic control strategies. A control strategy determines how an organization exerts influence and maintains the configuration of an IDS. It will also determine how the input and output of the IDS is to be managed. The three commonly utilized control strategies are centralized, partially distributed, and fully distributed. The IT industry has been exploring technologies and practices to enable the distribution of computer processing cycles and data storage for many years. These explorations have long considered the advantages and disadvantages of the centralized strategy versus those of strategies with varying degrees of distribution. In the early days of computing, all systems were fully centralized, resulting in a control strategy that provided high levels of security and control, as well as efficiencies in resource allocation and management. During the '80s and '90s, with the rapid growth in networking and computing capabilities, the IT industry's ideas about how to arrange computing systems swung to the other end of the pendulum-that is, the trend was to implement a fully distributed strategy. In the mid- '90s, however, the high costs of a fully distribute architecture became apparent, and the IT industry shifted toward a mixed strategy of partially distributed control. A strategy of partial distribution, where some features and components are distributed and others are centrally controlled, has now emerged as the recognized recommended practice for IT systems in general and for IDS control systems in particular.

Centralized Control Strategy: As Illustrated in Figure 7-4, with a centralized IDS control strategy all IDS control functions are implemented and managed in a central location. This is indicated, in the figure with the large square symbol labeled "IDS Console." The IDS console includes the management software; which collects information from the remote sensors (appearing in the figure as triangular symbols), analyzes the systems or networks monitored, and makes the determination as to whether the current situation has deviated from the preconfigured baseline. All reporting features are also implemented and managed from this central location. The primary advantages of this strategy are related to cost and control. With" one central implementation, there is one management system, one place to go to monitor the status of the systems or networks, one location for reports, and one set of administrative management. This centralization of IDS management supports specialization in tasks, since all managers are either located near the IDS management console or can acquire an authenticated remote connection to it, and technicians are located near the remote sensors. This means that each person can focus specifically on the assigned task at hand. In addition, the central control group can evaluate the systems and networks as a whole, and since it can compare pieces of information from all sensors, the group is better positioned to recognize a large-scale attack.

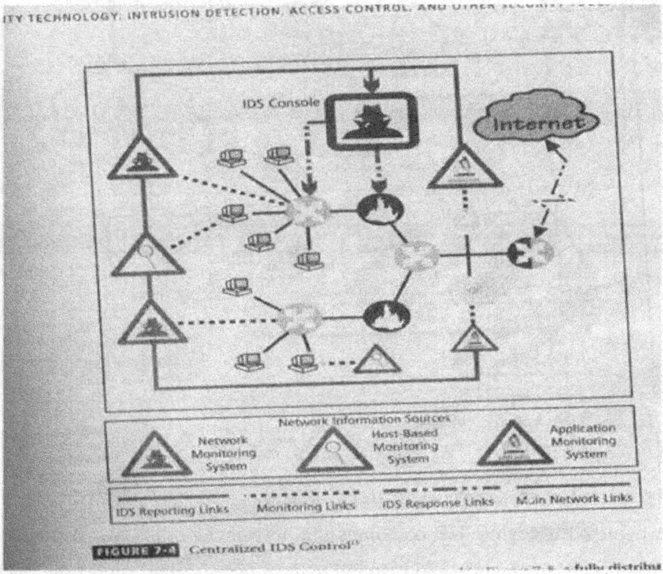

FIGURE 7-4 Centralized IDS Control

Fully Distributed Control Strategy. As presented in Figure 7-5, a **fully distributed IDS control strategy** is the opposite of the centralized strategy. Note in the figure that all control functions (which appear as small square symbols enclosing a computer icon) are applied at the physical location of each IDS component. Each monitoring site uses its own paired sensors to perform its own control functions to achieve the necessary detection, reaction, and response functions. Thus, each sensor/agent is best configured to deal with its own environment. Since the IDSs do not have to wait for a response from a centralized control facility, their reaction to individual attacks is greatly speeded up.

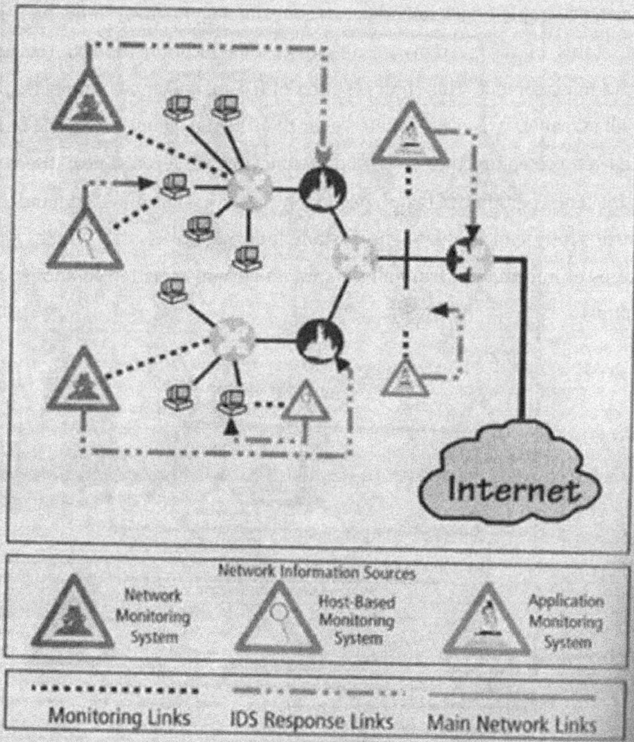

FIGURE 7-5 Fully Distributed IDS Control[11]

Partially Distributed Control Strategy. Finally, a partially distributed IDS control strategy, as depicted in Figure 7-6, combines the best of the other two strategies. While the individual agents can still analyze and respond to local threats, their reporting to a hierarchical central facility enables the organization to detect widespread attacks. This blended approach to reporting is one of the more effective methods of detecting intelligent attackers, especially those who probe an organization through multiple points of entry, trying to scope out the systems' configurations and weaknesses, before they launch a concerted attack. The partially distributed control strategy also allows the organization to optimize for economy of scale in the implementation of key management software and personnel, especially in the reporting areas. When the organization can create a pool of security managers to evaluate reports from multiple distributed IDS systems, it becomes better able to detect these distributed attacks before they become unmanageable.

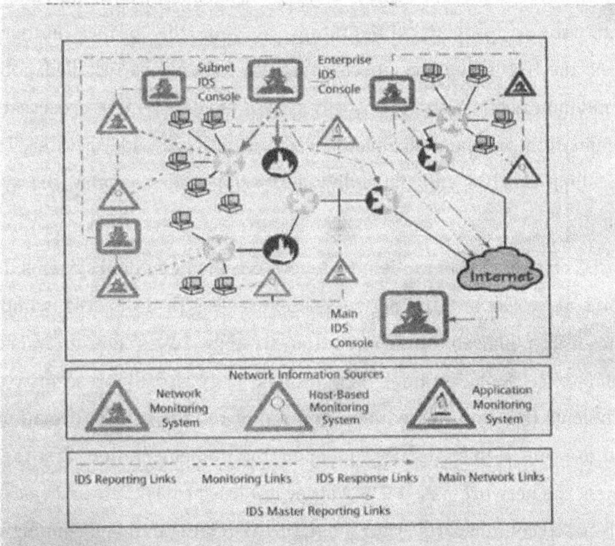

FIGURE 7-6 Partially Distributed IDS Control[1]

IDS Deployment Overview

Like the decision regarding control strategies, the decisions about where to locate the elements of the intrusion detection systems can be an art in itself. Given the highly technical skills required to implement and configure IDSs and the imperfection of the technology, great care must be made in the decisions about where to locate the components, both in their physical connection to the network and host devices and in how they will be logically connected to each other and the IDS administration team. Since IDSs are designed to detect, report, and even react to anomalous stimuli, placing IDSs in an area where such traffic is common can result in excessive reporting. Moreover, the administrators monitoring systems located in such areas can become desensitized to the high level of information flow and may fail to detect actual attacks in progress.

As an organization selects an IDS and prepares for implementation, planners must select a deployment strategy that is based on a careful analysis of the organization's information security requirements and that integrates with the organization's existing IT infrastructure but, at the same time, causes minimal impact. After all, the purpose of the IDS is to detect anomalous situations-not create them. One consideration for implementation is the skill level of the personnel required to install, configure, and maintain the systems. An IDS is a complex system in that it involves numerous remote monitoring agents (on both individual systems and networks) that require proper configuration to gain the proper authentication and authorization. As the IDS is deployed, each component should be installed, configured, fine-tuned, tested, and monitored. A problem in any step of the deployment process may produce a range of problems-from a minor inconvenience to a network-wide disaster. Thus, both the individuals installing the IDS and the individuals using and managing the system require proper training.

NIDS and HIDS can be used in tandem to cover both the individual systems that connect to an organization's networks and the networks themselves. To do this, it is important for an organization to use a phased implementation strategy so as not to impact the entire organization all at once. A phased implementation strategy also allows security technicians to resolve the problems that do arise without compromising the very information security the IDS is installed to protect. In terms of sequencing the implementation, first the organization should implement the network-based IDS, as they are less problematic and easier to configure than their host -based counterparts. After the NIDSs are configured and running without issue, the HIDSs can be installed to protect the critical systems on the host server. Next, after both are considered operational, it would be advantageous to scan the network with a vulnerability scanner like Nmap or Nessus to determine if a) the scanners pick up anything new or unusual, and b) if the IDS can detect the scans.

Deploying Network-Based IDSs. As discussed above, the placement of the sensor agents is critical to the operation of all IDSs, but this is especially critical in the case of Network IDSs. NIST recommends four locations for NIDS sensors:

Location 1: Behind each external firewall, in the network DMZ (See Figure 7-7, location 1)

Advantages

IDS sees attacks that originate from the outside world and may penetrate the network's perimeter defenses.

1) IDS can identify problems with the network firewall policy or performance.
2) IDS sees attacks that might target the Web server or fip server, both of which commonly reside in this DMZ.

Even if the incoming attack is not detected, the IDS can sometimes recognize, in the outgoing traffic, patterns that suggest that the server has been compromised.

Location 2: Outside an external firewall (See Figure 7-7, location 2)

Advantages:

1) IDS documents the number of attacks originating on the Internet that target the network.
2) IDS documents the types of attacks originating on the Internet that target the network.

Location 3: On major network backbones (See Figure 7-7, location 3)

Advantages

1) IDS monitors a large amount of a network's traffic, thus increasing its chances of spotting attacks.
2) IDS detects unauthorized activity by authorized users within the organization's security perimeter.

Location: On critical subnets (See Figure 7-7, location 4)

Advantages

1) IDS detects attacks targeting critical systems and resources.
2) Location allows organizations with limited resources to focus these resources on the network assets considered of greatest value[16].

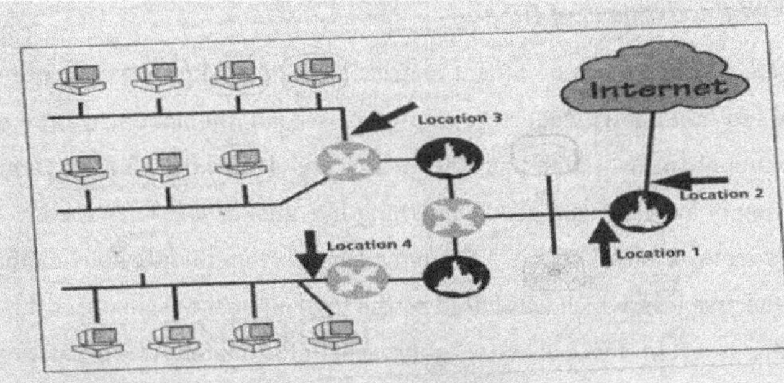

FIGURE 7-7 Network IDS Sensor Locations''

Deploying Host-Based IDSs. The proper implementation of HIDSs can be a painstaking and time-consuming task, as each HIDS must be custom configured to its host systems. Deployment begins with implementing the most critical systems first This poses a dilemma for the deployment team, since the first systems to be implemented are mission-critical and any problems in the installation could be catastrophic to the organization. As such, it may be beneficial to practice an implementation on one or more test servers configured on a network segment that resembles the mission-critical systems. Practicing will help the installation team gain experience and also help determine if the installation might trigger any unusual events. Gaining an edge on the learning curve by training on non-production systems will benefit the overall deployment process by reducing the risk of unforeseen complications.

Installation continues until either all systems are installed, or the organization reaches the planned degree of coverage it is willing to live with, with regard to the number of systems or percentage of network traffic. Lastly, to provide ease of management, control, and reporting, each HIDS should, as discussed earlier, be configured to interact with a central management console.

Just as technicians can install the HIDS in off-line systems to develop expertise and identify potential problems, users and managers can gain expertise and understanding of the operation of the HIDS by using a test facility. This test facility could use the off-line systems configured by the technicians, but also be connected to the organization's backbone to allow the HIDS to process actual network traffic. This setup Will also enable technicians to create a baseline of normal traffic for the organization. During the system testing process, training scenarios can be developed that will enable users to recognize and respond to common attack situations. Finally, to ensure effective and efficient operation, the management team can establish policy for the operation and monitoring of the HIDS.

Measuring the Effectiveness of IDSs

IDSs are evaluated using two dominant metrics: first, administrators evaluate the number of attacks detected in a known collection of probes; second, the administrators examine the level of use, commonly measured in megabits per second of network traffic, at which the IDSs fail. An evaluation of an IDS might read something like this: *at]00 Mb/s, the* IDS *was able* to *detect* 97% *of directed attacks.* This is a dramatic change from the previous method used for assessing IDS effectiveness, which was based on the total number of signatures the system was currently running-a sort of "more is better" approach. Unfortunately, this evaluation method of assessment was flawed for several reasons. Not all IDSs use simple signature-based detection. Some systems, as discussed earlier, can use the almost infinite combination of network performance characteristics of statistical-anomaly-based detection to detect a potential attack. Also, some more sophisticated signature-based systems actually use *fewer* signatures/rules than older, simpler versions-which, in direct contrast to the signature-based assessment method, suggests that less may actually be more. The recognition that the size of the signature base is an insufficient measure of an IDS' effectiveness led to the development of stress test measurements for evaluating IDS performance. These only work, however, if the administrator has a collection of known negative and positive actions that can be proven to elicit a desired response. Since developing this collection can be tedious, most IDS vendors provide testing mechanisms that verify that their systems are performing as expected. Some of these testing processes will enable the administrator to:

1) Record and retransmit packets from a real virus or worm scan.
2) Record and retransmit packets from a real virus or worm scan with incomplete TCP/IP session connections (missing SYN packets).
3) Conduct a real virus or worm scan against an invulnerable system.

This last measure is important, since future IDSs will probably include much more detailed information about the overall site configuration. According to experts in the field, "it may be necessary for the IDSs to be able to actively probe a potentially vulnerable machine, in order to either pre-load its configuration with correct information, or perform a retroactive assessment An IDS that performed some kind of actual system assessment would be a complete failure in today's generic testing labs, which focus on replaying attacks and scans against nonexistent machines.

With the rapid growth in technology, each new generation of IDSs will require new testing methodologies: However, the measured values that will continue to be of interest to IDS administrators and managers will, most certainly, include some assessment of how much traffic the IDS can handle, the numbers of false positives and false negatives it generates, and a measure of the IDSs ability to detect actual attacks. Vendors of IDSs systems could also include a report of the alarms sent and the relative accuracy of the system in correctly matching the alarm level to the true seriousness of the threat. Some planned metrics for IDSs may include the flexibility of signatures and detection policy customization.

IDS administrators may soon be able to purchase tools that test IDS effectiveness. Until these tools are available from a neutral third party, the diagnostics from the IDS vendors will always be suspect. No matter how reliable the vendor, no vendor would provide a test their system would fail.

One note of caution: there may be a strong tendency among IDS administrators to use common vulnerability assessment tools, like Nmap or Nessus, to evaluate the capabilities of an IDS. While this may seem like a good idea, it will in fact not work as expected, because most IDS systems are equipped to recognize the differences between a locally implemented vulnerability assessment tool and a true attack. In order to perform a true assessment of the effectiveness of IDS systems, the test process should be as realistic as possible in its simulation of an actual event. This means coupling realistic traffic loads with realistic levels of attacks. One cannot expect an IDS to respond to a few packet probes as if they represent a denial-of-service attack. In one reported example, a program was used to create a synthetic load of network traffic made up of many TCP sessions, with each session consisting of a SYN (or synchronization) packet, a series of data, and ACK (or acknowledgement) packets, but 110 FIN or connection termination packets. Of the several IDS systems tested, one of them crashed due to lack of resources while it waited for the sessions to be closed. Another IDS passed the test with flying colors because it did not perform state tracking on the connections. Neither of the tested IDS systems worked as expected, but the one that didn't perform state tracking was able to stay operational and was, therefore, given a better score on the test.

3.3. Honey Pots, Honey Nets, and Padded Cell system

A class of powerful security tools that go beyond routine intrusion detection is known variously as honey pots, honey nets, or padded cell systems. To realize why these tools are not yet widely used, you must understand how these products differ from a traditional IDS. Honey pots are decoy systems designed to lure potential attackers away from critical systems and encourage attacks against the themselves. Indeed, these systems are created for the sole purpose of deceiving potential attackers. In the industry, they are also known as decoys, lures, and fly-traps. When a collection of honey pots connects several honey pot systems on a subnet, it may be called a honey net. A honey pot system (or in the case of a honey net, an entire sub network) contains pseudo-services that emulate well-known services but is configured in ways that make it look vulnerable-that is, easily subject to attacks. This combination of attractants (i.e., attractive features such as the presence of both well-known services and vulnerabilities) is meant to lure potential attackers into committing an attack, and thereby revealing their existence-the idea being that once organizations have detected these attackers, they can better defend their networks against future attacks against real assets. In sum, honey pots are designed to:

- Divert an attacker from accessing critical systems
- Collect information about the attacker's activity
- Encourage the attacker to stay on the system long enough for administrators to document the event and, perhaps, respond

Honey pot systems are filled with information that is designed to appear valuable (hence the name honey pots), but this information is fabricated and would not even be useful to a legitimate user of the system. Thus, any time a honey pot is accessed, this constitutes suspicious activity. Honey pots are instrumented with sensitive monitors and event loggers that detect these attempts to access the system and collect information about the potential attacker's activities. A screenshot from a simple IDS that specializes in honey pot techniques, called Deception Toolkit, is shown in Figure 7-8. This screenshot shows the configuration of the honey pot as it is waiting for an attack.

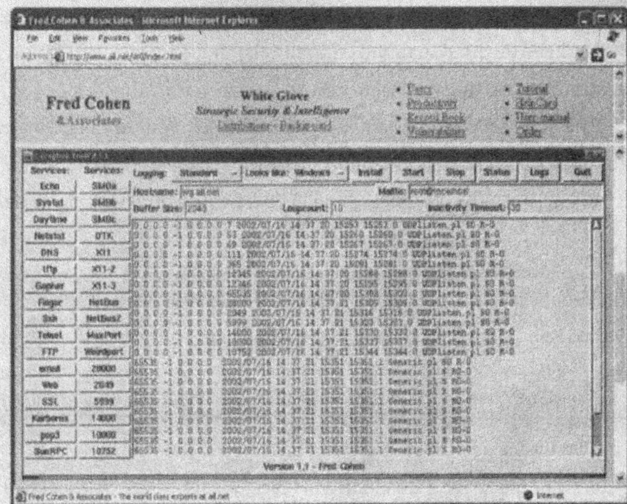

FIGURE 7-8 Deception Toolkit

Padded cells take a different approach. A **padded cell** is a honey poi that has been protected so that that it cannot be easily compromised. In other words, a padded cell is a hardened honey pot. In addition to attracting attackers with tempting data, a padded cell operates in tandem with a traditional IDS. when the IDS detects attackers, it seamlessly transfers them to a special simulated environment where they can cause no harm-the nature of this host environment is what gives the approach its name, padded cell. As in honey pots, this environment (an be filled with interesting data, some of which can be designed to convince an attacker that the attack is going according to plan. Like honey pots, padded cells are well-instrumented and offer unique opportunities for a would-be victim organization to monitor the actions of an attacker. IDS researchers have used padded cell and honey pot systems since the late 1980s, but until recently no commercial versions of these products were available. It is important to seek guidance from legal counsel before deciding to use either of these systems in your operational environment, since using an attractant and then launching a back-hack or counter strike might be construed as an illegal action and make the organization subject to a lawsuit or a criminal complaint.

The advantages and disadvantages of using the honey pot or padded cell approach are summarized below:

Advantages

1) Attackers can be diverted to targets that they cannot damage.
2) Administrators have time to decide how to respond to an attacker.
3) Attackers actions can be easily and more extensively monitored and the records can be used to refine threat models and improve system protections.
4) Honey pots may be effective at catching insiders who are snooping around a network.

Disadvantages

1) The legal implications of using such devices are not well defined.
2) Honey pots and padded cells have not yet been shown to be generally useful security technologies.
3) An expert attacker, once diverted into a decoy system, may become angry and launch a more hostile attack against an organization's systems.

Administrators and security managers will need a high level of expertise to use these systems.

Trap and Trace Systems

An extension of the attractant-based technologies in the preceding section, trap and trace applications are growing in popularity. These systems, often simply referred to as trap and trace, use a combination of techniques to detect an intrusion and then to trace incidents back to their sources. The trap usually consists of a honey pot or padded cell and an alarm.

While the intruders are distracted, or trapped, by what they perceive to be successful intrusions, the system notifies the administrator of their presence. The trace feature is an extension to the honey pot or padded cell approach. Similar in concept to caller ID, the trace is a process by which the organization attempts to determine the identity of someone discovered in unauthorized areas of the network or systems. If this individual turns out to be someone inside the organization, the administrators are completely within their power to track the individual down and turn them over to internal or external authorities. If the individual is outside the security perimeter of the organization, then numerous legal issues arise. One of the most popular professional trap and trace software suites is ManHunt, by Recourse Technologies

(www.recourse.com). It includes a companion product, ManTrap, which is the honey pot application and thus presents a virtual network running from a single server. ManHunt is an intrusion detection system with the capability of initiating a track back function that can trace a detected intruder *as* far as the administrator wishes. Although administrators usually trace an intruder back to their organization's information security boundary, it is possible, with this technology, for them to coordinate with an ISP that has similar technology and thus hand off a trace to an upstream neighbor.

On the surface, trap and trace systems seem like an ideal solution. Security is no longer limited to defense. Now the security administrators can go on the offense. They can track down the perpetrators and turn them over to the appropriate authorities. Under the guise of justice, some less scrupulous administrators may even be tempted to back-hack, or hack into a hacker's system to find out as much as possible about the hacker. Vigilante justice would be a more appropriate term for these activities, which are in fact deemed unethical by most codes of professional conduct. In tracking the hacker, administrators may end up wandering through other organizations' systems, especially when the wily hacker may have used IP spoofing, compromised systems, or a myriad of other techniques to throw trackers off the trail. The result is that the administrator becomes a hacker himself, and therefore defeats the purpose of catching hackers.

There are more legal drawbacks to trap and trace. The trap portion frequently involves the use of honey pots or honey nets. When using *honey* pots and honey nets, administrators should be careful not to cross the line between enticement and entrapment. **Enticement** is the process of attracting attention to a system by placing tantalizing bits of information in key locations.

Entrapment is the action of luring an individual into committing a crime to get a conviction. Enticement is legal and ethical, whereas entrapment is not. It is difficult to gauge the effect such a system can have on the average user, especially if the individual has been nudged into looking at the information. Administrators should also be wary of the *wasp trap syndrome.* In this syndrome, a concerned homeowner installs a wasp trap in his back yard to trap the few insects he sees flying about. Because these traps use scented bait, however, they wind up attracting far more wasps than were originally present. Security administrators should keep the wasp trap syndrome in mind before implementing honey pots, honey nets, padded cells, or trap and trace systems.

Active Intrusion Prevention

Some organizations would like to do more than simply wait for the next attack and implement active countermeasures to stop attacks. One tool that provides active intrusion prevention is known as LaBrea *(http://www.labreatechnologies.com)*. LaBrea works by taking up the unused IP address space within a network. When LaBrea notes an ARP request, it checks to see if the IP address requested is actually valid on the network. If the address is not currently being used by a real computer or network device, LaBrea will pretend to be a computer at that IP address and allow the attacker to complete the TCP/IP connection request, known as the three-way handshake. Once the handshake is complete, LaBrea will change the TCP sliding window size down to a low number to hold the TCP connection from the attacker open for many hours, days, or even months. Holding the connection open but inactive greatly slows down network-based worms and other attacks. It allows the LaBrea *system* time then to notify the system and network administrators about the anomalous behavior on the network.

3.4. Scanning and Analysis Tools

In order to secure a network, it is imperative that someone in the organization knows exactly where the network needs securing. This may sound like a simple and intuitive statement; however, many companies skip this step. They install a simple perimeter firewall, and then, lulled into a sense of security by this single layer of defense, they rest on their laurels. To truly assess the risk within a computing environment, one must deploy technical controls using a strategy of defense in depth. A strategy based on the concept of defense in depth is likely to include intrusion detection systems (IDS), active vulnerability scanners, passive vulnerability scanners, automated log analyzers, and protocol analyzers (commonly referred to as sniffers). As you've learned, the first item in this list, the IDS, helps to secure networks by detecting intrusions; the remaining items in the list also help secure networks, but they do this by helping administrators identify where the network needs securing. More specifically, scanner and analysis tools can find vulnerabilities in systems, holes in security components, and unsecured aspects of the network.

Although some information security experts may not perceive. them as defensive tools, scanners, sniffers, and other such vulnerability analysis tools can be invaluable to security administrators because they enable administrators to see what the attacker sees. Some of these tools are extremely complex and others are rather simple. The tools can also range from being expensive commercial products to those that are freely available at no cost. Many of the best scanning and analysis tools .are those that the attacker community has developed, and are available free on the Web. Good administrators should have several hacking Web sites' bookmarked and should try to keep up with chat room discussions on new vulnerabilities, recent conquests, and favorite assault techniques. There is nothing wrong with a security administrator using the tools that potential attackers use in order to examine his or her defenses and find areas that require additional attention. In the military, there is a long and distinguished history of generals inspecting the troops under their command before battle, walking down the line checking out the equipment and mental preparedness of each soldier. In a similar way, the security administrator can use vulnerability analysis tools to inspect the units (host computers and network devices) under his or her command. A word of caution, though, should be heeded: many of these scanning and analysis tools have distinct signatures, and Some Internet service providers (ISPs) scan for these signatures. If the ISP discovers someone using hacker tools, it can pull that person's access privileges. As such, it is probably best for administrators first to establish a working relationship with their ISPs and notify the ISP of their plans.

Scanning tools are, as mentioned earlier, typically used as part of an attack protocol to collect information that an attacker would need to launch a successful attack. The attack protocol is a series of steps or processes used by an attacker, in a logical sequence, to launch an attack against a target system or network. One of the preparatory parts of the attack protocol is the collection of publicly available information about a potential target, a process known as footprinting.

Footprinting is the organized research of the Internet addresses owned or controlled by a target organization. The attacker uses public Internet data sources to perform keyword searches to identify the network addresses of the organization. This research is augmented by browsing the organization's Web pages. Web pages usually contain quantities of information about internal systems, individuals developing Web pages, and other tidbit~, which can be used for social engineering attacks. The *View Source* option on most popular Web browsers allows the user to see the source code behind the graphics. A number of details in the source code of the Web page can provide clues to potential attackers and give them insight into the configuration of an internal network, such as the locations and directories for Common Gateway Interface (CGI) script bins and the names or possibly addresses of computers and servers. In addition, public business Web sites (such as Forbes, or Yahoo Business) will often reveal information about company structure, commonly used company names, and other information that attackers find useful. Furthermore, common search engines will allow attackers to query for any site that links to their proposed target. By doing a little bit of initial Internet research into a company, an attacker can often find additional Internet locations that are not commonly associated with the company-that is, Business to Business (B2B) partners and subsidiaries. Armed with this information, the attacker can find the "weakest link" into the target network.

For an example, consider Company X, which has a large data center located in Atlanta. The data center has been secured, and thus it will be very hard for an attacker to break into the data center via the Internet. However, the attacker has run a "link" query on the search engine *www.altavista.com* and found a small Web server that links to Company X's main Web server. After further investigation, the attacker learns that the small Web server was set up by an administrator at a remote facility and that the remote facility has, via its own leased lines, an unrestricted internal link into Company X's corporate data center. The attacker can now attack the weaker site at the remote facility and use this compromised network-which is an internal network-to attack the true target. While it may seem trite or cliche, the phrase *a chain is only as strong as its weakest link* is very relevant to network and computer security. If a company has a trusted network connection in place with 15 business partners, even one weak business partner can compromise all 16 networks.

To assist in the footprint intelligence collection process, another type of scanner can be used. This is an enhanced Web scanner that, among other things, can scan entire Web sites for valuable pieces of information, such as server names and e-mail addresses. One such scanner is called Sam Spade, the details of which can be found at *www.samspade.org.* A sample screenshot from Sam Spade is shown in Figure 7 -9. Sam Spade can also do a host of other scans and probes, such as sending multiple ICMP information requests (Pings), attempting to retrieve multiple and cross-zoned DNS queries, and performing network analysis queries (known, from the commonly used UNIX command for performing the analysis, as traceroutes). All of these are powerful diagnostic and hacking activities. Sam Spade is not, however, considered to be hackerware (or hacker-oriented software), but rather it is a utility that happens to be useful to network administrators and miscreants alike.

For Linux or BSD systems, there is a tool called "wget" that allows a remote individual to "mirror" entire Web sites. With this tool, attackers can copy an entire Web site and then go through the source HTML, JavaScript, and Web-based forms at their leisure, collecting and collating all of the data from the source code that will be useful to them for their attack.

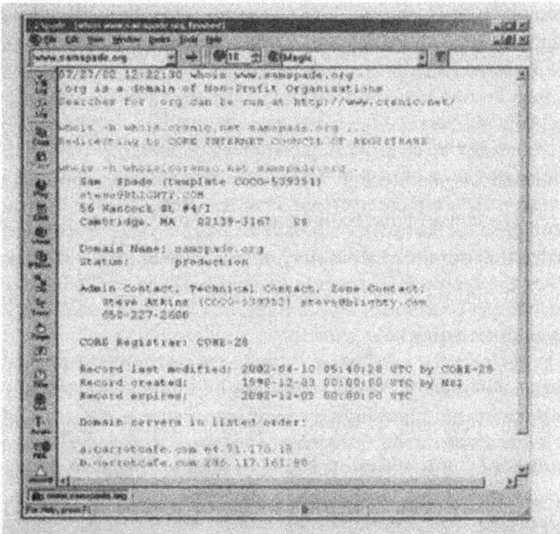

FIGURE 7-9 Sam Spade

The next phase of the attack protocol is a second intelligence or data-gathering process called fingerprinting. This is a systematic survey of all of the target organization's Internet addresses (which were collected during the foot printing phase described above); the survey is conducted to ascertain the network services offered by the hosts in that range. By using the tools discussed in the next section, fingerprinting reveals useful information about the internal structure and operational nature of the target system or network for the anticipated attack. Since these tools were created to find vulnerabilities in systems and networks quickly and with a minimum of effort, they are valuable for the network defender since they can quickly pinpoint the parts of the systems or network that need a prompt repair to close the vulnerability.

Port Scanners

Port scanning utilities (or port scanners) are tools used by both attackers and defenders to identify (or fingerprint) the computers that are active on a network, as well as the ports and services active on those computers. The functions and roles the machines are fulfilling, and other useful information. These tools can scan for specific types of computers, protocols, or resources, or their scans can be generic. It is helpful to understand the environment that exists in the network *you* are using. so that you can use the tool most suited to the data collection task at and. For instance, if you are trying to identify a Windows computer in a typical network, a built-in feature of the operating system, nbtstat, may be able to get the answer you need very quickly, without requiring the installation of a scanner. This tool will not work on other types of networks, however, so you must know your tools in order to make the best use of the features of each.

The more specific the scanner is, the better it can give attackers and defenders information that is detailed and will be useful later. However, it is also recommended that you keep a generic, broad-based scanner in your toolbox as well. This helps to locate and identify rogue nodes on the network that administrators may be unaware of. Probably the most popular port scanner is Nmap, which runs on both Unix and Windows systems. You can find out more about Nmap at *http://www.insecure.org.*

A port is a network channel or connection point in a data communications system. Within the TCP/IP networking protocol, TCP and User Datagram Protocol (UDP) port numbers differentiate the multiple communication channels that are used to connect to the network services being offered on the same network device. Each application within TCP/IP has a unique port number assigned. Some have default ports but can also use other ports. Some of the well-known port numbers are presented in Table 7-1. In all, there are 65,536 port numbers in use for TCP and another 65,536 port numbers for UDP. Services using the TCP/IP protocol can run on any port; however, the services with reserved ports generally run on ports 1-1023. Port 0 is not used. Ports greater than 1023 are typically referred to as ephemeral ports and may be randomly allocated to server and client processes.

Why secure open ports? Simply put, an open port can be used by an attacker to send commands to a computer, potentially gain access to a server, and possibly exert control over a networking device. The general rule of thumb is to remove from service or secure any port not absolutely necessary to conducting business. For example, if a business doesn't host Web services. there may be no need for port 80 to be available on its servers.

TABLE 7-1 Commonly Used Port Numbers

TCP Port Numbers	TCP Service
20 and 21	File Transfer Protocol (FTP)
22	Secure Shell (SSH)
23	Telnet
25	Simple Mail Transfer Protocol (SMTP)
53	Domain Name Services (DNS)
67 and 68	Dynamic Host Configuration Protocol (DHCP)
80	Hypertext Transfer Protocol (HTTP)
110	Post Office Protocol (POP3)
161	Simple Network Management Protocol (SNMP)
194	IRC chat port (used for device sharing)
443	HTTP over SSL
8080	Used for proxy services

Firewall Analysis Tools

Understanding exactly where an organization's firewall is located and what the existing rule sets on the firewall do are very important steps for any security administrator. There are several tools that automate the remote discovery of firewall rules and assist the administrator (or attacker) in analyzing the rules to determine exactly what they allow and what they reject.

The Nmap tool mentioned earlier has some advanced options that are useful for firewall analysis. The Nmap option called Idle scanning (which is run with the -I switch) will allow the Nmap user to bounce your scan across firewall by using one of the IDLE DMZ hosts as the initiator of the scan. More specifically, as most operating systems do not use truly random II' packet identification numbers (IP IDs), if there is more than one host in the DMZ and one host uses non-random IP IDs, then the attacker can query the server (server X) and obtain the currently used IP ID as well as the known algorithm for incrementing the IP IDs. The attacker can then spoof a packet that is allegedly &001 server X and destined ior an internal II' address behind the firewall. If the port is open on the internal machine, the internal machine will reply to server X with a SYN-ACK packet, which will force server X to respond with a TCI' RESET packet. In responding with the TCP RESET, server X increments its II' ID number. The attacker can now query server X a second time to see if the II' ID has incremented. If it has, the attacker knows that the internal machine is alive and that the internal machine has the queried service port open. In a nutshell, running the Nmap Idle scan allows an attacker to scan an internal network as if he or she were physically located on a trusted machine inside the DMZ.

Another tool that can be used to analyze firewalls is Firewalk. Written by noted author and network security expert Mike Schiffman, Firewalk uses incrementing Time-To-Live (TTL) packets to determine the path into a network as well as the default firewall policy. Running Firewalk against a target machine will reveal where routers and firewalls are filtering traffic to the target host. More information on Firewalk can be obtained from

http://www.packetfactory.net/.

A final firewall analysis tool worth mentioning is HI'ING, which is a modified Ping client. It supports multiple protocols and has a command-line means of specifying nearly any of the Ping parameter,. For instance, you can use HPING with modified TTL values to determine the infrastructure of a DMZ. You can use HPING with specific ICMP flags in order to bypass poorly configured firewalls (i.e., firewalls that allow all ICMP traffic to pass through) and find internal systems. HPING can be found at *http://www.hping.org/.*

Incidentally, administrators who fed wary of using the same tools that attackers use should remember two important points: regardless of the nature of the tool that is used to validate or analyze a firewall's configuration, it is the intent of the user that will dictate how the information gathered will be used; in order to defend a computer or network well, it is necessary to understand the ways it can be attacked. Thus, a tool that can help close up an open or poorly configured firewall will help the network defender minimize the risk from attack.

Operating System Detection Tools

Detecting a target computer's operating system is, very valuable to an attacker, because once the as is known, all of the vulnerabilities to which it is susceptible can easily be determined. There are many tools that use networking protocols to determine a remote computer's as. One specific tool worth mentioning is XProbe, which uses ICMP to determine the remote OS. This tool can be found at *http://wMi..sys-stcurity.cor/1/lrtmllprojectslX.html.* When it's run, XProbe sends a lot of different ICMP queries against the target host. As reply packets are received, XProbe matches these responses from the target's *TCP/IP* stack with its own internal database of known responses. As most ass have a unique way of responding to ICMP requests, Xprobe is very reliable in finding matches and thus detecting the operating systems of remote computers. System and network administrators should take note of this, and plan to restrict the use of ICMP through their organization's firewalls and, when possible, within its internal networks.

Vulnerability Scanners

Active vulnerability scanners scan networks for highly detailed information. An *active* scanner is one that initiates traffic on the network in order to determine security holes. As a class, this type of scanner identities exposed usernames and groups, shows open network shares, and exposes configuration problems and other vulnerabilities in servers. An example of a vulnerability scanner is GFI LAN guard Network Security Scanner (NSS), which is available as & freeware for non commercial use. Another example of a vulnerability scanner is Nessus, which is a professional & freeware utility that uses IP packets to determine the hosts available on the network, the services (ports) they are offering, the operating system and as version they are running, the type of packet filters and firewalls in use, and dozens of other characteristics of the network. Figures 7-10 and 7-11 show sample LAN guard and Nessus result screens.

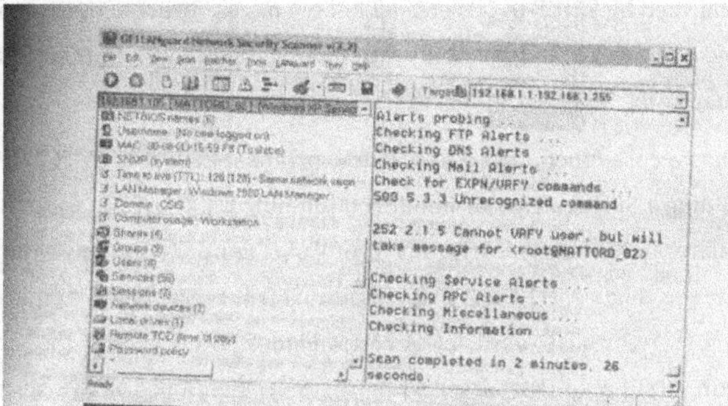

FIGURE 7-10 LANguard

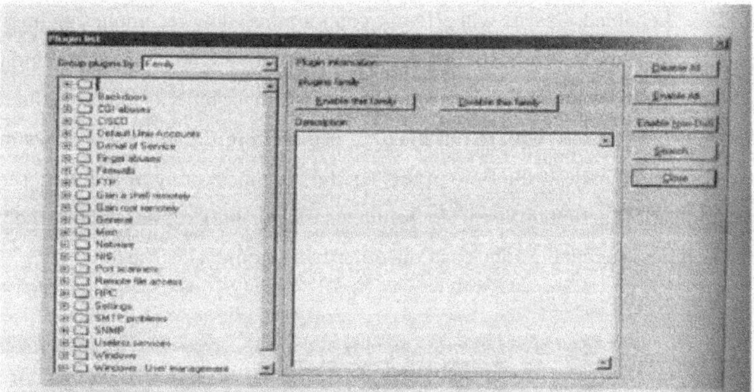

FIGURE 7-11 Nessus

Vulnerability scanners should be proficient in finding known, documented holes. But what happens if the Web server is from a new vendor, or the application was developed by an internal development team? There is a class of vulnerability scanners called *blackbox* scanners, or fuzzers. Fuzz testing is a straightforward testing technique that looks for vulnerabilities in a program or protocol by feeding random input to the program or a network running the protocol. Vulnerabilities can be detected by measuring the outcome of the random inputs. One example of fuzz scanner is SPIKE, which has two primary components. The first is the SPIKE Proxy, which is a full-blown proxy server. As Website visitors utilize the proxy, SPIKE builds a database of each of the traversed pages, forms, and web-specific information, When the web site owner determines that enough history has been collected to fully characterize the web sites, SPIKE can be used to check the web site for bugs- that is, administrators can use the usage history collected by SPIKE to traverse all known pages, forms, active programs (e.g., asp, cgi-bin),etc., and can test the system by attempting overflows, SQL injection, cross-site scripting, and many other classes of Web attacks.

SPIKE also has a core functionality to fuzz any protocol that utilizes TCP/IP. By sniffing a session and building a SPIKE script, or building a full-blown C program using the SPIKE API, a user can stimulate and —fuzz|| nearly any protocol. Figure 7-12 shows the spike PROXY configuration screen. Figure 7-13 shows a sample SPIKE script being prepared to fuzz the ISAKAMP protocol (which is used by VPNs). Figure 7-14 shows the spike program, generic_send_udp, fuzzing an IKE server using the aforementioned SPIKE script. As you can see, SPIKE can be used to quickly fuzz and find weakness in nearly any protocol.

Similar in function, the previously mentioned scanner has a class of attacks called DESTRUCTIVE. If enabled, Nessus will attempt common overflow techniques against a target host. Fuzzers or blackbox scanners and Nesses in destructive mode can be every dangerous tool and should only be used in a lab environment. In fact, these tools are so powerful that even system defenders who use them are not likely to use them in the most aggressive modes on their production networks. At the time of this writing, the most popular scanners seem to be Nessus(a commercial version of Nessus for windows is available), retina, and Internet scanner. The Nessus scanner is available at no cost: the other two require a license fee.

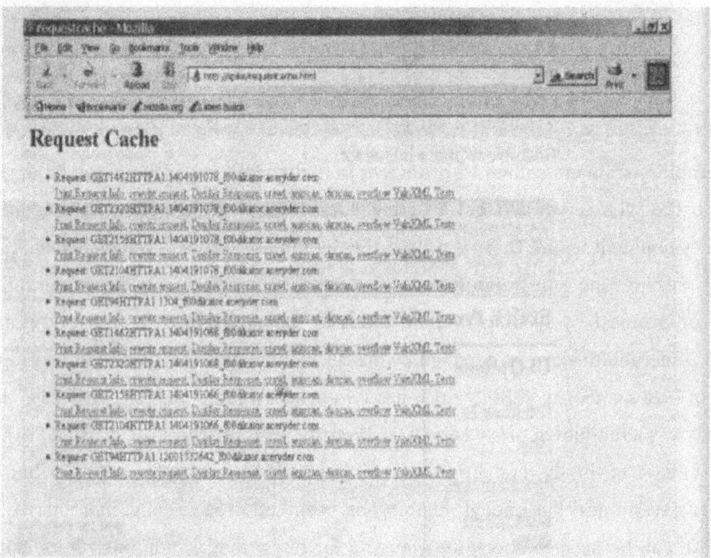

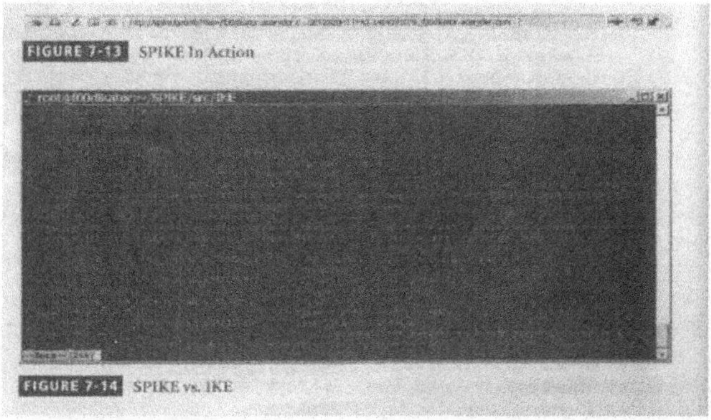

FIGURE 7-13 SPIKE In Action

FIGURE 7-14 SPIKE vs. IKE

Often times, some members of an organization will require proof that a system is actually vulnerable to c certain attack. They may require such proof in order to avoid having system administrators attempt to repair system that are not in fact broken, or because they have not yet built a satisfactory relationship with the vulnerability assessment team. In these instances, there exists a class of scanners that will actually exploit the remote machine and allow the vulnerability analyst (sometimes called penetration tester to create an account, modify a web page, or view data. These tools can be very dangerous and should only be used when absolutely necessary. Three tools that can perform this action are core Impact, Immunity's CANVAS, and the Metasploit Framework.

Of these three tools, only the Metasploit Framework is available without a license fee. The Metasploit Framework is a collection of exploits coupled with an interface that allows the penetration tester to automate the custom exploitation of vulnerable systems. So, for instance, if you wished to exploit a Microsoft Exchange server and run a single command (perhaps add the user —security|| into the administrators group), the tool would allow you to customize the overflow in this manner. See figure 7-15 for a screenshot of the Metasploit Framework in action.

FIGURE 7-15 Metasploit

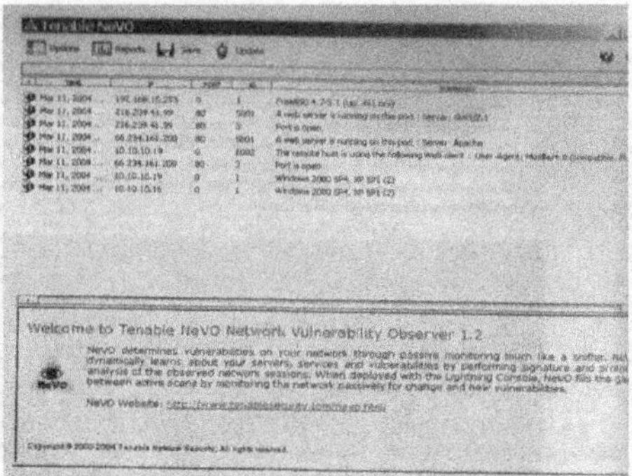

FIGURE 7-16 NeVO

Table 7-2 provides World Wide Web addresses for the products mentioned in the vulnerability scanners section.

Table 7-2 Vulnerability Scanner Products and Web Pages

Product	Web Page
Nessus	*http://www.nessus.org*
Nessus for Windows	*http://www.tenablesecurity.com*
GFI LANguard Network Security Scanner	*http://www.gfi.com/languard*
SPIKE - SPIKEproxy	*http://www.immunitysec.com*
Retina	*http://www.eeye.com*
Internet Scanner	*http://www.iss.net*
Core Impact	*http://www.coresecurity.com/home/home.php*
CANVAS	*http://www.immunitysec.com/CANVAS*
Metasploit Framework	*http://metasploit.com*

A Passive vulnerability scanner is one that listens in on the network and determines vulnerable versions of both server and client software. At the time of this writing, there are two primary vendors offering this type of scanning solution: Tenable Network Security with its NeVO product and Source fire with its RNA product. Passive scanners are advantageous in that they do not require vulnerability analysts to get approval prior for testing. These tools simply monitor the network connections to and from a server to gain a list of vulnerable applications. Furthermore, passive vulnerability scanners have the ability to find client-side Vulnerabilities that are typically not found in active scanners. For instance, an active scanner operating without DOMAIN Admin rights would be unable to determine the version of Internet Explorer running on a desktop machine, whereas a passive scanner will be able to make that determination by observing the traffic to and from the client. See Figure7-16 for a screenshot of the NeVO passive Vulnerability scanner running on Windows XP.

Packet Sniffers

Another tool worth mentioning here is the packet sniffer. A packet sniffer (sometimes called a network protocol analyzer) is a network tool that collects copies of packets from the network and analyzes them. It can provide a network administrator with valuable information for diagnosing and resolving networking issues. In the wrong hands, however, sniffer can be used to eavesdrop on network traffic. There are both commercial and open-source sniffers-more specifically, sniffer is a commercial product, and snort is open-source software. An excellent free, client-based network protocol analyzer is Ethereal *(www.ethereal.com)*.Ethereal allows the administrator to examine data from both live network traffic and captured traffic. Ethereal has several features, including a language filter and TCP session reconstruction utility. Figure 7-17 shows a sample screen from Ethereal. Typically, to use these types of programs most effectively, the user must be connected to a network from a central location. Simply tapping into an Internet connection floods with you more data than can be readily processed, and technically constitutes a violation of the wire tapping act. To use a packet sniffer legally, the administrator must: 1)be on a network that organization owns, 2)be under direct authorization of the owners of the network, and 3) have knowledge and consent of the content creators. If all three conditions are met, the administrator can selectively collect and analyze packets to identify and diagnose problems on the network. Conditions one and two are self-explanatory. The third, consent, is usually handled by having all system users sign a release when they are issued a user ID and passwords. Incidentally, these three items are the same requirements for employee monitoring in general, and packet sniffing should be constructed as a form of employee monitoring.

Many administrators feel that they are safe from sniffer attacks when their computing environment is primarily a switched network environment. This couldn't be farther from the truth. There are a number of open-source sniffers that support alternate networking approaches that can, in turn, enable packet sniffing in a switched network environment. Two of these alternate networking approaches are ARP- Spoofing and session hijacking (which uses tools like ettercap). To secure data in transit across any network, organizations must be encryption to be assured of content privacy.

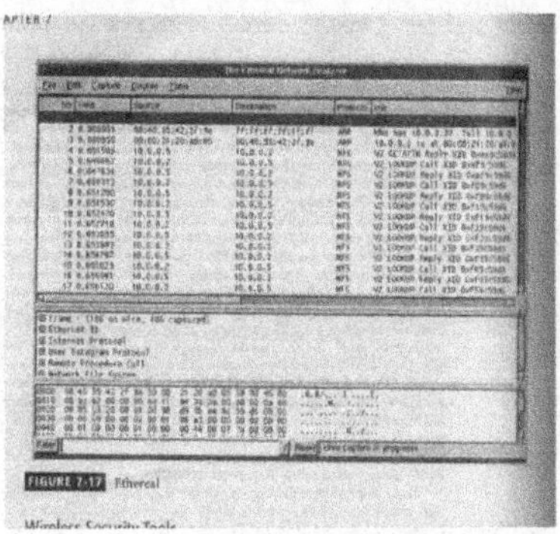

FIGURE 7-17 Ethereal

Wireless Security Tools

802.11 wireless networks have sprung up as subnets on nearly all large networks. A wireless connection, while convenient, has many potential security holes. An organization that spends all of its time securing the wired network and leaves wireless networks to operate in any manner is opening itself up for a security breach. As a security professional, you must access the risk of wireless networks A Wireless security toolkit should include the ability to sniff wireless traffic, scan wireless hosts, and asses the level of privacy or confidentiality afford on the wireless network. There is a suite of tools from dachb0dens labs *(http:// www. Dachb0den.com/bsd-airtools.html*) called bsd-airtools that automates all of the items noted above. The tools included within the bsd-airtools toolset are an access point detection tool, a sniffer, and a tool called dstumbler to crack Wired Equivalent Protocol (WEP) encryption keys. A windows version of the dstumbler tool called Netstumbler is also offered as freeware and can be found at http://www. Netstumbler.org. Figure 7-18 shows NetStumbler being run from a Windows XP machine. Another wireless tool worth mentioning is Airsnare. Airsnare is a free tool that can be run on a low-end wireless workstation. Airsnare monitors the airwaves for any new devices or Access Points. When it finds one Airsnarewill sound an alarm alerting the administrators that a new, potentially dangerous, wireless apparatus is attempting access on a closed wireless network. Figure 7-19 shows Airsnare in action.

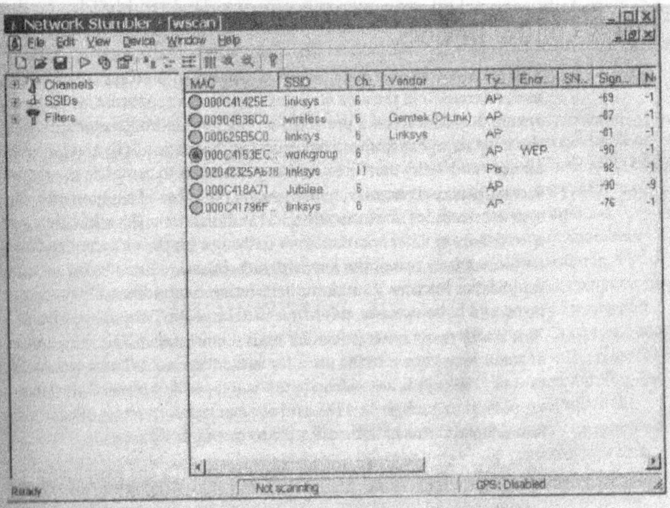

FIGURE 7-18 NetStumbler

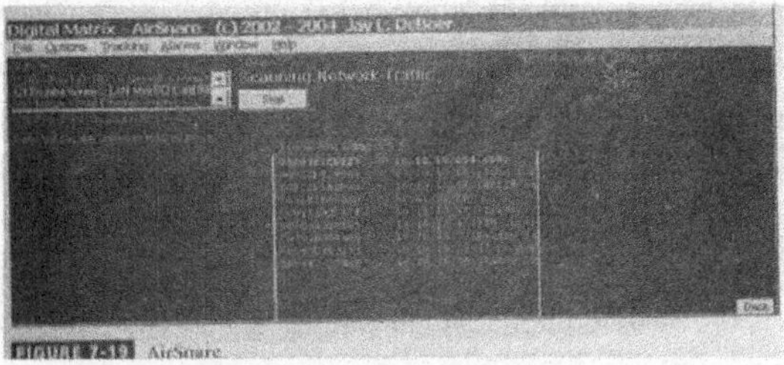

FIGURE 7-19 AirSnare

The tools discussed so far help the attacker and the defender prepare themselves to complete the next steps in the attack protocol: attack, compromise, and exploit. These steps are beyond the scope of this text, for they are usually covered in more advanced classes on computer and network attack and defense.

3.5. Access Control Devices

This section examines technologies associated with **access control.** When a prospective user, referred to in the area of access as a supplicant, seeks to use a protected system, logically access a protected service, or physically enter a protected space, he or she must engage in authentication and authorization activities to establish his or her identify and verify that he or she has permission to complete the requested activity. A successful access control system includes a number of components, depending on the system's needs for authentication and authorization.

Occasionally a system will have a need for strong authentication when verifying supplicant's identity. Strong authentication requires at least two of the forms of authentication listed below to authenticate the supplicant's identity. Routine authentication has traditionally made use of only one form; and in many cases, this happens to be of the –What a supplicant knows|| variety. This is why many systems familiar to us require a user ID and password (both examples of something known to the user) for authentication. When a second factor is required to verify the supplicant's identify. This is frequently a physical device, i.e., something the supplicant has, such as an ATM card or smart card. In terms of access control, there are four general forms of authentication to consider:

- What a supplicant knows: for example, user IDs and passphrases.
- What a supplicant has: often tokens and smart cards.
- Who a supplicant is : fingerprints, hand topography, hand geometry, retinal and iris recognition.
- What a supplicant produces: voice and signature pattern recognition.

The technology to manage authentication based on what a supplicant knows is widely integrated into the networking and security software systems in use across the IT industry. The last three forms of authentication are usually implemented as some form of identification technology and added to systems that require higher degrees of authentication.

Authentication

Authentication is the validation of a supplicant's identity. There are four general ways in which authentication is carried out . Each of these is discussed in detail in the following sections.

What a Supplicant Knows

This area of authentication deals with what the supplicant knows- for example , a password , passphrase , or other unique authentication code , such as a personal identification number (or PIN) – that could confirm his or her identity .

A **password** is a private word or combination of characters that only the user should know . One of the biggest debates in the information security industry concerns the complexity of passwords . On the one hand , a password should be difficult to guess, which means it cannot be a series of letters or word that is easily associated with the user, such as the name of the user's spouse , child, or pet . Nor should a password be a series of numbers commonly associated with the user , such as a phone number , Social Security number, or birth date. On the other hand , the password must be something the user can easily remember, which means it should be short or commonly associated with something the user can remember.

A **passphrase** is a series of characters, typically longer than a password, from which a **virtual password** is derived. For example, which a typical password might be —23skedoo,|| a typical passphrase can be—May The Force Be With You Always,|| which can also be represented as —MTFBWYA.||

What a Supplicant Has

The second area of authentication addresses something the supplicant carries in his or her possession-that is , something they have . These include **dumb cards,** such as ID cards or ATM cards with magnetic stripes containing the digital (and often encrypted) user personal identification number (PIN), against which the number a user inputs is compared. An improved version of the dumb card is the **smart card,** which contains a computer chip that can verify and validate a number of pieces of information instead of just a PIN . Another device often used is the token, a card or key fob with a computer chip and a liquid crystal display that shows a computer-generated number used to support remote login authentication . Tokens are synchronized with a server, both devices (server and token) use the same time or a time-based database to generate a number that is displayed and entered during the user login phase.

Asynchronous tokens use a challenge-response system, in which the server challenges the supplicant during login with a numerical sequence. The supplicant places this sequence into the token and receives a response. The prospective user then enters the response into the system to gain access . This system does not require the synchronization of the synchronous token system and therefore does not require the server and all the tokens to maintain the same exact time setting.

Who a Supplicant Is

The third area of authentication deals with a characteristic of the supplicant's person that is, something they are. This process of using body measurements is known as biometrics. Biometrics includes:

- Fingerprint comparison of the supplicant's actual fingerprint to a stored fingerprint
- Palm print comparison of the supplicant's actual palm print to a stored palm print
- Hand geometry comparison of the supplicant's actual hand to a stored measurement
- Facial recognition using a photographic ID card, in which a supplicant's face is compared to a stored image
- Retinal print comparison of the supplicant's actual retina to a stored image
- Iris pattern comparison of the supplicant's actual iris to a stored image

Among all possible biometrics, only three human characteristics are usually considered truly unique:

1) Fingerprints
2) Retina of the eye (blood vessel pattern) • Iris of the eye (random pattern of features in the iris including: freckles, pits, striations, vasculature, coronas, and crypts).

Most of the technologies that scan human characteristics convert these images to some form of minutiae. **Minutiae** are unique points of reference that are digitized and stored in an encrypted format when the user's system access credentials are created. Each subsequent access attempt results in a measurement that is compared with the encoded value to determine if the user is who he or she claims to be. A problem with this method is that some human characteristics can change over time, due to normal development, injury, or illness. This situation requires system designers to create fallback or failsafe authentication mechanisms to be used when the primary biometric procedure fails .

What a Supplicant Produces

The fourth and final area of authentication addresses something the supplicant performs or something he or she produces. This includes technology in the areas of signature recognition and voice recognition. Signature recognition has become commonplace. Retail stores use signature, or at least signature capture, for authentication during a purchase. The customer signs his or her signature on a digital pad with a special stylus that captures the signature. The signature is digitized and either simply saved for future reference, or compared with a signature on a database for validation. Currently, the technology for signature capturing is much more widely accepted than that for signature comparison, because signatures change due to a number of factors, including age, fatigue, and the speed with which the signatures is written. Voice recognition works in a similar fashion in that an initial voiceprint of the user reciting a phrase is captured and stored. Later, when the user attempts to access the system, the authentication process will require the user to speak this same pharse so that the technology can compare the current voiceprint against the stored value.

Effectiveness of Biometrics

Biometric technologies are evaluated on three basis criteria: first, the reject rate, which is the percentage of supplicants who are in fact authorized users but are denied access; second, the false accept rate, which is the percentage of supplicants who are unauthorized users but are granted access; finally, the crossover error rate, which is the level at which the number of false rejections equals the false acceptances. Each of these is examined in detail in the following sections.

False Reject Rate

The **false reject rate** is the percentage of or value associated with the rate at which supplicants who are authentic users are denied or prevented access to authorized areas as a result of a failure in the biometric device. This error rate is also known as a Type I error. While a nuisance to supplicants who are authorized users, this error rate is probably the one that least concerns security professionals since rejection of an authorized individual represents no threat to security , but is simply an impedance to authenticated use. As a result, the false reject rate is often ignored until it increases to a level high enough to irritate supplicants who, subsequently , begin complaining. Most people have experienced the frustration of having a frequently used credit card or ATM card fail to perform because of problems with the magnetic strip. In the field of biometrics, similar problems can occur when a system fails to pick up the various information points it uses to authenticate a prospective user properly.

False Accept Rate

The **false accept rate** is the percentage of or value associated with the rate at which supplicants who are not legitimate users are allowed access to systems or areas as a result of a failure in the biometric device. This error rate is also known as a Type II error. This type of error is unacceptable to security professionals, as it represents a clear breach of access.

Crossover Error Rate(CER)

The **crossover error rate(CER)** is the level at which the number of false rejections equals the false acceptances, also known as the equal error rate. This is possibly the most common and important overall measure of the accuracy of a biometric system. Most biometric systems can be adjusted to compensate for both false positive and false negative errors. Adjustment to one extreme creates a system that requires perfect matches and results in high false rejects, but almost no false accepts. Adjustment to the other extreme produces low false rejects, but almost no false accepts. The trick is to find the balance between providing the requisite level of security and minimizing the frustration level of authentic users. Thus, the optimal setting is found to be somewhere near the point at which these two error rates are equal-that is, at the crossover error rate or CER. CERs are used to compare various biometrics and may vary by manufacturer. A biometric device that provides a CER of 1% is a device for which the failure rate for false rejection and the failure rate for false acceptance are identical, at 1% failure of each type. A device with a CER of 1% is considered superior to a device with a CER of 5% .

Acceptability of Biometrics

As you've learned, a balance must be struck between how acceptable a security system is to its users and how effective it is in maintaining security. Many the biometric systems that are highly reliable and effective are considered somewhat intrusive to users. As a result, many information security professionals, in an effort to avoid confrontation and possible user boycott of the biometric controls, don't implement them. Table 7-3 shows how certain biometrics rank in terms of effectiveness and acceptance.

Interestingly, the order of effectiveness is nearly exactly opposite the order of acceptance.

TABLE 7-3 Ranking of Effectiveness and Acceptance[21]

Effectiveness of Biometric Authentication Systems—Ranked from Most Secure to Least Secure	Acceptance of Biometric Authentication Systems—Ranked from Most Accepted to Least Accepted
Retina pattern recognition	Keystroke pattern recognition
Fingerprint recognition	Signature recognition
Handprint recognition	Voice pattern recognition
Voice pattern recognition	Handprint recognition
Keystroke pattern recognition	Fingerprint recognition
Signature recognition	Retina pattern recognition

Questions

3a). How a firewall can be configured and managed? give example.

(December 2010) (10 marks)

3b). What is VPN? Explain the two modes of VPN.

(December 2010) (10 marks)

3 a). Differentiate between network based IDS and Host Based IDS emphasizing on their advantages and disadvantages.

(June 2012) (8 marks)

3b). With the help of schematic diagram explain the centralized control strategy implementation of IDS.

(June 2012) (6 marks)

3c). Enumerates the advantages and disadvantages of using honey pots.

(June 2012) (6 marks)

3a). How does a signature-based IDPs differ from a behavior based IDPs ?

(JUNE 2010) (6 marks)

3b). Explain the venerability scanners.

(JUNE 2010) (10 Marks)

3a). Explain network based intrusion detection and prevention system

(JUNE 2011) (10 Marks)

3b). Describe the need of operating system detection tools.

(JUNE 2011) (10 Marks)

3a). Define the following terms related to IDS :

- Alert
- False attack stimulus
- False negative
- False positive
- True attack stimulus

(Dec 2011) (5 Marks)

3b). Discuss the reasons for acquisition and use of IDSs by organizations.

(Dec 2011) (6 Marks)

UNIT-4

CRYPTOGRAPHY

Learning Objectives

Upon completion of this material, you should be able to

Describe the most significant events and discoveries from the history of cryptology.

Understand the basic principles of cryptography.

Understand the operating principles of the most popular tools in the area of cryptography.

List and explain the major protocols used for secure communications.

Understand the nature and execution of the dominant methods of attack used against cryptosystems.

4.1. Introduction

The science of cryptography is not as enigmatic as you might think. A variety of techniques related to cryptography are used regularly in everyday life. For example, open your newspaper to the entertainment section and you'll find the daily cryptogram, which is a word puzzle that makes a game out of unscrambling letters' to find a hidden message. Also, although it is a dying art, many secretaries still use stenography, a coded form of documentation, to take rapid dictation from their managers. Finally, a form of cryptography is used even in the hobby of knitting, where directions are written in a coded form, in such patterns as KIPI (knit I, pearl I), that only an initiate would be able to understand. Most of the examples above demonstrate the use of cryptography as a means of efficiently and rapidly conveying information. These aspects are only one important element of the science of cryptography. For the purposes of this chapter, the discussion of cryptography will be expanded to include the protection and verification of transmitted information.

In order to understand cryptography and its uses, you must become familiar with a number of key terms that are used across the information technology industry. The science of encryption, known as **cryptology**, encompasses *cryptography* and *cryptanalysis.* **Cryptography**, which comes from the Greek words *kryptos,* meaning "hidden," and *graphein,* meaning "to write," is the process of making and using codes to secure the transmission of information. Cryptanalysis is the process of obtaining the original message (called the **plaintext**) from an encrypted message (called the **ciphertext**) without knowing the algorithms and keys used to perform the encryption. **Encryption** is the process of converting an original message into a form that is unreadable to unauthorized individuals-that is, to anyone without the tools to convert the encrypted message back to its original format. **Decryption** is the process of converting the ciphertext into a message that conveys readily understood meaning.

The field of cryptology is so complex it can fill many volumes. *As* a result, this textbook seeks to provide only the most general overview of cryptology and some limited detail on the tools of cryptography. The early sections of this chapter, namely "A Short History of Cryptology,"Principles of Cryptography,|| and "Cryptography Tools," provide some background on cryptology and general definitions of the key concepts of cryptography, and discuss the usage of common cryptographic tools. Later sections discuss common cryptographic protocols and describe some of the attacks possible against cryptosystems.

4.2. A Short History of Cryptology

The creation and use of cryptology has a long history among the cultures of the world. Table provides an overview of the history of cryptosystems.

History of Cryptology

1900 B.C	Egyptian scribes used nonstandard hieroglyphs while inscribing clay tablets, this is the first documented use of written cryptography.
1500 B.C	Mesopotamian cryptography surpassed that of the Egyptians. This is demonstrated in a tablet that was discovered to contain an encrypted formula for pottery glazes; the tablet used special symbols that appear to have different meanings from the usual symbols used elsewhere.
500 B.C	Hebrew scribes writing the book of Jeremiah used a reversed alphabet substitution cipher known as the ATBASH.
487 B.C	The Spartans of Greece developed the Skytale, a system consisting of a strip of papyrus wrapped around a wooden staff. Messages were written down the length of the staff, and the papyrus was unwrapped. The decryption process involved wrapping the papyrus around a shaft of similar diameter.
50 B.C	Julius Caesar used a simple substitution cipher to secure military and government communications. To form an encrypted text, Caesar shifted the letter of the alphabet three places. In addition to this monoalphabetic substitution cipher, Caesar strengthened his encryption by substituting Greek letters for Latin letters.

Abu 'Abd al-Rahman al-Khalil ibn Ahman ibn 'Amr ibn Tammam al Farahidi al-Zadi at Yahmadi wrote a text (now lost) of cryptography; he also solved a Greek cryptogram by guessing the plaintext introduction.

855 Abu Wahshiyyaan-Nabati, a scholar, published several cipher alphabets that were used for encrypted writings of magic formulas.

1250 Roger Bacon, an English monk, wrote Epistle of Roger Bacon on the Secret Works of Art and of Nature and Also on the Nullity of Magic, in which he described several simple ciphers.

1392 The Equatorie of the Planetis, an early text possibly written by Geoffrey Chaucer, contained apassage in a simple substitution cipher.

1412 Subhalasha, a 14-volume Arabic encyclopedia, contained a section on cryptography, including both substitution and transposition ciphers, and ciphers with multiple substitutions, a technique that had never been used before.

1466 Leon Battista Alberti is considered the Father of Western cryptography because on his work with polyalphabetic substitution; he also designed a cipher disk.

1518 Johannes Trithemius wrote the first printed book on cryptography and invented a steganographic cipher, in which each Jetter was represented as a word taken from a succession of columns. He also described a polyalphabetic encryption method using a rectangular substitution format that is now commonly used. He is credited with the introduction of the method of changing substitution alphabets with each letter as it is deciphered.

1553 Giovan Batista Belaso introduced the idea of the passphrase (password) as a key for encryption; this polyalphabetic encryption method is misnamed for another person who later used the technique and thus is called "The Vigenere Cipher|| today.

1563 Giovanni Battista Porta wrote a classification text on encryption methods, categorizing them as transposition, substitution, and symbol substitution.

1623 Sir Francis Bacon described an encryption method by employing one of the first uses of steganography; he encrypted his messages by cipher was hidden within the text's letters.

1780s 1homas Jefferson created a 26-letter wheel cipher, which he used for official communications while ambassador to France; the concept of the wheel cipher would be reinvented in 1854, and again in 1913.

1854 Charles Babbage appears to have reinvented Thomas Jefferson's wheel cipher.

1861-5 During the U.S. Civil War, Union forces used a substitution encryption method based on specific words, and the Confederacy used a polyalphabetic cipher whose solution had been published before the start of the Civil War.

1914-17 World War I: The Germans, British, and French used a series of transposition and substitution ciphers in radio communications throughout the war. All sides spent considerable effort in trying to intercept and decode communications, and thereby brought about the birth of the science of cryptanalysis. British cryptographers broke the Zimmerman Telegram, in which the Germans offered Mexico U.S. territory in return for Mexico's support. This decryption helped to bring the United States into the war.

1917 William Frederick Friedman, the father of U.S. cryptanalysis, and his wife Elizabeth, were employed as civilian cryptanalysts by the U.S. government. Friedman later founded a school for cryptanalysis in Riverbank, Illinois.

1917 Gilbert S. Vernam, an AT&T employee, invented a polyalphabetic cipher machine that used a non-repeating random key.

1919 Hugo Alexander Koch filed a patent in the Netherlands for a rotor-based cipher machine; in 1927, Koch assigned the patent rights to Arthur Scherbius, the inventor of the Enigma Machine, which was a mechanical substitution cipher.

1927-33 During Prohibition, criminals in the U.S. began using cryptography to maintain the privacy of messages used in criminal activities.

1937 The Japanese developed the Purple machine, which was based on principles similar to Information network security those of Enigma and used mechanical relays from telephone systems to encrypt diplomatic messages.

By late 1940, a team headed by William Friedman had broken the code generated by this machine and constructed a machine that could quickly decode Purple's ciphers.

1939-42 The fact that the Allies secretly broke the Enigma cipher undoubtedly shortened World War II.

1942 Navajo Windtalkers entered World War II; in addition to speaking a language that was unknown outside a relatively small group within the United States, the Navajos developed code words for subjects and ideas that did not exist in their native tongue.

1948 Claude Shannon suggested using frequency and statistical analysis in the solution of substitution ciphers.

1970Dr. Horst Feistelled an IBM research team in the development of the Lucifer cipher.

1976 A design based upon Lucifer was chosen by the U.S. National Security Agency as the Data Encryption Standard and found worldwide acceptance.

1976 Whitefield Diffie and Martin Hellman introduced the idea of public key cryptography.

1977 Ronald Rivest, Adi Shamir, and Leonard Adleman developed a practical public key cipher for both confidentiality and digital signatures; the RSA family of computer encryption algorithms was born.

1978 The initial RSA algorithm was published in the Communication of ACM.

1991 Phil Zimmermann released the first version ofPGP (Pretty Good Privacy); PGP was released as freeware and became the worldwide standard for public cryptosystems.

2000 Rijndael's cipher was selected as the Advanced Encryption Standard.

4.3. Principles of Cryptography

Historically, cryptography was used in manual applications, such as handwriting. But with the emergence of automated technologies in the 20th century, the need for encryption in the IT environment vastly increased. Today, many common IT tools use embedded encryption technologies to protect sensitive information within applications.

For example, all the popular Web browsers use built -in encryption features that enable users to perform secure e-commerce applications, such as online banking and Web shopping.

Basic Encryption Definitions

To understand the fundamentals of cryptography, you must become familiar with the following definitions:

1) **Algorithm:** The programmatic steps used to convert an unencrypted message into an encrypted sequence of bits that represent the message; sometimes used as a reference to the programs that enable the cryptographic processes.
2) **Cipher or cryptosystem:** An encryption method or process encompassing the algorithm, key(s) or cryptovariable(s), and procedures used to perform encryption and decryption.
3) **Ciphertext or cryptogram:** The unintelligible encrypted or encoded message resulting from an encryption.
4) **Code:** The process of converting components (words or phrases) of an unencrypted message into encrypted components.
5) **Decipher:** To decrypt or convert ciphertext into the equivalent plaintext.
6) **Encipher:** To encrypt or convert plaintext into the equivalent ciphertext.
7) **Key or cryptovariable:** The information used in conjunction with an algorithm to create the ciphertext from the plaintext or derive the plaintext from the ciphertext; the key can be a series of bits used by a computer program, or it can be a passphrase used by humans that is then converted into a series of bits for use in the computer program.

8) **Keyspace:** The entire range of values that can possibly be used to construct an individual key.

9) **Link encryption:** A series of encryptions and decryptions between a number of systems, wherein each system in a network decrypts the message sent to it and then reencrypts it using different keys and sends it to the next neighbor, and this process continues until the message reaches the final destination.

10) **Plaintext or cleartext:** The original unencrypted message that is encrypted; also the name given to the results of a message that has been successfully decrypted.

11) **Steganography:** The process of hiding messages-for example, messages can be hidden within the digital encoding of a picture or graphic.

12) **Work factor:** The amount of effort (usually in hours) required to perform cryptanalysis. on an encoded message so that it may be decrypted when the key or algorithm (or both) are unknown

Cipher Methods

A plaintext can be encrypted through one of two methods, the bit stream method or the block cipher method. With the bit stream method, each bit in the plaintext is transformed into a cipher bit one bit at a time. In the case of the block cipher method, the message is divided into blocks, for example, sets of 8-,16-,32-, or 64-bit blocks, and then each block of plaintext. bits is transformed into an encrypted block of cipher bits using an algorithm and a key. Bit stream methods most commonly use algorithm functions like the exclusive OR operation (XOR), whereas block methods can use substitution, transposition, XOR, or some combination of these operations, as described in the following sections. As you read on, you should note that most encryption methods using computer systems will operate on data at the level of its binary digits (bits), but some operations may operate at the byte or character level.

Elements of Cryptosystems

Cryptosystems are made up of a number of elements or components. These are usually algorithms and data handling techniques as well as procedures and process steps, which are combined in multiple ways to meet a given organization's need to ensure confidentiality and provide specialized authentication and authorization for its business processes. In the sections that follow, you will first read about the technical aspects of a number of cryptographic techniques, often called ciphers. The chapter will continue with an exploration of some of the tools commonly used to implement cryptographic systems in the world of business. The discussion will then proceed to the security protocols used to bring communications security to the Internet and the world of e-commerce. Finally, the chapter will conclude with a discussion of the attacks that are often found being used against cryptosystems. Along the way, you will also encounter a number of Technical Details boxes that cover advanced material. Be sure to check with your instructor about how your course will include the Technical Details material.

Substitution Cipher

When using a substitution cipher, you substitute one value for another. For example, you can substitute a letter in the alphabet with the letter three values to the right. Or, you may substitute one bit for another bit that is four places to its left. A three-character substitution to the right would result in the following transformation of the standard English alphabet:

- Initial alphabet ABCDEFGHIJKLMNOPQRSTUVWXYZ
- yields Encryption alphabet DEFGHIJKLMNOPQRSTUVWXYZABC

Within this substitution scheme, the plaintext MOM would be encrypted into the ciphertext PRP. This is a simple enough method by itself but very powerful if combined with other operations. Incidentally, this type of substitution is based on a monoalphabetic substitution, since it only uses one alphabet. More advanced substitution ciphers use two or more alphabets, and are referred to as polyalphabetic substitutions.

To continue the previous example, consider the following block of text:

Substitution cipher 3 = JKLMNOPQRSTUVWXYZABCDEFGHI 4th

Substitution cipher 4 = MNOPQRSTUVWXYZABCDEFGHIJKL 5th

The first row here is the plaintext, and the next four rows are four sets of substitution ciphers, which taken together constitute a single polyalphabetic substitution cipher. To encode the word TEXT with this cipher, you substitute a letter from the second row for the first letter in TEXT, a letter from the third row for the second letter, and so on-a process that yields the ciphertext WKGF. Note how the plaintext letter T is transformed into a W or a F, depending on its order of appearance in the plaintext. Complexities like these make this type of encryption substantially more difficult to decipher when one doesn't have the algorithm (in this case, the rows of ciphers) and the key, which is the method used (in this case the use of the second row for first letter, third for second, and so on). A logical extension to this process would be to randomize the cipher rows completely in order to create a more complex operation.

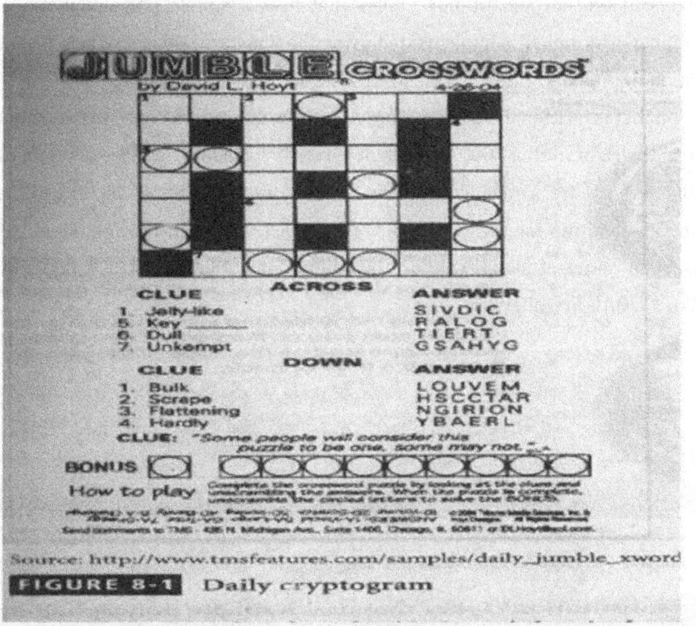

FIGURE 8-1 Daily cryptogram

One example of a substitution cipher is the cryptogram in the daily newspaper (see Figure 8-1); another is the once famous Radio Orphan Annie decoder pin (shown in Figure 8-2), which consisted of two alphabetic rings that could be rotated to a predetermined pairing to form a simple substitution cipher. The device was made to be worn as a pin so one could always be at the ready. As mentioned in Table 8-1, Caesar reportedly used a three-position shift to the right to encrypt his messages (so A became D, B became E, and so on), thus this particular substitution cipher was given his name-the Caesar Cipher.

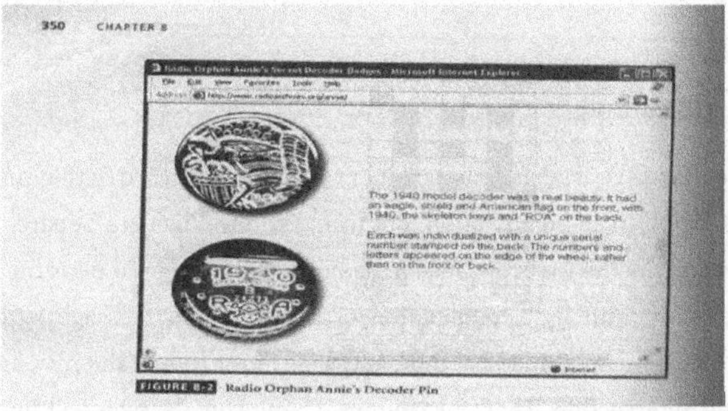

FIGURE 8-2 Radio Orphan Annie's Decoder Pin

An advanced type of substitution cipher that uses a simple polyalphabetic code is the Vigenere cipher. The cipher is implemented using the Vigenere Square. Which is made up of 26 distinct cipher alphabets. Table 8-2 illustrates the setup of the Vigenere Square. In the header row, the alphabet is written in its normal order. In each subsequent row, the alphabet is shifted one letter to the right until a 26 X 26 block of letters is formed. There are a number of ways to use the Vigenere square. You could perform an encryption by simply starting in the first row and finding a substitute for the first letter of plaintext, and then moving down the rows for each subsequent letter of plaintext. With this method, the word SECURITY in plaintext would become TGFYWOAG in ciphertext.

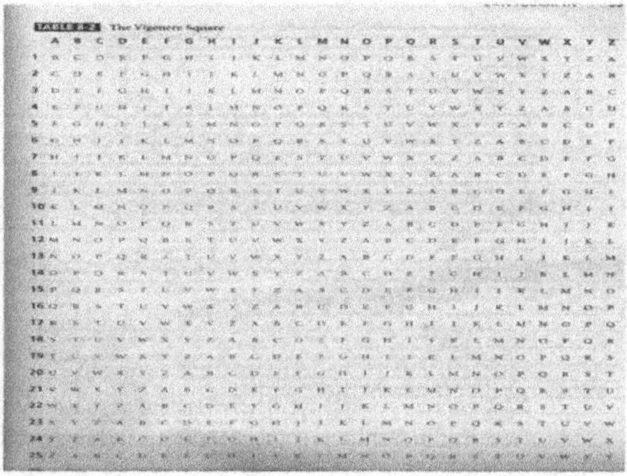

A much more sophisticated way to use the Vigenere Square would be to use a keyword to represent the shift. To accomplish this, you would begin by writing a keyword above the plaintext message. For example, suppose the plaintext message was "SACK GAUL SPARE NO ONE" and the keyword was ITALY. We thus end up with the

Following

ITALYITALYITALYITA

SACKGAULSPARENOONE

The idea behind this is that you will now use the keyword letter and the message (plaintext)letter below it in combination. Returning to the Vigenere Square, notice how the first column of text, like the first row, forms the normal alphabet. To perform the substitution of the message, start with first combination of keyword and message letters, IS. Use the keyword letter to locate the column, and the message letter to find the row, and then look for the letter at their intersection. Thus, for column "I" and row "S," you will find the ciphertext letter "JI||. After you follow this procedure for each of the letters in the message, you will produce the encrypted ciphertext ATCVEINLDNIKEYMWGE. Curiously, one weakness of this method is that any keyword-message letter combination containing an *"N'* row or column will reproduce the plaintext message letter. For example, the third letter in the plaintext message, the C (of SACK), has a combination of AC, and thus is unchanged in the ciphertext. To minimize the effects of this weakness, you should avoid choosing a keyword that contains the letter "A."

Transposition Cipher

The next type of cipher operation is the transposition. Just like the substitution operation, the transposition cipher is simple to understand, but it can, if properly used, produce ciphertext that is complex to decipher. In contrast to the substitution cipher, however, the **transposition cipher** (or **permutation cipher)** simply rearranges the values within a block to create the ciphertext.

This can be done at the bit level or at the byte (character) level. For an example, consider the following transposition key pattern.

Key Pattern

1-4, 2-8, 3-1, 4-5, 5-7, 6-2, 7-6, 8-3

In this key, the bit or byte (character) in position 1 (with position 1 being at the far *right)* moves to position 4 (counting from the right), and the bit or byte in position 2 moves to position 8, and so on. The following rows show the numbering of bit locations for this key; the plaintext message 00100101011010111001010101010100, which is broken into 8-bit blocks for ease of discussion; and the ciphertext that is produced when the transposition key depicted above is applied to the

plaintext:				
Bit locations:	87654321	87654321	87654321	87654321
Plaintext 8-bit blocks:	00100101	01101011	10010101	01010100
Ciphertext:	00001011	10111010	01001101	01100001

Reading from right to left in the example above, the first bit of plaintext (position 1 of the first byte) becomes the fourth bit (in position 4) of the first byte of the ciphertext. Similarly, the second bit of the plaintext (position 2) becomes the eighth bit (position 8) of the ciphertext, and "so on. To examine further how this transposition key works, let's see its effects on a plaintext message comprised of letters instead of bits. Replacing the 8-bit block of plaintext with the example plaintext message presented earlier, "SACK GAUL SPARE NO ONE," yields the following:

Letter locations:	87654321	87654321	87654321 87654321
Plaintext:	SACKGAUL	SPARENOO	N E
Key:	Same key as above, but characters transposed, not bits.		
Ciphertext:	UKAGLSCA	ORPEOSAN	E N

Here, reading again from right to left, the letter in position I of the first block of plaintext, "I.:', becomes the letter at position 4 in the ciphertext. In other words, the "L" that is the 8'h letter of the plaintext is the "L" at the 5th letter of the ciphertext. The letter in position 2 of the first block of plaintext, "U': becomes the letter at position 8 in the ciphertext. In other words, the "U" that is the 7th letter of the plaintext is the "U" at the 151 letter of the ciphertext. This process continues using the specified pattern.

In addition to being credited with inventing a substitution cipher, Julius Caesar was associated with an early version of the transposition cipher. As part of the Caesar block cipher, a courier would carry a message that when read normally would be unintelligible. However, the receiver of the message would know to fit the text to a prime number square (in practice, this meant that if there were fewer than 25 characters, the receiver would use a 5 x 5 square). For example, suppose you were the receiver and the ciphertext shown below arrived at your doorstep. Since it was from Caesar, you would know to make a square of 5 columns and 5 rows, and then to write the letters of the message into the square, filling the slots from left to right, top to bottom. Also, when you'd finished doing this, you'd know to read the message the opposite direction-that is, from top to bottom, left to right. Ciphertext:

SGS-NAAPNECUAO KLR EO

S G S - N

A A P N

E C U A 0

K L R_- -

-_-_E O -

Reading from top to bottom, left to right reveals the plaintext "SACK GAUL SPARE NO ONE': hen mechanical and electronic cryptosystems became more widely used, transposition ciphers and substitution ciphers began to be used in combinations to produce highly secure encryption processes. To make the encryption even stronger (more difficult to cryptanalyze) the keys and block sizes can be made much larger (upto 64 or 128 bits in size), which produces substantially more complex substitutions or transpositions.

Exclusive OR

The **exclusive OR operation** (XOR) is a function of Boolean algebra in which two bits are compared, and if the two bits are identical, the result is a binary 0. If the two bits are not the same, the result is a binary 1. XOR encryption is a very simple symmetric cipher that is used in many applications where security is not a defined requirement Table 8-3 shows a truth table for XOR with the results of all the possible combinations of two bits.

TABLE 8-3 XOR Truth Table

First Bit	Second Bit	Result
0	0	0
0	1	1
1	0	1
1	1	0

To see how XOR works, let's consider an example in which the plaintext we will start with is the word "CAT': The binary representation of the plaintext is "0 1110000 01100101 1000000". In order to encrypt the plaintext, a key value should be selected. In this case, the bit pattern for the letter "Y" (10000101) will be used and repeated for each character to be encrypted. Performing the XOR operation on the two bit streams (the plaintext and the key) will produce the following result:

TABLE 8-4 Example XOR Encryption

CAT as bits	0 1 1 1 0 0 0 0 0 1 1 0 0 1 0 1 1 0 0 0 0 0 0 0
VVV as key	1 0 0 0 0 1 0 1 1 0 0 0 0 1 0 1 1 0 0 0 0 1 0 1
Cipher	1 1 1 1 0 1 0 1 1 1 1 0 0 0 0 0 0 0 0 0 0 1 0 1

The row of Table 8-4 labeled "Cipher" contains the bit stream that will be transmitted; when this cipher is received, it can be decrypted using the key value of "y"'. Note that the XOR encryption method is very simple to implement and equally simple to break. The XOR encryption method should not be used by itself when an organization is transmitting or storing data that needs protection. Actual encryption algorithms used to protect data typically use the XOR operator as part of a more complex encryption pro<;ess, thus understanding XOR encryption is a necessary step on the path to becoming a cryptologist. Often, one can combine the XOR operation with a block cipher operation to produce a simple but powerful operation.

Consider the example that follows, the first row of which shows a character message "5E5+'" requiring encryption. The second row shows this message in binary notation. In order to apply an 8-bit block cipher method, the binary message is broken into 8-bit blocks in the. Row labeled "Message Blocks". The fourth row shows the 8-bit key (01010101) chosen for the encryption. To encrypt the message, you must perform the XOR operation on each 8-bit block by using the XOR function on the message bit and the key bit to determine the bits of the ciphertext until the entire message is enciphered. The result is shown in the row labelled message by simply knowing the algorithm (XOR) and the key (01010101).

"Ciphertext': Thi Message (text) :— 5E5+||

Message (binary): 0011001010001010011010100101011110010101

Message blocks: 00110101 01000101 00110101 00101011 10010101

Key: 01010101 01010101 01010101 01010101 01010101

Ciphertext: 01100000 00010000 01100000 01111110 11000000

s ciphertext can"Ciphertext': Thi Message (text) : — 5E5+||

Message (binary): 0011001010001010011010100101011110010101

Message blocks: 00110101 01000101 00110101 00101011 10010101

Key: 01010101 01010101 01010101 01010101 01010101

Ciphertext: 01100000 00010000 01100000 01111110 11000000

s ciphertext can now be sent to a receiver, who will be a ble to decipher the message by simply knowing the algorithm (XOR) and the key (01010101)

Message (text) :	— 5E5+||
Message (binary):	0011001010001010011010100101011110010101
Message blocks:	00110101 01000101 00110101 00101011 10010101
Key:	01010101 01010101 01010101 01010101 01010101
Ciphertext:	01100000 00010000 01100000 01111110 11000000

If the receiver cannot apply the key to the ciphertext and derive the original message, either the cipher was applied with an incorrect key or the cryptosystem was not used correctly.

Vernam Cipher

Also known as the one-time pad, the Vernam dpher, which was developed at AT&T, uses a set of characters only one time for each encryption process (hence, the name one- time pad). The pad in the name comes from-the days of manual encryption and decryption when the key values for each ciphering session were prepared by hand and bound into an easy-to-use form-i.e., a pad of paper. To peiform the Yernam cipher encryption operation, the pad values are added to numeric values that represent the plaintext that needs to be encrypted. So, each character of the plaintext is turned into a number and a pad value for that position is added to it. The resulting sum for that character is then converted back to a ciphertext letter for transmission. If the sum of the. two values exceeds 26, then 26 is subtracted from the total (Note that the process of keeping a computed number within a specific range is called a modulo; thus, requiring that all numbers be in the range 1-26 is referred to as Modulo 26. In Modulo 26, if a number is larger than 26, then 26 is repeatedly subtracted from it until the number is in the proper range.).

To examine the Yernam cipher and its use of modulo, consider the following example, which uses the familiar "SACK GAUL SPARE NO ONE" as plaintext. In the first step of this encryption process, the letter "S" will be converted into the number 19 (because it is the 19th letter of the alphabet), and the same conversion will be applied to the rest of the letters of the plaintext message, as shown below.

Plain Text:	S	A	C	K	G	A	U	L	S	P	A	R	E	N	O	O	N	E
Plain Text Value:	19	01	03	11	07	01	21	12	19	16	01	18	05	14	15	15	14	05
One-Time Pad text:	F	P	Q	R	N	S	B	I	E	H	T	Z	L	A	C	D	G	J
One-Time Pad Value:	06	16	17	18	14	19	02	09	05	08	20	26	12	01	03	04	07	10
Sum of Plaintext and Pad:	25	17	20	29	21	20	23	21	24	24	21	44	17	15	18	19	21	15
After Modulo Substraction				03								18						
				CUTW		UXXURQ		ORSU	O									
Ciphertext:	Y	Q	P															

Rows three and four in the example above show, respectively, the one-time pad text that was chosen for this encryption and the one time pad value. As you can see, the pad value is, like the plaintext value, derived by considering the position of each pad text letter in the alphabet, thus the pad text letter "F" is assigned the position number of 06. This conversion process is repeated for the entire one-time pad text. Next, the plaintext value and the one time pad value are added together-the first such sum is 25. Since 25 is in the range of 1 to 26, no Modulo- 26 subtraction is required. The sum remains 25, and yields the cipher text "Y'; as shown above. Skipping ahead to the fourth character of the plaintext, "K'; we find that the plaintext value for it is 11. The pad text is "R" and the pad value is 18. Adding 11 and 18 will result in a sum of 29.

Since 29 is larger than 26, 26 is Subtracted from it, which yields the value 3. The cipher text for this plaintext character will then be the third letter of the alphabet, "C||.

Decryption of any cipher text generated from a one-time pad will require either knowledge of the pad values or the use of elaborate and (the encrypting party hopes)very difficult cryptanalysis. Using the pad values and the cipher text, the decryption process would happen as follows; "Y" becomes the number 25 from which we subtract the pad value for the first letter of the message, 06. This yields a value of 19, or the letter—S||. This pattern continuous until the fourth letter of the cipher text where the cipher text letter is —c|| and the pad value is 18. Subtracting 18 from 3 will give a difference of negative 15. Since modulo- 26 is employed, it requires that all numbers are in the range of that fourth letter of the message is —K||.

Book or Running Key Cipher

One encryption method made popular by spy movies involves using the text in a book as the key to decrypt a message. The ciphertext consists of a list of codes representing the page number, line number, and word number of the plaintext word. The algorithm is the mechanical process of looking up the references from the ciphertext and converting each reference to a word by using the cipher text's value and the key (the book). For example, from a copy of a particular popular novel, one may send the message: 259,19,8; 22,3,8;375,7,4; 394,17,2. Although almost any book will work just fine, dictionaries and thesauruses are typically the most popular sources as they can guarantee having almost every word that might be needed. Returning to the example, the receiver must first know which novel is used-in this case, suppose it is the science fiction novel, *A Fire Upon the Deep,* the 1992 TOR edition. To decrypt the ciphertext, the receiver would acquire the book and begin by turning to page 259, finding line 19, and selecting the eighth word in that line (which happens to be "sack"). Then the receiver would go to page 22, line 3, and select the eighth word again, and so forth. For this example, the resulting message will be" SACK ISLAND SHARP PATH". If dictionaries are used, the message would be made up of only the page number and the number of the word on the page. An even more sophisticated version might use multiple books, perhaps even in a particular sequence for each word or phrase.

Hash Functions

In addition to ciphers, another important encryption technique that is often incorporated into cryptosystems is the hash function. Hash functions are mathematical algorithms that generate a message summary or digest (sometimes called a fingerprint) to confirm the identity of a ~pacific message and to confirm that there have not been any changes to the content

While not directly related to the creation of a ciphertext, hash functions are used to confirm message identity and integrity, both of which are critical functions in e-commerce.

Hash algorithms are publicly known functions that create a hash value, also known as a message digest, by converting variable-length messages into a single fixed-length value. The message digest is a fingerprint of the author's message that is to be compared with the receiver's locally calculated hash of the same message If both hashes are identical after transmission, the message has arrived without modification. Hash functions are considered one-way operations in that the message will always provide the same hash value if it is the same message, but the hash value itself cannot be used to determine the contents of the message.

Hashing functions do not require the use of keys, but **a message authentication code(MAC),** which is a key-dependent, and one-way hash function, may be attached to a message to allow only specific recipients to access the message digest The MAC is essentially a one-way hash value that is encrypted with a symmetric key. The recipients must possess the key to access the message digest and to confirm message integrity.

Because hash functions are one-way, they are used in password verification systems to confirm the identity of the user. In such systems, the hash value, or message digest, is calculated based upon the originally issued password, and this message digest is stored for later comparison. When the user logs on for the next session, the system calculates a hash value based on the user's inputted password. The newly calculated hash value is compared against the stored value to confirm identity.

The Secure Hash Standard (SHS) is a standard issued by the National Institute of Standards and Technology (NIST). Standard document FIPS 180-1 specifies SHA-l (Secure Hash Algorithm 1) as a secure algorithm for computing a condensed representation of a message or data file. SHA-I produces a 160-bit message digest, which can then be used as an input to a digital signature algorithm. SHA-I is based on principles modeled after MD4 (which is part of the MDx family of hash algorithms created by Ronald Rivest). New hash algorithms (SHA-256, SHA-384, and SHA-512) have been proposed by NIST as standards for 128, 192, and 156 bits, respectively. The number of bits used in the hash algorithm is a measurement of the strength of the algorithm against collision attacks. SHA-256 is essentially a 256-bit block cipher algorithm that creates a key by encrypting the intermediate hash value with the message block functioning as the key. The compression unction operates on each 512-bit message block and a 256-intermediate message digest'

Cryptographic Algorithms

In general, cryptographic algorithms are often grouped into two broad categories-symmetric and asymmetric-but in practice, today's popular crypto systerns use a hybrid combination of symmetric and asymmetric algorithms. Symmetric and asymmetric algorithms can be distinguished by the types of keys they use for encryption and decryption operations. The upcoming section discusses both of these algorithms, and includes Technical Details boxes that provide supplemental information on cryptographic notation and advanced encryption standards.

Symmetric Encryption. A method of encryption that requires the same secret key to encipher and decipher the message is known as **private key encryption or symmetric encryption.** Symmetric encryption methods use mathematical operations that can be programmed into extremely fast computing algorithms so that the encryption and decryption processes are done quickly by even small computers. As you can see in Figure 8- 3, one of the challenges is that both the sender and the receiver must have the secret key. Also, if either copy of the key falls into the wrong hands, messages can be decrypted by others and the sender and intended receiver may not know the message was intercepted. The primary challenge of symmetric key encryption is getting the key to the receiver, a process that must be conducted out of band (meaning through a channel or band other than the one carrying the cipher text) to avoid interception.

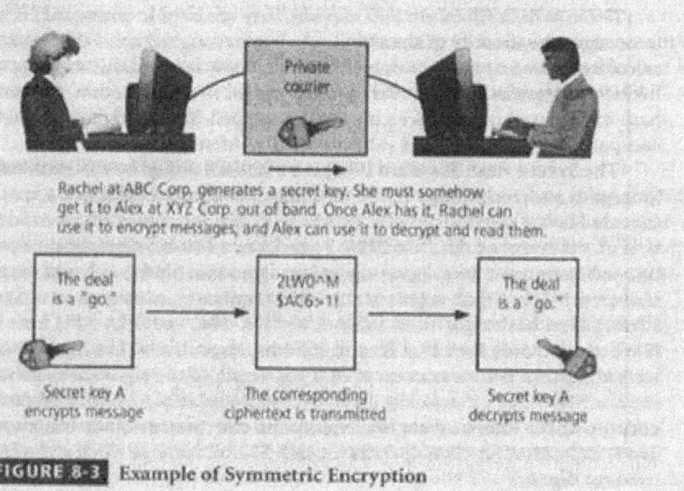

FIGURE 8-3 Example of Symmetric Encryption

Cryptographic Notation

The notation used to describe the encryption process varies, depending on its source. The notation chosen for the discussion in this text uses the letter M to represent the original message, C to represent the ending ciphertext, and E to represent the encryption process: thus, E(M) = C.[2] This formula represents the application of encryption (E) to a message (M) to create ciphertext (C). Also in this notation scheme, the letter D represents the decryption or deciphering process, thus the formula D[E(M)] = M states that if you decipher (D) an enciphered an message (E(M)), you should get the original message (M). This could also be stated as D[C]=M, or the deciphering of the ciphertext (remember that C=E(M)) results in the original message M. Finally the letter K is used the represent the key, therefore(M,K) = C suggests that encrypting (E) the message (M) with the key (K) results in the ciphertext (C). Similarly, D(C,K) = D[E(M,K),K] = M, or deciphering the ciphertext with key K results in the original plaintext message—or, to translate this formula even more precisely, deciphering with key K the message encrypted eith key K results in the original message.

To encrypt a plaintext set of data, you can use one of two methods: bit stream and block cipher. With the bit stream method, the message is divided into blocks, e.g., 8-,16-,32-, or 64-bit blocks, and then each block is transformed using the algorithm and key. Bit stream methods most commonly use algorithm functions like XOR, whereas block methods can use XOR, transposition, or substitution.

There are a number of popular symmetric encryption cryptosystem. One of the most widely known is the DATA ENCRYPTION STANDARDS (DES)., which was developed by IBM and I based on the company's Lucifer algorithm, which uses a key length of 128 bits. As implemented , DES uses a 64-bit block size and a 56-bit key.DES was adopted by nIST in 1976 as a federal standard for encryption of non-classified information. With this approval, DES became widely employed in commercial applications as the encryption standard of choice. DES enjoyed increasing popularity for almost 20 years, until 1997, when users realized that using a 56-bit key size was no longer sufficient as an acceptable level of secure communications. And soon enough, in 1998, a group called Electronic Frontier Foundation (www.eff.org), using a specially designed computer, broke a DES key in less than three days(just over 56 hours, to be precise). Since then, it has been theorized that a dedicated attack supported by the proper hardware (thus, not even a specialized computer like that of Electronic Frontier Foundation) can break a DES key in less than four hours. As DES became known as being too weak for highly classified communications, Triple DES (3DES) was created to provide a level of security far beyond that of DES. 3 DES was an advanced application of DES, and was in fact originally designed to replace DES. While 3DES did deliver on its promise of encryption strength beyond DES, it too was soon proven too weak to survive indefinitely-especially as computing power continued to double every 18 months. Within just few years, 3DES needed to be replaced.

Triple DES (3DES)

As it was demonstrated that DES was not strong enough for highly classified communication, 3DES was created to provide a level of security far beyond that of standard DES. (In between, there was a 2DES; however, it was statistically shown that the double DES did not provide significantly stronger security than that of DES). 3DES takes three 64-bit keys for an overall key length of 192 bits. Triple DES encryption is the same as that of standard DES; however, it is repeated three times. Triple DES can be employed using two or three keys, and a combination of encryption or decryption to obtain additional security. The most common implementations involve encrypting and /or decrypting with two or three different keys, a process that is described below. 3DES employs 48 rounds in its encryption computation, generating ciphers that are approximately 2^{56}. (72 quadrillion) times stronger than standard DES ciphers but require only three times longer to process. One example of 3DES encryption is illustrated here:

1) In the first operation, 3DES encrypts the message with key 1, then decrypts it with key 2, and then it encrypts it again with key 1. In cryptographic notation terms, this would be [E{D[E(M,K1)],K2},K1]. Decrypting with a different key is essentially another encryption, but it reverses the application of the traditional encryption operations.
2) In the second operation, 3DES encrypts the message with key 1, then it encrypts it again with key2, and then it encrypts it a third time with key 1 again, or [E{E[E(M,K1)],K2},K1].

In the third operation, 3DES encrypts the message three times with three different keys; [E{E[E(M,K1)],K2},K3].This is the most secure level of encryption possible with 3DES.

The successor to 3DES is Advanced Encryption Standard (AES). AES is a Federal Information Processing Standard (FIPS) that specifies a cryptographic algorithm that is used within the U.S. government to protect information at federal agencies that are not a part of the national defense infrastructure. (Agencies that are considered a part of national defense use other, more secure methods of encryption, which are provided by the National Security Agency.) The requirements for AES stipulate that the algorithm should be unclassified, publicly disclosed, and available royalty-free worldwide. AES has been developed to replace both DES and 3DES. While 3DES remains an approved algorithm for some uses, its expected useful life is limited. Historically, cryptographic standards approved by FIPS have been adopted on a voluntary basis by organizations outside government entities. The AES selection process involved cooperation between the U.S. government, private industry, and academia from around the world. AES was approved by the Secretary of Commerce as the official federal governmental standard on May 26, 2002.

The AES implements a block cipher called the Rijndael Block Cipher with a variable block length and a key length of 128, 192, or 256 bits. Experts estimate that the special computer used by the Electronic Frontier Foundation to crack DES within a couple of days would require approximately 4,698,864 quintillion years (4,698,864,000,000,000,000,000) to crack AES. To learn more about the AES, See the Technical Details box entitled "Advanced Encryption Standard(AES).||

Advanced Encryption Standard (AES)

Of the many ciphers that were submitted (from across the world) for consideration in the AES selection process, five finalists were chosen: MARS, RC6, Rijndael, Serpent, and Two fish. On October 2, 2000, NIST announced the selection of Rijndael as the cipher to be used as the basis for the AES, and this block cipher was approved by the Secretary of Commerce as the official federal governmental standard as of May 26, 2002.

The AES version of Rijndael can use a multiple round based system. Depending on the key size, the number of rounds varies between 9 and 13: for a l28.bit key, 9 rounds plus one end round are used; for a 192-bit key, 11 rounds plus one end round are used; and for a 256-bit key, 13 rounds plus one end round are used. Once Rijndael was adopted as the AES, the ability to use variable sized blocks was standardized to a single l28-bit block for simplicity.

There are four steps within each Rijndael round, and these are described in "The Advanced Encryption Standard (Rijndael)" by John Savard as follows:

1) The Byte Sub step. Each byte of the block is replaced by its substitute in an S-box (Substitution box). [Author's Note: The S-box consists of a table of computed values, the calculation of which is beyond the scope of this text.].
2) The Shift Row step. Considering the block to be made up of bytes 1 to 16, these bytes are arranged in a rectangle, and shifted as follows:

from				to			
1	5	9	13	1	5	9	13
2	6	10	14	6	10	14	2
3	7	11	15	11	15	3	7
4	8	12	16	16	4	8	12

Other shift tables are used for larger blocks.

3) The Mix Column step. Matrix multiplication is performed: each column is multiplied by the matrix:

   2 3 1 1

   1 2 3 1

   1 1 2 3

   3 1 1 2

4) The Add Round Key step. This simply XORs in the subkey for the current round.

The extra final round omits the Mix Column step, but is otherwise the same as a regular round."3

Asymmetric Encryption. Another category of encryption techniques is asymmetric encryption. Whereas the symmetric encryption systems are based on using a single key to both encrypt and decrypt a message, **asymmetric encryption** uses two different but related keys, and either key can be used to encrypt or decrypt the message. If, however, Key A is used to encrypt the message, only Key B can decrypt it, and if Key B is used to encrypt a message, only Key A can decrypt it. Asymmetric ~ncryption can be used to provide elegant solutions to problems of secrecy and verification. This technique has its highest value when one key is used as a private key, which means that it is kept secret (much like the key of symmetric encryption), known only to the owner of the key pair, and the other key serves as a public key, which means that it is stored in a public location where anyone can use it. This is why the more common name for asymmetric encryption is **public key encryption.**

Consider the following example, illustrated in Figure 8-4. Alex at XYZ Corporation wants to send an encrypted message to Rachel at ABC Corporation. Alex goes to a public key registry and obtains Rachel's public key. Remember that the foundation of asymmetric encryption is that the same key cannot be used to both encrypt and decrypt the same message. So. when Rachel's public key is used to encrypt the message, only Rachel's private key can be used to decrypt the message and that private key is held by Rachel alone. Similarly, if Rachel wants to respond to Alex's message, she goes to the registry where Alex's public key is held, and uses it to encrypt her message, which of course can only be read by Alex's private key. This approach, which keeps private keys secret and encourages the sharing of public keys in reliable directories, is an elegant solution to the key management problems found in symmetric key applications.

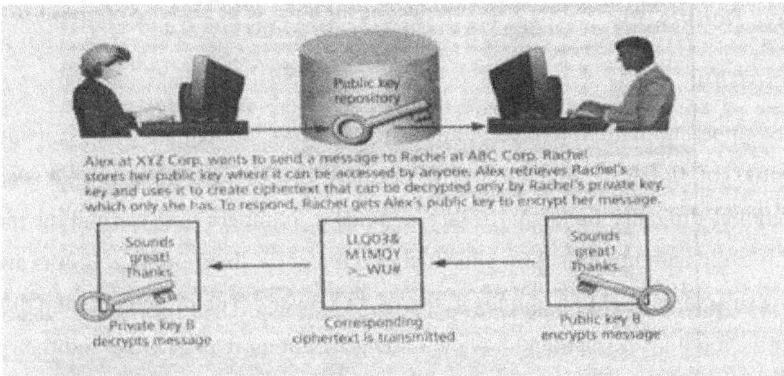

FIGURE 8-4 Example of Asymmetric Encryption

Asymmetric algorithms are based on one-way functions. A one-way function is simple to compute in one direction, but complex to compute in the opposite. This is the foundation of public-key encryption. Public-key encryption is based on a hash value, which, as you learned earlier in this chapter, is calculated from an input number using a hashing algorithm. This hash value is essential summary of the original input values. It is virtually impossible to derive the original values without knowing how the values were used to create the hash value. For example. if you multiply 45 by 235 you get 10,575. This is simple enough. But if you are simply given the number 10,575, can you determine which two numbers were multiplied to determine this number? Now assume that each multiplier is 200 digits long and prime. The resulting multiplicative product would be up to 400 digits long. Imagine the time you'd need to factor that out There is a shortcut, however. In mathematics, it is known as a trapdoor (which is different from the software trapdoor). A mathematical **trapdoor** is a "secret mechanism that enables you to easily accomplish the reverse function in a one-way function."4 With a trapdoor, you can use a key to encrypt or decrypt the ciphertext, but not both, thus requiring two keys. The public key becomes be the true key, and the private key is to be derived from the public key using the trapdoor.

One of the most popular public key cryptosystems is RSA, whose name is derived from Rivest-Shamir-Adleman, the algorithm's developers. The **RSA algorithm** was the first public key encryption algorithm developed (in 1977) and published for commercial use. It is very popular and has been embedded in both Microsoft's and Netscape's Web browsers to enable them to provide security for e-commerce applications. The patented RSA algorithm has in fact become the de facto standard for public use encryption applications. To see how this algorithm works, see the Technical Details box "RSA Algorithm."

Technical Details Box

RSA Algorithm

If you understand modulo If you understand modulo mathematics, you can appreciate the complexities of the RSA algorithm. The security of the RSA algorithm is based on the computational difficulty of factor in lare composite numbers and computing the eth roots modulo, a composite number for a specified odd integer *e.* Encryption in RSA is accomplished by raising the message *M* to a nonnegative integer power *e.* The product is then divided by the nonnegative modulus *n* (n should have a bit length of at least *1024* bits), and the remainder is the ciphertext *C.* This process results in one-way operation (shown below) when n is a very large number.

$$IC = Me / \bmod n$$

In the decryption process, the ciphertext C is raised to the power d, a nonnegative integer, as follows:

$$d = e^{-l} \bmod((p-l)(q-1))$$

C is then reduced by modulo n. In order for the recipient to calculate the decryption key, the p and q factors must be known. The modulus n, which is a composite number, is determined by multiplying two large nonnegative prime numbers, p and q:

$$n=p\infty q$$

In RSA's asymmetric algorithm, which is the basis of most modern Public Key Infrastructure (PKI) systems (a topic covered later in this chapter), the public and private keys are generated using the following procedure, which is from the RSA Corporation:

"Choose two large prime numbers, p and q, of equal length, and compute !

p x q = n, which is the public modulus. !

Choose a random public key, e, so that e and (p-1)(q-l) are relatively prime. I Compute e x d = 1 mod (p -l)(q - 1), where d is the private key. Thus d = e-lmod[(p - l)(q -1)]."

Where "(d, n) is the private key; (e, n) is the public key. P is encrypted to generate ciphertext C as C = p^e mod n, and is decrypted to recover the plaintext, P as P = Cd. Essentially, the RSA algorithm can be divided into three steps:

1) Key generation: Prime factors p and q are statistically selected by a technique known as i probabilistic primality testing and then multiplied together to form n. The encryption exponent e is selected, and the decryption exponent d is calculated.

2) Encryption: M is raised to the power of e, reduced by modulo n, and remainder C is the ciphertext.

3) Decryption: C is raised to the power of d and reduced by modulo n.

The sender publishes the public key, which consists of modulus n and exponent e. The remaining variables d, p, and q are kept secret.

A message can then be encrypted by: $C = M^e$(recipient) mod n(recipient)

Digitally signed by:	$C = M'^d$(sender) mod n(sender)
Verified by:	$M' = C'^e$(sender) mod n(sender)
Decrypted by:	$M = C^d$(recipient) mod n(recipient)

Example Problems

Because this Technical Details box presents complex information, the following sections contain practice examples to help you better understand the machinations of the various algorithms.

RSA Algorithm Example: Work through the following steps to better understand how the RSA algorithm functions:

1) Choose randomly two large prime numbers: P, Q (usually P, Q > 10^100)→t This means 10 to the power 100.
2) Compute:

   N=PXQ

   Z=(P-1)(Q-l)
3) Choose a number relatively prime with Z and call it *D*.

   D < N; relatively prime means that *D* and Z have no common factors, except 1
4) Find number E, such that ->*EX D* = 1 mod Z;
5) The public key is: (N, E); the private Key is (N, D).
6) Create Cipher (Encrypted Text): C=|TEXT|E(MOD N)

   C→ Encrypted text -t this is the text that's transmitted

   | TEXT |→ Plaintext to be encrypted (its numerical correspondent)
7) Decrypt the message:

   D = Plaintext = CD (MOD N), C = Ciphertext from part 6.

Note that it is almost impossible to obtain the private key, knowing the public key, and it's almost impossible to factor N into P and Q.

RSA Numerical Example: 13 Work through the following steps to better understand RSA Numericals:

1) Choose P = 3, Q = 11 (two prime numbers). Note that small numbers have been chosen for the example, so that you can easily work with them. In real life encryption, they:are larger than 10^100.
2) N= P∞Q =3 ∞11 = 33; Z = (P-1)(Q-l) =2∞10 = 20
3) Choose a number for D that is relatively prime with Z, for example, D = 7→ (20 and 7 have no common divisors, except 1).
4) E = ? such as E∞D = I MOD Z (I MOD Z means that the remainder of E/D division is 1).

   E ∞ D / Z → E ∞7 /20→E=3

   Check E∞D/Z-+ *3007/* 20→2l/20→ Remainder = 1
5) So, the public key is (N,E) = (33,3) → This key will be used to encrypt the message. The private key is (N,D) = (33,7)→This key will be used to decrypt the message

English Alphabet and Corresponding Numbers *for* Each Letter:[7] In real life applications, the ASCII code is used to represent each of the characters of a message. For this example, the position of the letter in the alphabet is used instead to simplify the calculations:

A=01,B=02,etc.....Z=26.

Encrypt The Word "Technology" as illustrated in Table 8-5:[8] Now you can use the corresponding numerical and the previous calculations to calculate values for the public ke

(N,E) = (33,3) and the private key (N,D) = (33,7).

Table 8-5: Encryption

Plaintext	**Text value**	**(Text)AE**	**(Text)AE MOD N = Ciphertext**
T	20	8000	8000 MOD 33 = 14
E	05	125	125 MOD 33 = 26
C	03	27	27 MOD 33 = 27
H	08	512	512MOD33=17
N	14	2744	2744 MOD 33 = 05
O	15	3375	3375 MOD 33 = 09
L	12	1728	1728 MOD 33 = 12
O	15	3375	3375 MOD 33 = 09
G	07	343	343 MOD 33 = 13
Y	25	15625	15625 MOD 33 = 16

So, the cipher (encrypted message) is: 14262717050912091316. This is what is trans. mitted over unreliable lines. Note that there are two digits per letter. To decrypt the transmitted message we apply the private key *(AD)* and re-MOD the product, the result *of* which is the numerical equivalent *of* the original plaintext.

Table 8-6: Decryption

Ciphertext	(Cipher)AD	(Cipher)AD MOD N = |Text|	Plaintext
14	105413504	105413504 MOD 33 = 20	T
26	8031810176	8031810176 MOD 33 = 05	E
27	10460353203	10460353203 MOD 33 = 03	C
17	410338673	410338673 MOD 33 = 08	H
05	78125	78125 MOD 33 = 14	N
09	4782969	4782969 MOD 33 = 15	O
12	35831808	35831808 MOD 33 = 12	L
09	4782969	4782969 MOD 33 = 15	O
13	62748517	62748517 MOD 33 = 07	G
16	268435456	268435456 MOD 33 = 25	Y

As you can see in Table 8.6, although very small P and Q numbers were used, the numbers required for decrypting the message are relatively large. Now you have a good idea of what kind *of* numbers are needed when P and Q are large (that is, in the 10^{100} range).

If P and Q are not big enough for the cipher to be secure, P and Q must be increased. The strength of this encryption algorithm relies on how difficult it is to factor P and Q from N if N is known. If N is not known, the algorithm is even harder to break, of course.

The problem with asymmetric encryption, as is shown by the example ill Figure 8-4, is that holding a single conversation between two parties requires four keys. Moreover, if four organizations want to exchange communications frequently, each party must manage its private key and four public keys. In such scenarios, determining which public key is needed to encrypt a particular message can become a rather confusing problem, and with more organizations in the loop, the problem expands. This is why asymmetric encryption is sometimes regarded by experts as an inefficient endeavor. Compared to symmetric encryption, asymmetric encryption is also not as efficient in terms of CPU computations. Consequently, hybrid systems, such as those described in the section of this chapter titled "Public Key Infrastructure (PKI);' are more com-monly used than pure asymmetric system.

Encryption Key Size

When using ciphers, one of the decisions that has to be made is the size of the crypto variable or key. This will prove to be very important, because the strength of many encryption applications and cryptosystems is measured by key size. But does the size of the encryption key really matter? And how exactly does key size affect the strength of an algorithm? Typically, the length of the key increases the number of random selections that will have to be guessed in order to break the code. Creating a larger universe of possibilities that need to be checked increases the time required to make guesses, and thus a longer key will directly influence the strength of the encryption.

It may surprise you to learn that when it comes to cryptosystems, the security of encrypted data is *not* dependent on keeping the encrypting algorithm secret; in fact, algorithms should be (and often are) published, so that research to uncover their weaknesses can be done. Instead the security of any cryptosystem depends on keeping some or all of the elements of the crypto variable (s) or key(s) secret, and effective security is maintained by manipulating the size (bit length) of the keys and by following proper procedures and policies for key management.

For a simple example of how key size is related to encryption strength, suppose you have an algorithm that uses a three-bit key. You may recall from earlier in the chapter that key space is the amount of space from which the key can be drawn. Also, you may recall that in binary notation, three bits can be used to represent values from 000. to Ill, which correspond to the numbers 0 to 7 in decimal, and thus a key space of eight keys. This means that with an algorithm that uses a three-bit key you have eight possible keys to choose from (the numbers 0 to 7 in binary are 000, 001, 010, 011, 100, 101, 110,111). If you know how many keys you have to choose from, you can program a computer simply to try all the keys and see if it can crack the encrypted message.

The preceding statement presumes a few things: I) you know the algorithm, 2) you have the encrypted message, and 3) you have time on your hands. It is easy to satisfy the first criterion. The encryption tools that use the Data Encryption Standard (DES) can be purchased over the counter. Many of these tools are based on encryption algorithms that are standards, as is DES itself, therefore it is relatively easy to get a cryptosystem based on DES that would enable you to decrypt an encrypted message if you possess the key. The second criterion requires the interception of an encrypted message, which is illegal, but not impossible. As for the third criterion, the task required is a brute force attack, in which a computer randomly (or sequentially) selects possible keys of the known size and applies them to the encrypted text, or a piece of the encrypted text. If the result is plaintext-bingo! But as indicated earlier in this chapter, it can take quite a long time to exert brute force on the more advanced cryptosystems. In fact, the strength of an algorithm is determined by how long it takes to guess the key.

Luckily, however, once set to a task, computers do not require much adult supervision, so you probably won't have to quit your day job.

But when it comes to keys, how big is big? From the example at the beginning of this section, you learned that a three-bit system has eight keys to guess. An eight-bit system has 256 keys to guess. Note, however, that if you use a 32-bit key, puny by modem standards, you have to guess almost 16.8 million keys. Even so, a modern PC, such as the one described in

Table 8-7, could do this in mere seconds. But, as Table 8-7 shows, the amount of time needed to crack a cipher by guessing its key grows very quickly-that is, exponentially with each additional bit.

One thing to keep in mind here is that even though the estimated time to crack grows so rapidly with respect to the number of bits in the encryption key and the odds of cracking seem at first glance to be insurmountable, Table 8-7 doesn't account for the fact that computing power has increased (and continues to increase). Therefore, these days even the once-standard 56-bit encryption can't stand up to brute force attacks by personal computers, especially if multiple computers are used together to crack these keys. Each additional computer reduces the amount of time needed. Two computers can divide the possibilities and crack the key in approximately half the time and so on. Thus, two hundred and eighty five computers can crack a 56-bit key in one year, ten times as many would do it in a little over a month.

Encryption Key Power

Number of its In Key	Odds of Cracking:1 in	Estimated Time to Crack*
8	256	
16	65,536	.000032 seconds
24	16,777,216	
		.008192 seconds
32	4,294,967,296	
56	72,057,594,037,927,900	2.097 seconds
64	18,446,744,073,709,600,00	
		8 minutes 56.87 seconds
	0	
128	3.40282E+38	285 years 32 weeks 1 day
256	1.15792E+77	
		8,090,677,225 years
512	1.3408E+154	
		5,257,322,061,209,440,000,000 years
		2,753,114,795,116,330,000,000,000,0 00,000,00, 000,000,000,000,000,000 years
		608,756,305,260,875,000,000,000,000 ,000, 000,000,000,000,000,000,000,000,000 ,000, 000,000,000,000,000,000,000,000,000 ,000, 000,000,000,000 years

[Note]* Estimated Time to crack is based on a general purpose personal computer performing eight million guesses per second

4.4. Cryptography Tools

Public key Infrastructure

Public Key Infrastructure (PKI) is an integrated system of software, encryption methodologies protocols, legal agreements, and third party services that enable users to communicate security. PKI systems are based on public key cryptosystems and include digital certificates and certificate authorities (CAs). Digital certificates are public key container files that allow computer programs to validate the key and identify to whom it belongs.PKI and the digital certificate registries they contain enable the protection of information assets by making verifiable digital certificates readily available to business applications. This, in turn , allows the applications to implement several of the key characteristics of information security and to integrate these characteristics into business processes across an organization. These processes include the following:

1) Authentication: Individuals, organizations, and web servers can validate the identity of each of the parties in an internet transaction.
2) Integrity: Content signed by the certificate is known to be unaltered while being moved from host to host or server to client.
3) Privacy: Information is protected from being intercepted during transmission.
4) Authorization: The validated identity of users and programs can be used to enable authorization rules that remain in place for the duration of a transaction; this reduces some of the overhead required and allows for more control of access privileges for specific transactions.

A typical PKI solution protects the transmission and reception of secure information by integrating the following components.

1) A certificate authority (CA), which issues, manages, authenticates, signs, and revokes user's digital certificates, which typically contain the user's name,public key, and other identifying information.
2) A registration authority (RA), which operates under the trusted collaboration of the certificate authority and can be delegated day-to-day certification functions, such as verifying registration information about new registrants, generating end-user keys, revoking certificates, and validating that users possess a valid certificate.
3) Certificate directories, which are central locations for certificate storage that provide a single access point for administration and distribution.
4) Management protocols, which organize and manage the communications between CAs,

RAs, and end users. This includes the functions and procedures for setting up new users, issuing keys, recovering keys, updating keys, revoking keys, and enabling the transfer of certificates and status information among the parties involved in the PKI's area of authority.

Policies and procedures that assist an organization in the application and management of certificates, the formalization of legal liabilities and limitations, and actual business practice use. Common implementations of PKI include: systems to issue digital certificates to users and servers; directory enrolment, key issuing systems; tools for managing the key issuant and verification and return of certificates. These systems enable organizations to apply an enterprise-wide solution that provides users within the PKI's area of authority the means to implement authenticated and secure communications and transactions.

Digital Signatures

Digital signatures were created in response to the rising need to verify information transferred using electronic system. Currently, asymmetric encryption processes are used to create digital signatures. When an asymmetric cryptographic process uses the senders private key to encrypt a message, the sender's public key must be used to decrypt the message –when the decryption happens successfully, it provides verification that the message was sent by the sender and cannot be refused. This process is known as non-repudiation and is the principle of cryptography that gives credence to the authentication mechanism collectively known as a digital signature. Digital signatures are, therefore, encrypted messages that can be mathematically proven to be authentic. The management of digital signatures has been built into most web browsers. As an example, the Internet Explorer digital management screen is shown in Figure 8-5.

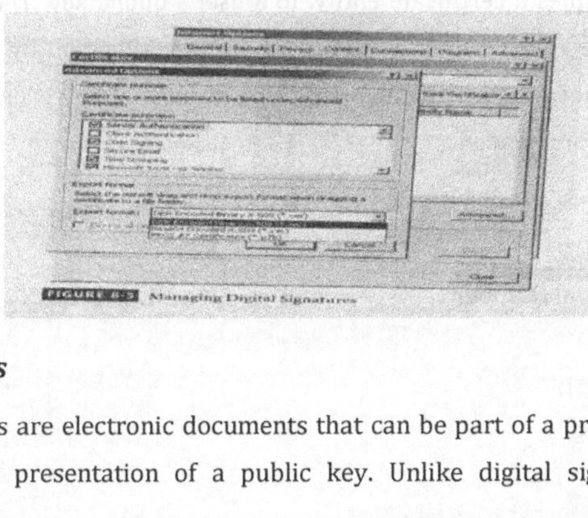

FIGURE 8-5 Managing Digital Signatures

Digital Certificates

Digital certificates are electronic documents that can be part of a process of identification associated with the presentation of a public key. Unlike digital signatures, which help authenticate the origin of a message, digital certificates authenticate the cryptographic key that is embedded in the certificate. When used properly these certificates enable diligent users to verify the authenticity of any organization's certificates. This is much like what happens when the Federal Deposit Insurance Corporation issues its "FDIC" logo to banks to help assure bank customers that their bank is authentic. Different client-server applications use different types of digital certificates to accomplish their assigned functions:

1) The CA application suite issues and uses certificates that identify and establish a trust relationship with a CA to determine what additional certificates can be authenticated.
2) Mail applications use Secure/Multipurpose Internet Mail Extension (S/MIME) certificates for signing and encrypting e-mail as well as for signing forms.
   - Development applications use object-signing certificates to identify signers of object-oriented code and scripts.
   - Web servers and Web application servers use Secure Socket Layer (SSL) certificates to authenticate servers via the SSL protocol (which is described in an upcoming section) in order to establish an encrypted SSL session.
   - Web clients use client SSL certificates to authenticate users, sign forms, and participate in single sign-on solutions via SSL.

Two popular certificate types in use today are those created using Pretty Good Privacy (PGP) and those created using applications that conform to International Telecommunication Union' (ITU-T) x.509 version 3. You should know that X.S09 v3, whose structure is outlined in Table 8-8, is an ITU- T recommendation that essentially defines a directory service that maintains a database (also known as a repository) of information about a group of users holding X.SOY v3 certificates. An X.S09 v3 certificate binds a **distinguished name (DN)**, which uniquely identifies a certificate entity, to a user's public key. The certificate is signed and placed in the directory by the CA for retrieval and verification by the user's associated public key. X.S09 v3 does not specify an encryption algorithm; however, RSA with its hashed digital signature is recommended.

Table 8-8: X.509 v3 Certificate Structure

Version
Certificate Serial Number
Algorithm ID
    Algorithm ID
    Parameters
Issuer Name

Validity

Not Before

Not After

Subject Name

Subject Public Key Info

Public Key Algorithm

Parameters

Subject Public Key

Issuer Unique Identifier (Optional)

Subject Unique Identifier (Optional)

Extensions (Optional)

Type

Criticality

Value

Certificate Signature Algorithm

Certificate Signature

Hybrid Cryptography Systems

Except in the case of digital certificates, pure asymmetric key encryption is not widely used.

Asymmetric key encryption is more often used in conjunction with symmetric key encryption-thus, as part of a hybrid encryption system. The most common hybrid system is based on the **Diffie-Hellman Key Exchange method**, which is a method for exchanging private keys using public key encryption. With Diffie-Hellman, asymmetric encryption is used to exchange session keys. These are limited-use symmetric keys for temporary communications; they allow two organizations to conduct quick, efficient, secure communications based on symmetric encryption. Diffie-Hellman provided the foundation for subsequent developments in public key encryption. Because symmetric encryption is more efficient than asymmetric for sending messages, and asymmetric encryption doesn't require out-of-band key exchange, asymmetric encryption can be used to transmit symmetric keys in a hybrid approach. Diffie-Hellman avoids the exposure of data to third parties that is sometimes associated with out-of-band key exchanges. A hybrid encryption approach is illustrated in Figure 8-7, and it works as follows:

Alex at XYZ Corp. wants to communicate with Rachel at ABC Corp., so Alex first creates a session key. Alex encrypts a message with this session key, and then gets Rachel's public key.

Alex uses Rachel's public key to encrypt both the session key and the message, which is already encrypted. Alex transmits the entire package to Rachel, who uses her private key to decrypt the package containing the session key and the encrypted message, and then uses the session key to decrypt the message. Rachel can then continue to use only this session key for electronic communications until the session key expires. The asymmetric session key is used in the much more efficient asymmetric encryption and decryption processes. After the session key expires (usually in just a few minutes) a new session key will be chosen and shared using the same process.

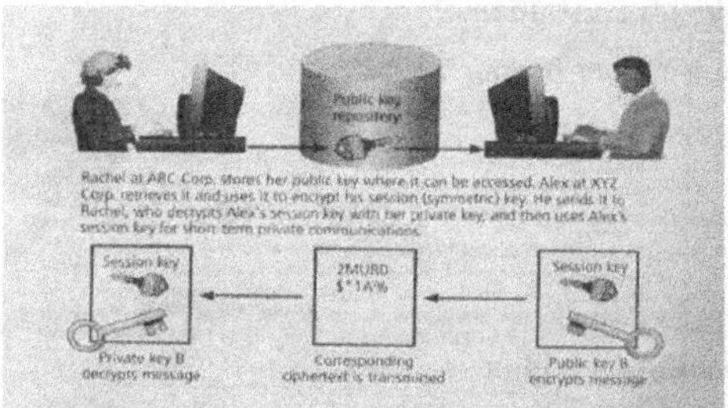

FIGURE 8-7 Example of Hybrid Encryption

Steganography

Steganography is a process of hiding information and has been in use for a long time. In fact the word "steganography" is derived from the Greek words steganos meaning "covered" and graphein meaning "to write." The Greek historian Herodotus reported on one of the first steganographers when he described a fellow Greek sending a message to warn of an imminent invasion by writing it on the wood beneath a wax writing tablet. If the tablet were intercepted, it would appear blank.[11] While steganography is technically not a form of cryptography, it is related to cryptography in that it ~ also a way of transmitting information so that the information is not revealed wl1i1e it's in transit. The most popular modem version of steganography involves hiding information within files that appear to contain digital pictures or other images.

4.5. Attacks on Cryptosystems

Man-in-the-Middle Attack

A man-in-the-middle attack, as discussed in Chapter 2, is designed to intercept the transmission of a public key or even to insert a known key structure in place of the requested public key. Thus, attackers attempt to place themselves between the sender and receiver, and once they've intercepted the request for key exchanges, they send each participant a valid public key, which is known only to them. From the perspective of the victims of such attacks, their encrypted communication appears to be occurring normally, but in fact the attacker is receiving each encrypted message and decoding it (with the key given to the sending party), and then encrypting signatures can prevent the traditional man-in-the-middle attack, as the attacker cannot duplicate

Dictionary Attacks

In a **dictionary attack**, the attacker encrypts every word in a dictionary using the same cryptosystem as used by the target. The attacker does this in an attempt to locate a match between the target ciphertext and the list of encrypted words from the same cryptosystem. Dictionary attacks can be successful when the ciphertext consists of relatively few characters, as for example files which contain encrypted usernames and passwords. If an attacker acquires a system password file, the individual can run hundreds of thousands of potential passwords from the dictionary he or she has prepared against the stolen list. Most computer systems use a well-known one-way hash function to store passwords in such files, but this can almost always allow the attacker to find at least a few matches in any stolen password file. After a match is located, the attacker has essentially identified a potential valid password for the system under attack.

Timing Attacks

In a **timing attack**, the attacker eavesdrops during the victim's session and uses statistical analysis of the user's typing patterns and inter-keystroke timings to discern sensitive session information. While timing analysis may not directly result in the decryption of sensitive data, it can be used to gain information about the encryption key and perhaps the cryptosystem in use. It may also eliminate' some algorithms as possible candidates, thus narrowing the attacker's search. In this narrower field of options, the attacker can increase the odds of eventual success. Once the attacker has successfully broken an encryption, he or she may launch a **replay attack**, which is an attempt to resubmit a recording of the deciphered authentication to gain entry into a secure source.

Defending From Attacks

Encryption is a very useful tool in protecting the confidentiality of information that is in storage and/or transmission. However, it is just that-another tool in the information security administrator's arsenal of weapons against threats to information security. Frequently, unenlightened individuals describe information security exclusively in terms of encryption (and possibly firewalls and antivirus software). But encryption is simply the process of hiding the true meaning of information. Over the millennia, mankind has developed dramatically more sophisticated means of hiding information from those who should not see it. No matter how sophisticated encryption and cryptosystems have become, however, they have retained the same flaw that the first systems contained thousands of years ago: If you discover the key, that is, the method used.

Questions

4a). What is an intrusion? Briefly write about eight IDPS terminologies.

(December 2010)(10 marks)

4b). What is an encryption? Discuss the asymmetric and symmetric methods.

(December 2010)(10 marks)

4a). What are the fundamental differences between asymmetric and symmetric encryption

(June 2012) (6 marks)

4b). Explain the different categories of attacks on cryptosystem.

(June 2012) (8 marks)

4c). Define the following with relation to cryptography

(June 2012) (6 marks)

4a). What are the difference between digital signature and digital certificate?

(JUNE 2010) (10 Marks)

4 b. Explain the two methods of encrypting plaintext.

(JUNE 2010) (10 Marks)

Cipher Methods

4a). List out the elements of cryptosystems and explain transposition cipher technique

(July 2011) (10Marks)

4b). Who can attack cryptosystems? Discuss different categories of attacks on cryptosystems

(July 2011) (10 Marks)

4a). Define the following with relation to cryptography

(Dec 2011) (6 marks)

4b). What is an encryption? Discuss the asymmetric and symmetric methods

(10 marks)

UNIT-5

INTRODUCTION TO NETWORK SECURITY, AUTHENTICATION

Applications

Information: is defined as–knowledge obtained from investigation, Study or Instruction, Intelligence, news, facts, data, a Signature or Character representing data||.

Security: is defined as –freedom from Danger||, or Safety: –Freedom from Fear or Anxiet y||.

Information Security: "Measures adopted to prevent the unauthorized use, misuse, modification, Denial of use of knowledge, Facts, data or Capabilities".

From the above definition, Information Security does guarantees protection.

Computer security: With the introduction of the computer, the need for automated tools for protecting files and other information stored on the computer became evident. This is especially the case for a shared system, and the need is even more acute for systems that can be accessed over a public telephone network, data network, or the Internet. The generic name for the collection of tools designed to protect data and to thwart hackers is **computer security.**

Internet security: Security is affected with the introduction of distributed systems and the use of networks and communications for carrying data between terminal user and computer and between computer and computer. Network security measures are needed to protect data during their transmission. In fact, the term **network security** is somewhat misleading, because virtually all business, government, and academic organizations interconnect their data processing equipment with a collection of interconnected networks. Such a collection is often referred to as an internet, and the term **internet security** is used.

There are no clear boundaries between the above said forms of security.

5.1. The OSI Security Architecture

The International Telecommunication Union (ITU) Telecommunication Standardization Sector (ITU-T) Recommends X.800, Security Architecture for OSI, defines a systematic approach. The OSI security architecture provides overview of many of the concepts and it focuses on security attacks, mechanisms, and services.

Security attack: Any action that compromises the security of information owned by an organization.

Security mechanism: A process (or a device incorporating such a process) that is designed to detect, prevent, or recover from a security attack.

Security service: A processing or communication service that enhances the security of the data processing systems and the information transfers of an organization. The services are intended to counter security attacks, and they make use of one or more security mechanisms to provide the service. The terms threat and attack are commonly used to mean more or less the same thing and the actual definitions are:

Threat: A potential for violation of security, which exists when there is a circumstance, capability, action, or event that could breach security and cause harm. That is, a threat is a possible danger that might exploit vulnerability.

Attack: An assault on system security that derives from an intelligent threat; that is, an intelligent act that is a deliberate attempt (especially in the sense of a method or technique) to evade security services and violate the security policy of a system.

5.2. Security Attacks

Security attacks, used both in X.800 and RFC 2828, are classified as passive attacks and active attacks.

A passive attack attempts to learn or make use of information from the system but does not affect system resources.

An active attack attempts to alter system resources or affect their operation.

Passive Attacks

Passive attacks are in the nature of eavesdropping on, or monitoring of, transmissions. The goal of the opponent is to obtain information that is being transmitted. Two types of passive attacks are release of message contents and traffic analysis.

The **release of message** contents is easily understood (Figure 1.3a). A telephone conversation, an electronic mail message, and a transferred file may contain sensitive or confidential information. To prevent an opponent from learning the contents of these transmissions.

A second type of passive attack, **traffic analysis**, is subtler (Figure 1.3b). Suppose that we had a way of masking the contents of messages or other information traffic so that opponents, even if they captured the message, could not extract the information from the message. The common technique for masking contents is encryption. If we had encryption protection in place, an opponent might still be able to observe the pattern of these messages. The opponent could determine the location and identity of communicating hosts and could observe the frequency and length of messages being exchanged. This information might be useful in guessing the nature of the communication that was taking place.

Passive attacks are very difficult to detect because they do not involve any alteration of the data. Typically, the message traffic is sent and received in an apparently normal fashion and neither the sender nor receiver is aware that a third party has read the messages or observed the traffic pattern. However, it is feasible to prevent the success of these attacks, usually by means of encryption. Thus, the emphasis in dealing with passive attacks is on prevention rather than detection.

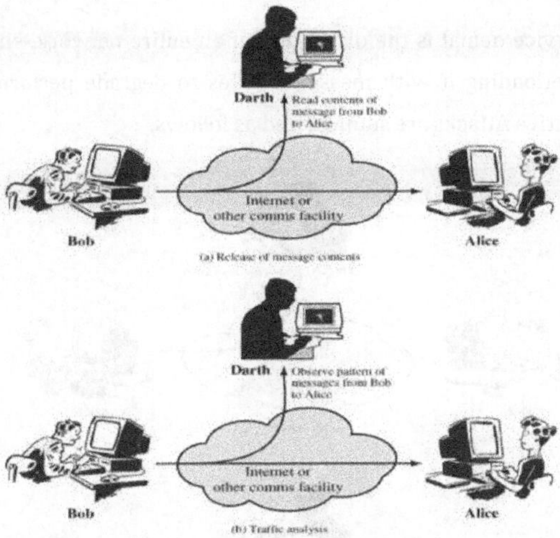

Figure 1.3: Passive Attacks

Active Attacks

Active attacks involve some modification of the data stream or the creation of a false stream and can be subdivided into four categories: Masquerade, Replay, Modification of messages, and Denial of service. A **masquerade** takes place when one entity pretends to be a different entity (Figure 1.4a). A masquerade attack usually includes one of the other forms of active attack. For example, authentication sequences can be captured and replayed after a valid authentication sequence has taken place, thus enabling an authorized entity with few privileges to obtain extra privileges by impersonating an entity that has those privileges.

Replay involves the passive capture of a data unit and its subsequent retransmission to produce an unauthorized effect (Figure 1.4b).

Modification of messages simply means that some portion of a legitimate message is altered, or that messages are delayed or reordered, to produce an unauthorized effect (Figure 1.4c). For example, a message meaning "Allow John Smith to read confidential file accounts" is modified to mean "Allow Fred Brown to read confidential file accounts."

The **denial of service** prevents or inhibits the normal use or management of communications facilities (Figure 1.4d). This attack may have a specific target; for example, an entity may suppress all messages directed to a particular destination (e.g., the security audit service).

Another form of service denial is the disruption of an entire network, either by disabling the network or by overloading it with messages so as to degrade performance difference between passive and Active Attacks are summarized as follows.

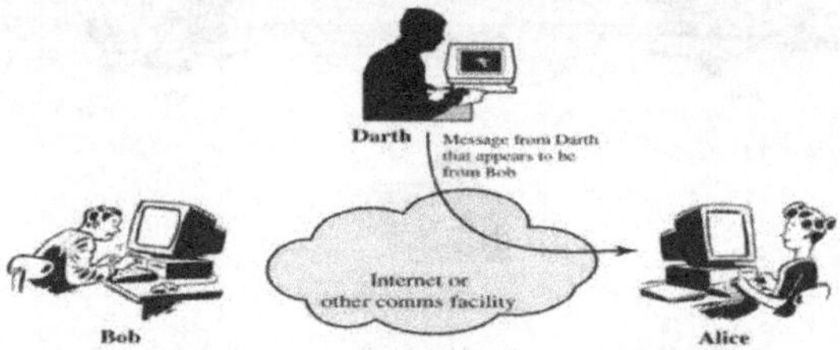

(a) Masquerade

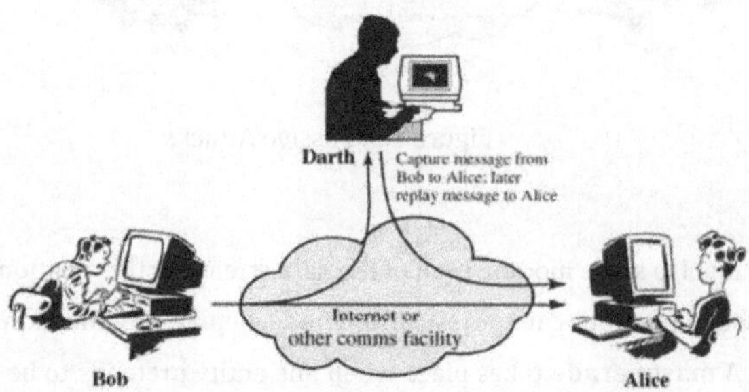

(b) Replay

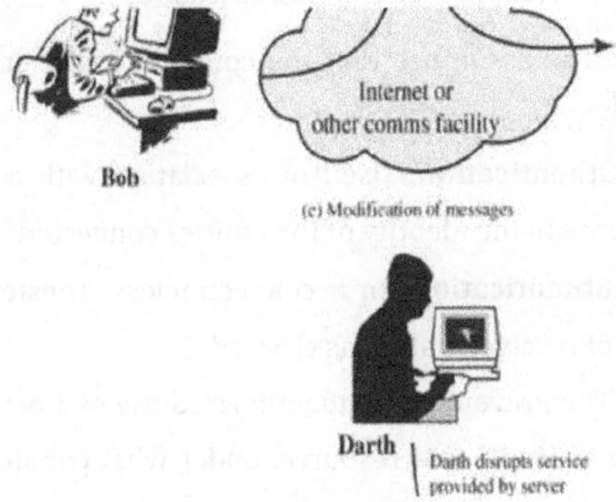

Figure 1.4

Sl.No	Passive Attacks	Active Attacks
1	Very Difficult to Detect and Measures are Available to prevent their Success	Very easy to Detect and Very difficult to Prevent.
2	The Attacker merely needs to be able to observe Transmissions.	The Attacker needs to gain Physical control of a portion of the link and be able to Insert and Capture Transmission.
3	The Entity is unaware of the Attack.	The Entity gets aware of it, when attacked.
4	Don't involve any modification of the contents of original message.	Involve modification of the original contents
5	No Such changes	The Attacks may be Masquerade Modification Replay DOS

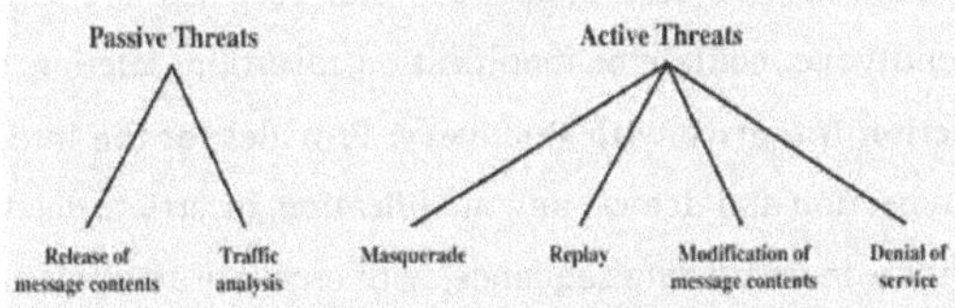

Active and Passive Threats

5.3. Security Services

X.800 defines a security service as a service provided by a protocol layer of communicating open systems, which ensures adequate security of the systems or of data transfers. Also the RFC 2828 defines security services as a processing or communication service that is provided by a system to give a specific kind of protection to system resources. *Security Services implement security policies and are implemented by security mechanisms.*

X.800 divides these services into **five categories** and **fourteen specific services** as shown in the below Table.

Table: Security Services (X.800)

1) **AUTHENTICATION:** The assurance that the communicating entity is the one that it laims to be.
   - **Peer Entity Authentication:** Used in association with a logical connection to provide confidence in the identity of the entities connected.
   - **Data Origin Authentication:** In a connectionless transfer, provides assurance that the source of received data is as claimed.
2) **ACCESS CONTROL:** The prevention of unauthorized use of a resource (i.e., this service controls who can have access to a resource, under what conditions access can occur, and what those accessing the resource are allowed to do).
3) **DATA CONFIDENTIALITY:** The protection of data from unauthorized disclosure.
   - **Connection Confidentiality:** The protection of all user data on a connection.
   - **Connectionless Confidentiality:** The protection of all user data in a single data block
   - **Selective-Field Confidentiality:** The confidentiality of selected fields within the user Data on a connection or in a single data block.
   - **Traffic Flow Confidentiality:** The protection of the information that might be Derived from observation of traffic flows.
4) **DATA INTEGRITY:** The assurance that data received are exactly as sent by an authorized entity (i.e., contain no modification, insertion, deletion, or replay).
   - **Connection Integrity with Recovery:** Provides for the integrity of all user data on a connection and detects any modification, insertion, deletion, or replay of any data within an entire data sequence, with recovery attempted.
   - **Connection Integrity without Recovery:** As above, but provides only detection without recovery.
   - **Selective-Field Connection Integrity:** Provides for the integrity of selected fields within the user data of a data block transferred over a connection and takes the form of determination of whether the selected fields have been modified, inserted, deleted, or replayed.
   - **Connectionless Integrity:** Provides for the integrity of a single connectionless data block and may take the form of detection of data modification. Additionally, a limited form of replay detection may be provided.
   - **Selective-Field Connectionless Integrity:** Provides for the integrity of selected fields within a single connectionless data block; takes the form of determination of

whether the selected fields have been modified.

5) **NONREPUDIATION:** Provides protection against denial by one of the entities involved in a communication of having participated in all or part of the communication.

- **Nonrepudiation, Origin:** Proof that the message was sent by the specified party.
- **Nonrepudiation, Destination:** Proof that the message was received by the specified party.

Security Mechanisms

The following Table lists the security mechanisms defined in X.800. The security mechanisms are divided into those that are implemented in a specific protocol layer and those that are not specific to any particular protocol layer or security service. X.800 distinguishes between reversible encipherment mechanisms and irreversible encipherment mechanisms.

A reversible encipherment mechanism is simply an encryption algorithm that allows data to be encrypted and subsequently decrypted.

Irreversible encipherment mechanisms include hash algorithms and message authentication codes, which are used in digital signature and message authentication applications.

Below table indicates the relationship between Security Services and Security Mechanisms.

Relationship between Security Services and Security Mechanisms (X.800)

Service	Encipherement	Digital Signature	Access Control	Data Integrity	Authentication Exchange	Traffic Padding	Routing Control	Notarization
Peer Entity Authentication		Y	Y			Y		
Data origin Authentication		Y	Y					
Access Control			Y					
Confidentiality		Y						Y
Traffic Flow Confidentiality		Y					Y	Y
Data Integrity		Y	Y		Y			
Non-repudation Availability		Y			Y			
Y					Y	Y		

Specific Security Mechanisms

Incorporated into the appropriate protocol layer in order to provide some of the OSI security services.

1) **Encipherment:** The use of mathematical algorithms to transform data into a form that is not readily intelligible. The transformation and subsequent recovery of the data depend on an algorithm and zero or more encryption keys.

2) **Digital Signature:** Data appended to, or a cryptographic transformation of, a data unit

that allows a recipient of the data unit to prove the source and integrity of the data unit and protect against forgery.

3) **Access Control:** A variety of **mechanisms** that enforce access rights to resources.

4) **Data Integrity:** A variety of mechanisms used to assure the integrity of a data unit or stream of data units.

5) **Authentication Exchange:** A mechanism intended to ensure the identity of an entity by means of information exchange.

6) **Traffic Padding:** The insertion of bits into gaps in a data stream to frustrate traffic analysis attempts.

7) **Routing Control:** Enables selection of particular physically secure routes for certain data and allows routing changes, especially when a breach of **security** is suspected.

8) **Notarization:** The use of a trusted third party to assure certain **properties** of a data exchange.

Pervasive Security Mechanisms

Mechanisms that are not specific to any particular OSI security service or protocol layer.

1) **Trusted Functionality:** That which is perceived to be correct with respect to some criteria (e.g., as established by a security policy).

2) **Security Label:** The marking bound to a resource (which may be a data unit) that names or designates the security attributes of that resource.

3) **Event Detection:** Detection of security-relevant events.

4) **Security Audit Trail:** Data collected and potentially used to facilitate a security audit, which is an independent review and examination of system records and activities.

5) **Security Recovery:** Deals with requests from mechanisms, such as event handling and management functions, and takes recovery actions.

5.4. A Model for Network Security

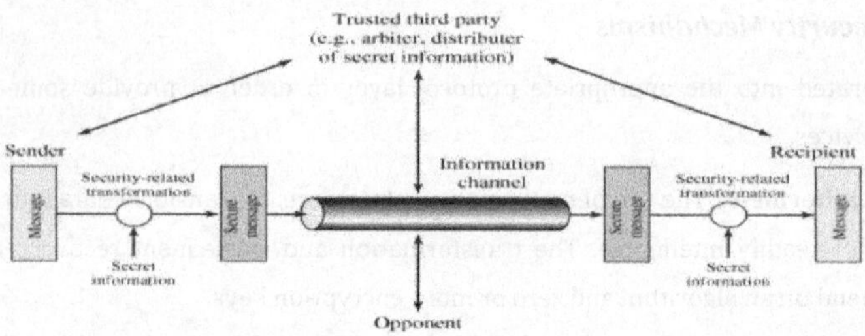

Model for Network Security

A message is to be transferred from one party to another across some sort of internet. The two parties, who are the principals in this transaction, must cooperate for the exchange to take place. A logical information channel is established by defining a route through the internet from source to destination and by the cooperative use of communication protocols (e.g., TCP/IP) by the two principals. Security aspects come into play when it is necessary or desirable to protect the information transmission from an opponent who may present a threat to confidentiality, authenticity, and so on. All the techniques for providing security have two components:

A security-related transformation on the information to be sent. Examples include the encryption of the message, which scrambles the message so that it is unreadable by the opponent, and the addition of a code based on the contents of the message, which can be used to verify the identity of the sender Some secret information shared by the two principals and, it is hoped, unknown to the opponent. An example is an encryption key used in conjunction with the transformation to scramble the message before transmission and unscramble it on reception. The general model shows that there are four basic tasks in designing a particular security service:

1) Design an algorithm for performing the security-related transformation. The algorithm should be such that an opponent cannot defeat its purpose.
2) Generate the secret information to be used with the algorithm.
3) Develop methods for the distribution and sharing of the secret information.
4) Specify a protocol to be used by the two principals that makes use of the security algorithm and the secret information to achieve a particular security service.

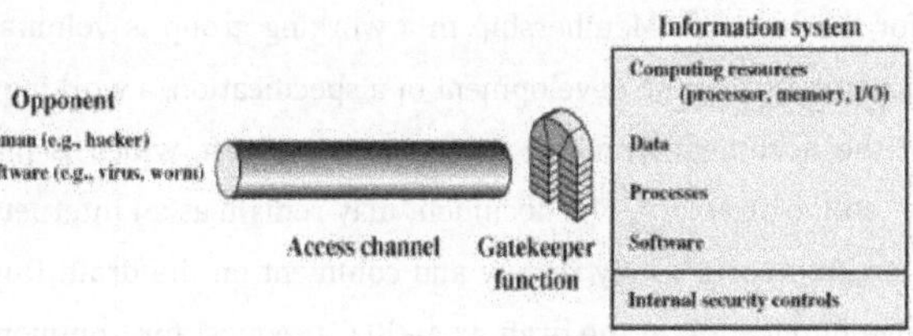

Network Access Security Model

A general model is illustrated by the above Figure, which reflects a concern for protecting an information system from unwanted access. Most readers are familiar with the concerns caused by the existence of hackers, who attempt to penetrate systems that can be accessed over a network. The hacker can be someone who, with no malign intent, simply gets satisfaction from breaking and entering a computer system. Or, the intruder can be a disgruntled employee who wishes to do damage, or a criminal who seeks to exploit computer assets for financial gain.

5.5. Internet Standards and the Internet Society

Many of the protocols that make up the TCP/IP protocol suite have been standardized or are in the process of standardization. By universal agreement, an organization known as the Internet Society is responsible for the development and publication of these standards.

The Internet Society is a professional membership organization that oversees a number of boards and task forces involved in Internet development and standardization.

The Internet Organizations and RFC Publication

The Internet Society is the coordinating committee for Internet design, engineering, and management. Areas covered include the operation of the Internet itself and the standardization of protocols used by end systems on the Internet for interoperability. Three organizations under the Internet Society are responsible for the actual work of standards development and publication:

1) **Internet Architecture Board (IAB):** Responsible for defining the overall architecture of the Internet, providing guidance and broad direction to the IETF.
2) **Internet Engineering Task Force (IETF):** The protocol engineering and development arm of the Internet.
3) **Internet Engineering Steering Group (IESG):** Responsible for technical management of IETF activities and the Internet standards process.

Working groups chartered by the IETF carry out the actual development of new standards and protocols for the Internet. Membership in a working group is voluntary; any interested party may participate. During the development of a specification, a working group will make a draft version of the document available as an Internet Draft, which is placed in the IETF's "Internet Drafts" online directory. The document may remain as an Internet Draft for up to six months, and interested parties may review and comment on the draft. During that time, the IESG may approve publication of the draft as an RFC (Request for Comment). If the draft has not progressed to the status of an RFC during the six-month period, it is withdrawn from the directory. The working group may subsequently publish a revised version of the draft. The IETF is responsible for publishing the RFCs, with approval of the IESG. The RFCs are the working notes of the Internet research and development community. A document in this series may be on essentially any topic related to computer communications and may be anything from a meeting report to the specification of a standard.

The work of the IETF is divided into eight areas, each with an area director and each composed of numerous working groups. Table A.1 shows the IETF areas and their focus.

A.1

IETF Area	Theme	Example Working Groups
General	IETF processes and procedures	Policy Framework Process for Organization of Internet Standards
Applications	Internet applications	Web-related protocols (HTTP) EDI-Internet integration LDAP
Internet	Internet infrastructure	IPv6 PPP extensions
Operations and management	Standards and definitions for network	SNMPv3 Remote Network Monitoring
Routing	Protocols and management for routing information	Multicast routing OSPF QoS routing
Security	Security protocols and technologies	Kerberos IPSec X.509 S/MIME TLS
Transport	Transport layer protocols	Differentiated services IP telephony NFS RSVP
User services	Methods to improve the quality of information available to users of the Internet	Responsible Use of the Internet User services FYI documents

The Standardization Process

The decision of which RFCs become Internet standards is made by the IESG, on the recommendation of the IETF. To become a standard, a specification must meet the following criteria:

1) Be stable and well understood.
2) Be technically competent.
3) Have multiple, independent, and interoperable implementations with substantial operational experience.
4) Enjoy significant public support.
5) Be recognizably useful in some or all parts of the Internet.

The key difference between these criteria and those used for international standards from ITU is the emphasis here on operational experience.

The left-hand side of Below figure shows the series of steps, called the *standards track,* that a specification goes through to become a standard; this process is defined in RFC 2026. The steps involve increasing amounts of scrutiny and testing. At each step, the IETF must make a recommendation for advancement of the protocol, and the IESG must ratify it. The process begins when the IESG approves the publication of an Internet Draft document as an RFC with the status of Proposed Standard.

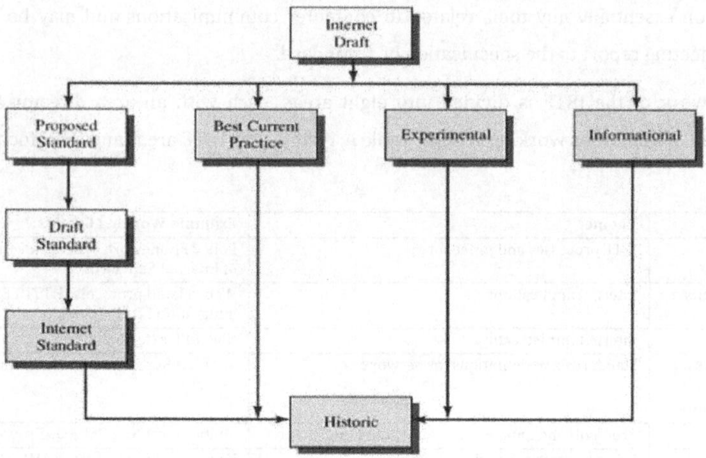

Internet RFC Publication Process

The white boxes in the diagram represent temporary states, which should be occupied for the minimum practical time. However, a document must remain a Proposed Standard for at least six months and a Draft Standard for at least four months to allow time for review and comment. The gray boxes represent long-term states that may be occupied for years.

For a specification to be advanced to Draft Standard status, there must be at least two independent and interoperable implementations from which adequate operational experience has been obtained. After significant implementation and operational experience has been obtained, a specification may be elevated to Internet Standard. At this point, the Specification is assigned an STD number as well as an RFC number. Finally, when a protocol becomes obsolete, it is assigned to the Historic state.

Internet Standards Categories

All Internet standards fall into one of two categories:

Technical specification (TS): A TS defines a protocol, service, procedure, convention, or format. The bulk of the Internet standards are TSs.

Applicability statement (AS): An AS specifies how, and under what circumstances, one or more TSs may be applied to support a particular Internet capability. An AS identifies one or more TSs that are relevant to the capability, and may specify values or ranges for particular parameters associated with a TS or functional subsets of a TS that are relevant for the capability.

Other RFC Types

There are numerous RFCs that are not destined to become Internet standards. Some RFCs standardize the results of community deliberations about statements of principle or conclusions about what is the best way to perform some operations or IETF process function. Such RFCs are designated as Best Current Practice (BCP). Approval of BCPs follows essentially the same process for approval of Proposed Standards. Unlike standards-track documents, there is not a three-stage process for BCPs; a BCP goes from Internet draft status to approved BCP in one step.

A protocol or other specification that is not considered ready for standardization may be published as an Experimental RFC. After further work, the specification may be resubmitted. If the specification is generally stable, has resolved known design choices, is believed to be well understood, has received significant community review, and appears to enjoy enough community interest to be considered valuable, then the RFC will be designated a Proposed Standard. Finally, an Informational Specification is published for the general information of the Internet community.

Kerberos

Kerberos is an authentication service developed by MIT. The problem that Kerberos addresses is this: Assume an open distributed environment in which users at workstations wish to access services on servers distributed throughout the network. We would like for servers to be able to restrict access to authorized users and to be able to authenticate requests for service. In this environment, a workstation cannot be trusted to identify its users correctly to network services. In particular, the following three threats exist:

1) A user may gain access to a particular workstation and pretend to be another user operating from that workstation.
2) A user may alter the network address of a workstation so that the requests sent from the altered workstation appear to come from the impersonated workstation.
3) A user may eavesdrop on exchanges and use a replay attack to gain entrance to a server or to disrupt operations.

In any of these cases, an unauthorized user may be able to gain access to services and data that he or she is not authorized to access. Rather than building in elaborate authentication protocols at each server, Kerberos provides a centralized authentication server whose function is to authenticate users to servers and servers to users. Unlike most other authentication schemes, Kerberos relies exclusively on symmetric encryption, making no use of public-key encryption.

Two versions of Kerberos are in common use. Version 4 implementations still exist. Version 5 corrects some of the security deficiencies of version 4 and has been issued as a proposed Internet Standard (RFC 1510).

Today the more commonly used architecture is a distributed architecture consisting of dedicated user workstations (clients) and distributed or centralized servers. In this environment, three approaches to security can be envisioned:

1) Rely on each individual client workstation to assure the identity of its user or users and rely on each server to enforce a security policy based on user identification (ID).
2) Require that client systems authenticate themselves to servers, but trust the client system concerning the identity of its user.
3) Require the user to prove his or her identity for each service invoked. Also require that servers prove their identity to clients.

In a small, closed environment, in which all systems are owned and operated by a single organization, the first or perhaps the second strategy may suffice. But in a more open environment, in which network connections to other machines are supported, the third approach is needed to protect user information and resources housed at the server. Kerberos supports this third approach.

Kerberos assumes distributed client/server architecture and employs one or more Kerberos servers to provide an authentication service and Version 4 is the "original" Kerberos.

Kerberos Version 4

Version 4 of Kerberos makes use of DES, to provide the authentication service. Viewing the protocol as a whole, it is difficult to see the need for the many elements contained therein. Therefore, we adopt a strategy used by Bill Bryant of Project Athena and build up to the full protocol by looking first at several hypothetical dialogues. Each successive dialogue adds additional complexity to counter security vulnerabilities revealed in the preceding dialogue.

A Simple Authentication Dialogue

In any network environment, any client can apply to any server for service. The obvious security risk is that of impersonation. An opponent can pretend to be another client and obtain unauthorized privileges on server machines. To counter this threat, servers must be able to confirm the identities of clients who request service.

Each server can be required to undertake this task for each client/server interaction, but in an open environment, this places a substantial burden on each server.

An alternative is to use an authentication server (AS) that knows the passwords of all users and stores these in a centralized database. In addition, the AS shares a unique secret key with each server. These keys have been distributed physically or in some other secure manner.

[The portion to the left of the colon indicates the sender and receiver; the portion to the right indicates the contents of the message, the symbol || indicates concatenation.]

(1) C →AS:IDC||PC||IDV

(2) AS→ C:Ticket

(3) C →V: IDC||Ticket

Ticket = E(*Kv*,
[*IDC*||*ADC*||*IDV*])
where
C = client
AS =
authentication
server V
=server
IDC = identifier of user on C
IDV = identifier of V
PC = password of user on C
ADC = network address of C
Kv = secret encryption key shared by AS and V

In this scenario, the user logs on to a workstation and requests access to server V. The client module C in the user's workstation requests the user's password and then sends a message to the AS that includes the user's ID, the server's ID, and the user's password. The AS checks its database to see if the user has supplied the proper password for this user ID and whether this user is permitted access to server V. If both tests are passed, the AS accepts the user as authentic and must now convince the server that this user is authentic. To do so, the AS creates a ticket that contains the user's ID and network address and the server's ID. This ticket is encrypted using the secret key shared by the AS and this server. This ticket is then sent back to C. Because the ticket is encrypted, it cannot be altered by C or by an opponent. With this ticket, C can now apply to V for service. C sends a message to V containing C's ID and the ticket.

V decrypts the ticket and verifies that the user ID in the ticket is the same as the unencrypted user ID in the message. If these two match, the server considers the user authenticated and grants the requested service.

A More Secure Authentication Dialogue

First, we would like to minimize the number of times that a user has to enter a password. Suppose each ticket can be used only once. If user C logs on to a workstation in the morning and wishes to check his or her mail at a mail server, C must supply a password to get a ticket for the mail server. If C wishes to check the mail several times during the day, each attempt requires re entering the password. We can improve matters by saying that tickets are reusable. For a single logon session, the workstation can store the mail server ticket after it is received and use it on behalf of the user for multiple accesses to the mail server.

The second problem is that the earlier scenario involved a plaintext transmission of the password [message (1)]. An eavesdropper could capture the password and use any service accessible to the victim.

To solve these additional problems, we introduce a scheme for avoiding plaintext passwords and a new server, known as the ticket-granting server (TGS). The new but still hypothetical scenario is as follows:

Once per user logon session:		
(1)	C→ AS	*IDC*||*IDtgs*
(2)	AS→ C:	E(*Kc, Tickettgs*)
Once per type of service:		
(3)	C →TGS	*IDC*||*IDV*||*Tickettgs*
(4)	TGS→ C	*Ticketv*
Once per service session:		
(5)	C→ V	*IDC*||*Ticketv*

Tickettgs = E(*Ktgs*, [*IDC*||*ADC*||*IDtgs*||*TS*1||*Lifetime*1])
Ticketv = E(*Kv*, [*IDC*||*ADC*||*IDv*||*TS*2||*Lifetime*2])

The new service, TGS, issues tickets to users who have been authenticated to AS. Thus, the user first requests a ticket-granting ticket (Tickettgs) from the AS. The client module in the user workstation saves this ticket. Each time the user requires access to a new service, the client applies to the TGS, using the ticket to authenticate itself. The TGS then grants a ticket for the particular service. The client saves each service-granting ticket and uses it to authenticate its user to a server each time a particular service is requested. Let us look at the details of this scheme.

1. The client requests a ticket-granting ticket on behalf of the user by sending its user's ID and password to the AS, together with the TGS ID, indicating a request to use the TGS service.
2. The AS responds with a ticket that is encrypted with a key that is derived from the user's password. When this response arrives at the client, the client prompts the user for his or her password, generates the key, and attempts to decrypt the incoming message. If the correct password is supplied, the ticket is successfully recovered.

The Version 4 Authentication Dialogue

The first problem is the lifetime associated with the ticket-granting ticket. If this lifetime is very short (e.g., minutes), then the user will be repeatedly asked for a password. If the lifetime is long (e.g., hours), then an opponent has a greater opportunity for replay.

The second problem is that there may be a requirement for servers to authenticate themselves to users. Without such authentication, an opponent could sabotage the configuration so that messages to a server were directed to another location. The false server would then be in a position to act as a real server and capture any information from the user and deny the true service to the user.

The following Table which shows the actual Kerberos protocol

- **C→ AS** *IDc||IDtgs||TS*1
- **AS →C** E(*Kc*,[*Kc,tgs*||*IDtgs*||*TS*2||*Lifetime*2||*Tickettgs*])

Tickettgs = E(K*tgs*, [Kc,*tgs*||IDc||ADc||IDtgs||TS2||Lifetime2])

(a) Authentication Service Exchange to obtain ticket-granting ticket

- **C →TGS** *IDv*||*Tickettgs*||*Authenticatorc*
- **TGS→ C** E(*Kc,tgs*, [*Kc,v*||*IDv*||*TS*4||*Ticketv*])

Tickettgs = E(K*tgs*, [Kc,*tgs*||ID*C*||AD*C*||ID*tgs*||TS2||Lifetime2])

Ticketv = E(K*v*, [Kc,*v*||ID*C*||AD*C*||ID*v*||TS4||Lifetime4])

Authenticatorc = E(Kc,*tgs*, [ID*C*||AD*C*||TS3])

(b) Ticket-Granting Service Exchange to Obtain Service-granting Ticket

C →V *Ticketv*||*Authenticatorc*

V→ C E(*Kc,v*, [*TS*5 + 1]) (for mutual authentication)

Ticketv = E(K*v*, [Kc,*v*||IDc||AD*c*||ID*v*||TS4||Lifetime4])

Authenticatorc = E(Kc,*v*,[IDc||AD*C*||TS5])

(C) Client/Server Authentication Exchange to Obtain Service

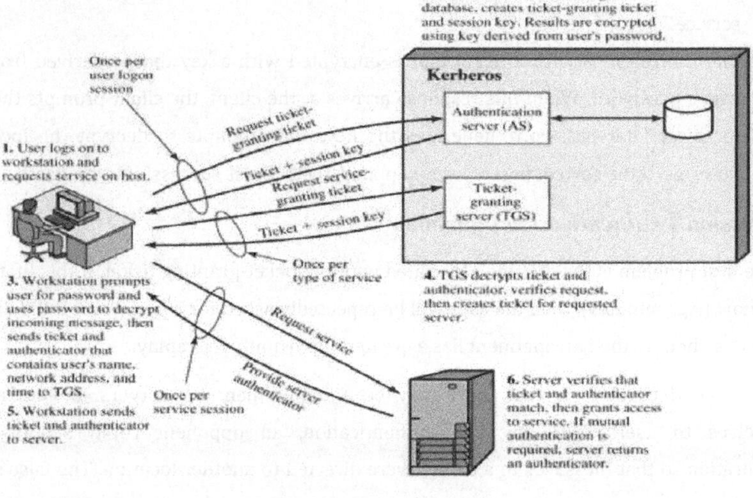

Overview of Kerberos

Kerberos Realms and Multiple Kerberi

A full-service Kerberos environment consisting of a Kerberos server, a number of clients, and a number of application servers requires the following:

- The Kerberos server must have the user ID and hashed passwords of all participating users in its database. All users are registered with the Kerberos server.
- The Kerberos server must share a secret key with each server. All servers are registered with the Kerberos server.
- The Kerberos server in each interoperating realm shares a secret key with the server in the other realm. The two Kerberos servers are registered with each other.

Such an environment is referred to as a **Kerberos realm**. A Kerberos realm is a set of managed nodes that share the same Kerberos database. Networks of clients and servers under different administrative organizations typically constitute different realms. The scheme requires that the Kerberos server in one realm trust the Kerberos server in the other realm to authenticate its users. Furthermore, the participating servers in the second realm must also be willing to trust the Kerberos server in the first realm. With these ground rules in place, we can describe the mechanism as shown in the below Figure.

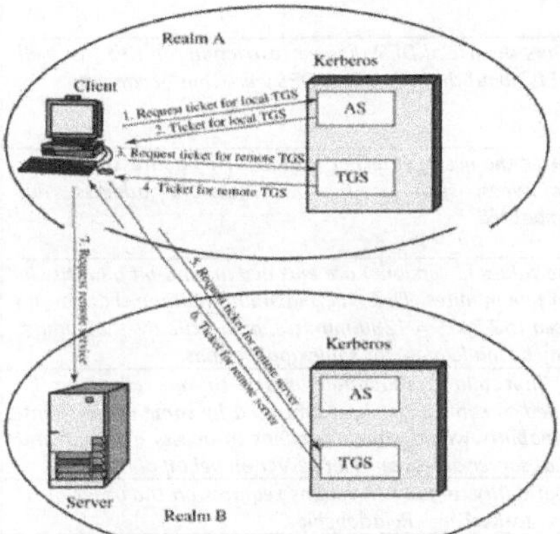

Request for Service in another Realm

The details of the exchanges are as follows

(1) C→ AS: *IDc*||*IDtgs*||*TS*1

1. AS→ C: E(*Kc*, [*Kc,tgs*||*IDtgs*||*TS*2||*Lifetime*2||*Tickettgs*])
2. C→ TGS: *IDtgsrem*||*Tickettgs*||*Authenticatorc*
3. TGS→ C: E(*Kc,tgs*, [*Kc,tgsrem*||*IDtgsrem*||*TS*4||*Tickettgsrem*])
4. C →TGSrem: *IDvrem*||*Tickettgsrem*||*Authenticatorc*
5. TGSrem →C: E(*Kc,tgsrem*, [*Kc,vrem*||*IDvrem*||*TS*6||*Ticketvrem*])
6. C→ Vrem: *Ticketvrem*||*Authenticatorc*

The ticket presented to the remote server (*Vrem*) indicates the realm in which the user was originally authenticated. The server chooses whether to honor the remote request.

Kerberos Version 5

Kerberos Version 5 is specified in RFC 1510 and provides a number of improvements over version 4.

Differences between Versions 4 and 5

Version 5 is intended to address the limitations of version 4 in two areas: environmental shortcomings and technical deficiencies. Let us briefly summarize the improvements in each area. Kerberos Version 4 was developed for use within the Project Athena environment and, accordingly, did not fully address the need to be of general purpose. This led to the following

Environmental Shortcomings

Encryption system dependence	*Version 4*	*Version 5*
Internet protocol dependence	*It requires the use of DES. Export restriction on DES as well as doubts about the strength of DES were thus of concern*	*Ciphertext is tagged with an encryption type identifier so that any encryption technique may be used.*
Message byte ordering	*It requires the use of Internet Protocol (IP) addresses. Other address types, such as the ISO network address, not accommodated.*	*Network addresses are tagged with type and length, allowing any network address type to be used. are*
Ticket lifetime	*Lifetime values in version 4 are encoded in an 8-bit quantity in units of five minutes. Thus, the maximum lifetime that can be expressed is $2^8 \times 5 = 1280$ minutes, or a little over 21 hours. This may be inadequate for some applications.*	*Tickets include an explicit start time and end time, allowing tickets with arbitrary lifetimes.*
Authentication forwarding	*It does not allow credentials issued to one client to be forwarded to some other host and used by some other client. This capability would enable a client to access a server and have that server access another server on behalf of the client*	*It provides this capability*
Inter realm authentication	*interoperability among N realms requires on the order of N^2 Kerberos-to-Kerberos Relationships.*	*Supports a method that Relationships.*

Apart from these environmental limitations, there are technical deficiencies in the version 4 protocol itself. Most of these deficiencies were documented and version 5 attempts to address these. The deficiencies are the following:

1) PCBC encryption: Encryption in version 4 makes use of a nonstandard mode of DES known as propagating cipher block chaining (PCBC).It has been demonstrated that this mode is vulnerable to an attack involving the interchange of ciphertext blocks PCBC was intended to provide an integrity check as part of the encryption operation. Version 5 provides explicit integrity mechanisms, allowing the standard CBC mode to be used for encryption. In particular, a checksum or hash code is attached to the message prior to encryption using CBC.
2) Session keys: Each ticket includes a session key that is used by the client to encrypt the authenticator sent to the service associated with that ticket. In addition, the session key may subsequently be used by the client and the server to protect messages passed during that session. However, because the same ticket may be used repeatedly to gain service from a particular server, there is the risk that an opponent will replay messages from an old session to the client or the server. In version 5, it is possible for a client and server to negotiate a subsession key, which is to be used only for that one connection. A new access by the client would result in the use of a new subsession key.
3) Password attacks: Both versions are vulnerable to a password attack. The message from the AS to the client includes material encrypted with a key based on the client's password. An opponent can capture this message and attempt to decrypt it by trying various passwords. If the result of a test decryption is of the proper form, then the

opponent has discovered the client's password and may subsequently use it to gain authentication credentials from Kerberos. This is the same type of password attack, with the same kinds of countermeasures being applicable. Version 5 does provide a mechanism known as preauthentication, which should make password attacks more difficult, but it does not prevent them.

4) Double encryption: the tickets provided to clients are encrypted twice, once with the secret key of the target server and then again with a secret key known to the client. The second encryption is not necessary and is computationally wasteful.

X.509 Authentication Service

ITU-T recommendation X.509 is part of the X.500 series of recommendations that define a directory service. The directory is a server or distributed set of servers that maintains a database of information about users.

- X.509 defines a framework for the provision of authentication services by the X.500 directory to its users. The directory may serve as a repository of public-key certificates.
- X.509 defines alternative authentication protocols based on the use of public-key certificates.
- X.509 is an important standard because the certificate structure and authentication protocols defined in X.509 are used in a variety of contexts.
- X.509 is based on the use of public-key cryptography and digital signatures.

The digital signature scheme is assumed to require the use of a hash function. Again, the standard does not dictate a specific hash algorithm. The below Figure illustrates the generation of a public-key certificate.

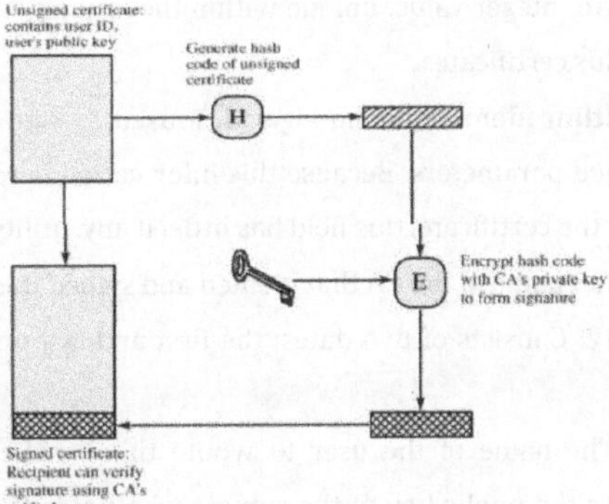

Public-Key Certificate Use

Certificates

The heart of the X.509 scheme is the public-key certificate associated with each user. These user certificates are assumed to be created by some trusted certification authority (CA) and placed in the directory by the CA or by the user. The directory server itself is not responsible for the creation of public keys or for the certification function; it merely provides an easily accessible location for users to obtain certificates. Below Figure shows the general format of a certificate, which includes the following elements:

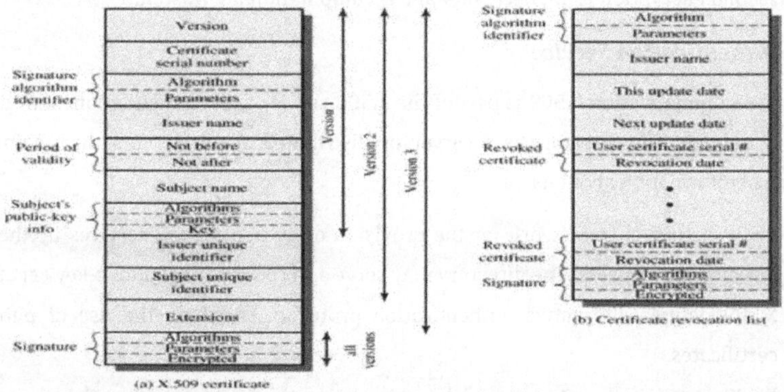

X.509 Formats

- **Version:** Differentiates among successive versions of the certificate format; the default is version 1. If the Issuer Unique Identifier or Subject Unique Identifier are present, the value must be version 2. If one or more extensions are present, the version must be version 3.
- **Serial number:** An integer value, unique within the issuing CA, that is unambiguously associated with this certificate.
- **Signature algorithm identifier:** The algorithm used to sign the certificate, together with any associated parameters. Because this information is repeated in the Signature field at the end of the certificate, this field has little, if any, utility.
- **Issuer name:** X.500 name of the CA that created and signed this certificate.
- **Period of validity:** Consists of two dates: the first and last on which the certificate is valid.
- **Subject name:** The name of the user to whom this certificate refers. That is, this certificate certifies the public key of the subject who holds the corresponding private key.

- **Subject's public-key information:** The public key of the subject, plus an identifier of the algorithm for which this key is to be used, together with any associated parameters.
- **Issuer unique identifier:** An optional bit string field used to identify uniquely the issuing CA in the event the X.500 name has
- been reused for different entities.
- **Subject unique identifier:** An optional bit string field used to identify uniquely the subject in the event the X.500 name has been reused for different entities.
- **Extensions:** A set of one or more extension fields. Extensions were added in version 3 and are discussed later in this section.
- **Signature:** Covers all of the other fields of the certificate; it contains the hash code of the other fields, encrypted with the CA's private key. This field includes the signature algorithm identifier.

The unique identifier fields were added in version 2 to handle the possible reuse of subject and/or issuer names over time. These fields are rarely used. The standard uses the following notation to define a certificate:

CA<<A>> = CA {V, SN, AI, CA, TA, A, Ap}

where

Y <<X>> = the certificate of user X issued by certification authority Y

Y {I} = the signing of I by Y. It consists of I with an encrypted hash code appended

The CA signs the certificate with its private key. If the corresponding public key is known to a user, then that user can verify that a certificate signed by the CA is valid.

Obtaining a User's Certificate

User certificates generated by a CA have the following characteristics:

- Any user with access to the public key of the CA can verify the user public key that was certified.
- No party other than the certification authority can modify the certificate without this being detected.

Because certificates are unforgeable, they can be placed in a directory without the need for the directory to make special efforts to protect them. Below Figure, taken from X.509, is an example of hierarchy. The connected circles indicate the hierarchical relationship among the CAs; the associated boxes indicate certificates maintained in the directory for each CA entry. The directory entry for each CA includes two types of certificates:

1) Forward certificates: Certificates of X generated by other CAs.

2) Reverse certificates: Certificates generated by X that are the certificates of other CAs.

In this example, user A can acquire the following certificates from the directory to establish a certification path to B:

X<<W>> W <<V>> V <<Y>> <<Z>> Z <<B>>

When A has obtained these certificates, it can unwrap the certification path in sequence to recover a trusted copy of B's public key. Using this public key, A can send encrypted messages to B. If A wishes to receive encrypted messages back from B, or to sign messages sent to B, then B will require A's public key, which can be obtained from the following certification path:

Z<<Y>> Y <<V>> V <<W>> W <<X>>X <<A>>

B can obtain this set of certificates from the directory, or A can provide them as part of its initial message to B.

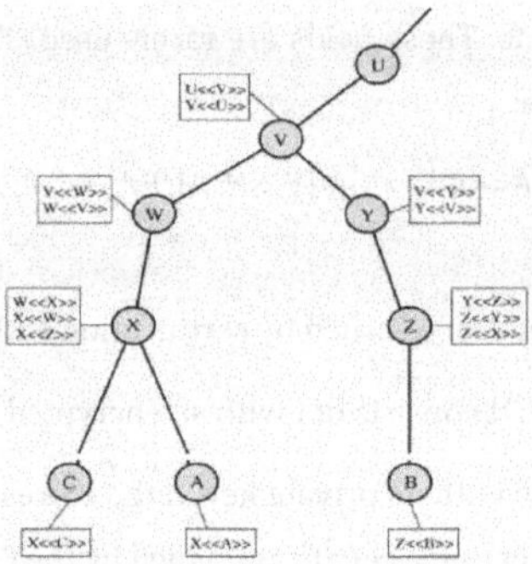

X.509 Hierarchy: A Hypothetical Example

Revocation of Certificates

Recall from Figure 1.4 that each certificate includes a period of validity, much like a credit card. Typically, a new certificate is issued just before the expiration of the old one. In addition, it may be desirable on occasion to revoke a certificate before it expires, for one of the following reasons:

1) The user's private key is assumed to be compromised.

2) The user is no longer certified by this CA.

3) The CA's certificate is assumed to be compromised.

Each CA must maintain a list consisting of all revoked but not expired certificates issued by that CA, including both those issued to users and to other CAs. These lists should also be posted on the directory.

Each certificate revocation list (CRL) posted to the directory is signed by the issuer and includes (Figure 1.4b) the issuer's name, the date the list was created, the date the next CRL is scheduled to be issued, and an entry for each revoked certificate. Each entry consists of the serial number of a certificate and revocation date for that certificate. Because serial numbers are unique within a CA, the serial number is sufficient to identify the certificate.

When a user receives a certificate in a message, the user must determine whether the certificate has been revoked. The user could check the directory each time a certificate is received. To avoid the delays (and possible costs) associated with directory searches, it is likely that the user would maintain a local cache of certificates and lists of revoked certificates.

Authentication Procedures

X.509 also includes three alternative authentication procedures that are intended for use across a variety of applications. All these procedures make use of public-key signatures. It is assumed that the two parties know each other's public key, either by obtaining each other's certificates from the directory or because the certificate is included in the initial message from each side. Figure illustrates the three procedures.

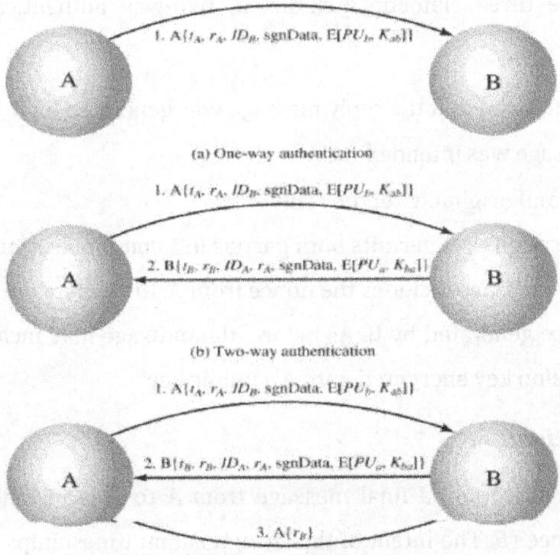

X.509 Strong Authentication Procedures

One-Way Authentication

One way authentication involves a single transfer of information from one user (A) to another (B), and establishes the following:

- The identity of A and that the message was generated by A
- That the message was intended for B
- The integrity and originality (it has not been sent multiple times) of the message

Note that only the identity of the initiating entity is verified in this process, not that of the responding entity. At a minimum, the message includes a timestamp *tA*, a nonce *rA* and the identity of B and is signed with A's private key. The timestamp consists of an optional generation time and an expiration time. This prevents delayed delivery of messages. The nonce can be used to detect replay attacks. The nonce value must be unique within the expiration time of the message. Thus, B can store the nonce until it expires and reject any new messages with the same nonce. For pure authentication, the message is used simply to present credentials to B. The message may also include information to be conveyed. This information, signData, is included within the scope of the signature, guaranteeing its authenticity and integrity. The message may also be used to convey a session key to B, encrypted with B's public key.

Two-Way Authentication

In addition to the three elements just listed, two-way authentication establishes the following elements:

- The identity of B and that the reply message was generated by B
- That the message was intended for A
- The integrity and originality of the reply

Two-way authentication thus permits both parties in a communication to verify the identity of the other. The reply message includes the nonce from A, to validate the reply. It also includes a timestamp and nonce generated by B. As before, the message may include signed additional information and a session key encrypted with A's public key

Three-Way Authentication

In three-way authentication, a final message from A to B is included, which contains a signed copy of the nonce *rB*. The intent of this design is that timestamps need not be checked: Because both nonces are echoed back by the other side, each side can check the returned nonce to detect replay attacks. This approach is needed when synchronized clocks are not available.

X.509 Version 3

The X.509 version 2 format does not convey all of the information that recent design and implementation experience has shown to be needed. The following requirements not satisfied by version 2:

- The Subject field is inadequate to convey the identity of a key owner to a public-key user. X.509 names may be relatively short and lacking in obvious identification details that may be needed by the user.
- The Subject field is also inadequate for many applications, which typically recognize entities by an Internet e-mail address, a URL, or some other Internet-related identification.
- There is a need to indicate security policy information. This enables a security application or function, such as IPSec, to relate an X.509 certificate to a given policy.
- There is a need to limit the damage that can result from a faulty or malicious CA by setting constraints on the applicability of a particular certificate.
- It is important to be able to identify different keys used by the same owner at different times. This feature supports key life cycle management, in particular the ability to update key pairs for users and CAs on a regular basis or under exceptional circumstances.

Rather than continue to add fields to a fixed format, standards developers felt that a more flexible approach was needed. Thus, version 3 includes a number of optional extensions that may be added to the version 2 format. Each extension consists of an extension identifier, a criticality indicator, and an extension value. The criticality indicator indicates whether an extension can be safely ignored. If the indicator has a value of TRUE and an implementation does not recognize the extension, it must treat the certificate as invalid. The certificate extensions fall into three main categories: key and policy information, subject and issuer attributes, and certification path constraints.

Key and Policy Information

These extensions convey additional information about the subject and issuer keys, plus indicators of certificate policy. A certificate policy is a named set of rules that indicates the applicability of a certificate to a particular community and/or class of application with common security requirements. For example, a policy might be applicable to the authentication of electronic data interchange (EDI) transactions for the trading of goods within a given price range.

This area includes the following:

- **Authority key identifier:** Identifies the public key to be used to verify the signature on this certificate or CRL. Enables distinct keys of the same CA to be differentiated. One use of this field is to handle CA key pair updating.
- **Subject key identifier:** Identifies the public key being certified. Useful for subject key pair updating. Also, a subject may have multiple key pairs and, correspondingly, different certificates for different purposes (e.g., digital signature and encryption key agreement).
- **Key usage:** Indicates a restriction imposed as to the purposes for which, and the policies under which, the certified public key may be used. May indicate one or more of the following: digital signature, non repudiation, key encryption, data encryption, key agreement, CA signature verification on certificates, CA signature verification on CRLs.
- **Private-key usage period:** Indicates the period of use of the private key corresponding to the public key. Typically, the private key is used over a different period from the validity of the public key. For example, with digital signature keys, the usage period for the signing private key is typically shorter than that for the verifying public key.
- **Certificate policies:** Certificates may be used in environments where multiple policies apply. This extension lists policies that the certificate is recognized as supporting, together with optional qualifier information.
- **Policy mappings:** Used only in certificates for CAs issued by other CAs. Policy mappings allow an issuing CA to indicate that one or more of that issuer's policies can be considered equivalent to another policy used in the subject CA's domain.

Certificate Subject and Issuer Attributes

These extensions support alternative names, in alternative formats, for a certificate subject or certificate issuer and can convey additional information about the certificate subject, to increase a certificate user's confidence that the certificate subject is a particular person or entity. For example, information such as postal address, position within a corporation, or picture image may be required.

The extension fields in this area include the following:

1) **Subject alternative name:** Contains one or more alternative names, using any of a variety of forms. This field is important for supporting certain applications, such as electronic mail, EDI, and IPSec, which may employ their own name forms.
2) **Issuer alternative name:** Contains one or more alternative names, using any of a variety of forms.
3) **Subject directory attributes:** Conveys any desired X.500 directory attribute values for the subject of this certificate.

Certification Path Constraints

These extensions allow constraint specifications to be included in certificates issued for CAs by other CAs. The constraints may restrict the types of certificates that can be issued by the subject CA or that may occur subsequently in a certification chain.

The extension fields in this area include the following:

1) **Basic constraints:** Indicates if the subject may act as a CA. If so, a certification path length constraint may be specified.
2) **Name constraints:** Indicates a name space within which all subject names in subsequent certificates in a certification path must be located.
3) **Policy constraints:** Specifies constraints that may require explicit certificate policy identification or inhibit policy mapping for the remainder of the certification path.

Public-Key Infrastructure

RFC 2822 (*Internet Security Glossary*) defines public-key infrastructure (PKI) as the set of hardware, software, people, policies, and procedures needed to create, manage, store, distribute, and revoke digital certificates based on asymmetric cryptography. The principal objective for developing a PKI is to enable secure, convenient, and efficient acquisition of public keys. The Internet Engineering Task Force (IETF) Public Key Infrastructure X.509 (PKIX) working group has been the driving force behind setting up a formal (and generic) model based on X.509 that is suitable for deploying a certificate-based architecture on the Internet. This section describes the PKIX model. Below Figure shows the interrelationship among the key elements of the PKIX model. These elements are

1) **End entity:** A generic term used to denote end users, devices (e.g., servers, routers), or any other entity that can be identified in the subject field of a public key certificate. End entities typically consume and/or support PKI-related services.

2) **Certification authority (CA):** The issuer of certificates and (usually) certificate revocation lists (CRLs). It may also support a variety of administrative functions, although these are often delegated to one or more Registration Authorities.
3) **Registration authority (RA):** An optional component that can assume a number of administrative functions from the CA. The RA is often associated with the End Entity registration process, but can assist in a number of other areas as well.
4) **CRL issuer:** An optional component that a CA can delegate to publish CRLs.
5) **Repository:** A generic term used to denote any method for storing certificates and CRLs so that they can be retrieved by End Entities.

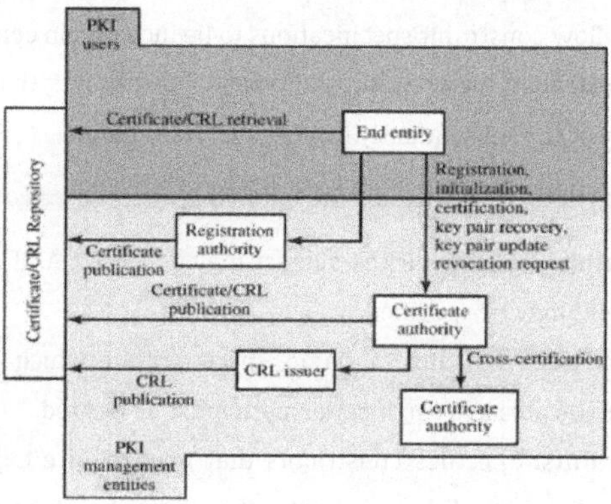

PKIX Architectural Model

PKIX Management Functions

PKIX identifies a number of management functions that potentially need to be supported by management protocols. These are indicated in Figure 1.7 and include the following:

1) **Registration:** This is the process whereby a user first makes itself known to a CA (directly, or through an RA), prior to that CA issuing a certificate or certificates for that user. Registration begins the process of enrolling in a PKI. Registration usually involves some offline or online procedure for mutual authentication. Typically, the end entity is issued one or more shared secret keys used for subsequent authentication.
2) **Initialization:** Before a client system can operate securely, it is necessary to install key materials that have the appropriate relationship with keys stored elsewhere in the infrastructure. For example, the client needs to be securely initialized with the

public key and other assured information of the **trusted** CA(s), to be used in validating certificate paths.

3) **Certification:** This is the process in which a CA issues a certificate for a user's public key, and returns that certificate to the user's client system and/or posts that certificate in a repository.

4) **Key pair recovery:** Key pairs can be used to support digital signature creation and verification, encryption and decryption, or both. When a key pair is used for encryption/decryption, it is important to provide a mechanism to recover the necessary decryption keys when normal access to the keying material is no longer possible, otherwise it will not be possible to recover the encrypted data. Loss of access to the decryption key can result from forgotten passwords/PINs, corrupted disk drives, damage to hardware tokens, and so on. Key pair recovery allows end entities to restore their encryption/decryption key pair from an authorized key backup facility (typically, the CA that issued the End Entity's certificate).

5) **Key pair update:** All key pairs need to be updated regularly (i.e., replaced with a new key pair) and new certificates issued. Update is required when the certificate lifetime expires and as a result of certificate revocation.

6) **Revocation request:** An authorized person advises a CA of an abnormal situation requiring certificate revocation. Reasons for revocation include private key compromise, change in affiliation, and name change.

7) **Cross certification:** Two CAs exchange information used in establishing a cross-certificate. A cross-certificate is a certificate issued by one CA to another CA that contains a CA signature key used for issuing certificates.

Questions

5a). what is meant by information secutiry? Discuss the three aspects of information security.

(December 2010) (10 marks)

5b). Briefly explain the four types of security attacks? That are normally encountered. also distinguish between active and passive attacks.

(December 2010) (10 marks)

5a). Discuss Active security attack.

(June 2012) (10 marks)

5b). With the help of neat diagram explain the general format of a X.509 public key certificate.

(June 2012) (10 marks)

5a). What are the difference between active and passive security attacks?

(June/July 2010) (10 Marks)

5b). Explain the different authentication procedures in X.509 certificate.

(June 2010) (9 Marks)

5c). Write the summary of Kerberos version five message exchange.

(June 2010) (6 Marks)

5a). With a neat diagram, explain network security model.

(June 2011) (07 Marks)

5b). List out the difference between Kerberos version 4 and version 5.

(July 2011) (8 Marks)

5a). Describe the various security attacks and specific mechanisms covered by X.800

(Dec 2011) (14 Marks)

5b). Explain the different authentication procedures in X.509 certificate.

(Dec 2011) (10 marks)

UNIT-6

ELECTRONIC MAIL SECURITY

Electronic Mail is the most heavily used Network- application and it is also the only distributed application used across all architectures and vendor platforms. Users expect to send mails to others who are connected directly or indirectly to the internet, regardless of host operating systems or communication systems.

With the fast growing reliance on electronic mail for every purpose, there grows a demand for security services such as authentication and confidentiality.

Two schemes, Pretty Good Service (PGP) and S/MIME (Secure/Multipurpose Internet Mail Extension) are used to provide security services to E-mails.

6.1. Pretty Good Service (PGP)

PGP is largely the effort of a single person, Phil Zimmermann, PGP provides a confidentiality and authentication service that can be used for electronic mail and file storage applications. The properties of PGP are:

PGP is an open-source freely available software package for e-mail security.

It provides authentication through the use of digital signature, confidentiality through the use of symmetric block encryption.

It is available free worldwide in versions that run on a variety of platforms, including Windows, UNIX, Macintosh, and many more.

It is based on algorithms are considered extremely secure. Specifically, the package includes RSA, DSS, and Diffie-Hellman for public-key encryption; CAST-128, IDEA, and 3DES for symmetric encryption; and SHA-1 for hash coding.

It has a wide range of applicability, from corporations to individuals who wish to communicate securely with others worldwide over the Internet and other networks.

It was not developed by, nor is it controlled by, any governmental or standards organization. PGP is now on an Internet standards track (RFC 3156).

Operational Description

The actual operation of PGP consists of five services: authentication, confidentiality, Compression, e-mail compatibility, and segmentation as shown in the following Table.

Summary of PGP Services

Sl.No	Function	Algorithms	Used Description
1	Digital signature	DSS/SHA or RSA/SHA	A hash code of a message is created using SHA-1. This message digest is encrypted using DSS or RSA with the sender's private key and included with the message.
2	Message encryption	CAST or IDEA or Three-key Triple DES with Diffie-Hellman or RSA.	A message is encrypted using CAST-128 or IDEA or 3DES with a one-time session key generated by the sender. The session key is encrypted using Diffie- Hellman or RSA with the recipient's public key and included with the message.
3	Compression	Zip	A message may be compressed, for storage or transmission, using ZIP.
4	Email compatibility	Radix 64 conversion	To provide transparency for email applications, an encrypted message may be converted to an ASCII string using radix 64 conversion.
5	Segmentation		To accommodate maximum message size limitations, PGP performs segmentation and reassembly.

Authentication

Figure 1.1a illustrates the digital signature service provided by PGP and the sequence is as follows:

[Digital signatures provide the ability to:

1) Verify author, date & time of signature.
2) Authenticate message contents.
3) Be Verified by third parties to resolve disputes.

Hence include authentication function with additional capabilities]

a) The sender creates a message.
b) SHA-1 is used to generate a 160-bit hash code of the message.
c) The hash code is encrypted with RSA using the sender's private key, and the result is prepended to the message.
d) The receiver uses RSA with the sender's public key to decrypt and recover the hash code.

The receiver generates a new hash code for the message and compares it with the decrypted hash code. If the two match, the message is accepted as authentic.

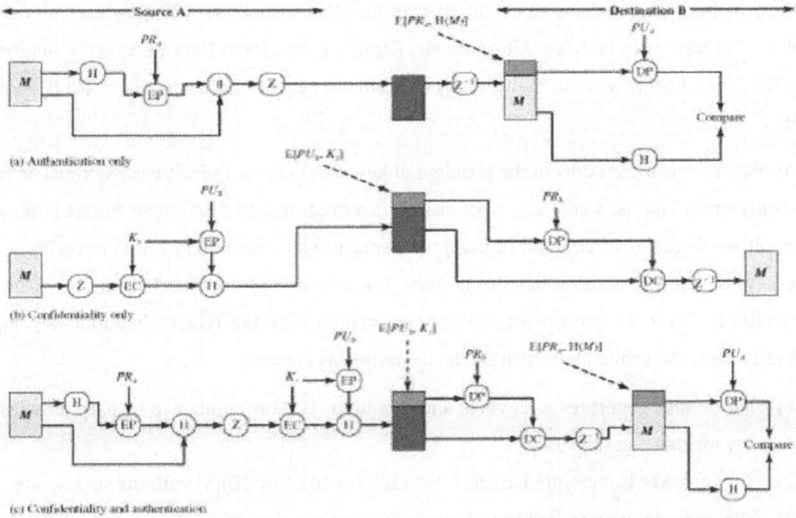

Figure 1.1: PGP Cryptographic Functions

The combination of SHA-1 and RSA provides an effective digital signature scheme. Because of the strength of RSA, the recipient is assured that only the possessor of the matching private key can generate the signature. Because of the strength of SHA-1, the recipient is assured that no one else could generate a new message that matches the hash code and, hence, the signature of the original message.

Although signatures normally are found attached to the message or file, this is not always the case: Detached signatures are also supported. A detached signature may be stored and transmitted separately from the message it signs.

Detached Signatures are useful in several contexts.

A user may wish to maintain a separate signature log of all messages sent or received. A detached signature of an executable program can detect subsequent virus infection.

A detached signature can be used when more than one party must sign a document, such as a legal contract. Each person's signature is independent and therefore is applied only to the document. Otherwise, signatures would have to be nested, with the second signer signing both the document and the first signature, and so on.

Confidentiality

Confidentiality is provided by encrypting messages to be transmitted or to be stored locally as files. In both cases, the symmetric encryption algorithm CAST-128 (Carlisle Adams and Stafford Tavares) may be used. Alternatively, IDEA (International Data Encryption Algorithm) or 3DES (Data Encryption Standards) may be used. The 64-bit cipher feedback (CFB) mode is used.

As always, one must address the problem of key distribution. In PGP, each symmetric key is used only once. That is, a new key is generated as a random 128-bit number for each message. Thus, although this is referred to in the documentation as a session key, it is in reality a one-time key. Because it is to be used only once, the session key is bound to the message and transmitted with it. To protect the key, it is encrypted with the receiver's public key. Figure 1.1b illustrates the sequence, which can be described as follows:

1) The sender generates a message and a random 128-bit number to be used as a session key for this message only.
2) The message is encrypted, using CAST-128 (or IDEA or 3DES) with the session key.
3) The session key is encrypted with RSA, using the recipient's public key, and is prepended to the message.
4) The receiver uses RSA with its private key to decrypt and recover the session key.
5) The session key is used to decrypt the message.

As an alternative to the use of RSA for key encryption, PGP provides an option referred to as

Diffie-Hellman

Several observations may be made:

First, to reduce encryption time the combination of symmetric and public-key encryption is used in preference to simply using RSA or ElGamal to encrypt the message directly: CAST-128 and the other symmetric algorithms are substantially faster than RSA or ElGamal.

Second, the use of the public-key algorithm solves the session key distribution problem, because only the recipient is able to recover the session key that is bound to the message. Note that we do not need a session key exchange protocol because we are not beginning an ongoing session. Rather, each message is a one-time independent event with its own key.

Furthermore, given the store-and-forward nature of electronic mail, the use of handshaking to assure that both sides have the same session key is not practical. Finally, the use of one-time symmetric keys strengthens what is already a strong symmetric encryption approach. Only a small amount of plaintext is encrypted with each key, and there is no relationship among the keys. Thus, to the extent that the public-key algorithm is secure, the entire scheme is secure. To this end, PGP provides the user with a range of key size options from 768 to 3072 bits.

Confidentiality and Authentication

As Figure 1.1c illustrates, both services may be used for the same message.

First, a signature is generated for the plaintext message and prepended to the message. Then the plaintext message plus signature is encrypted using CAST-128 (or IDEA or 3DES), and the session key is encrypted using RSA.

In summary, when both services are used, the sender first signs the message with its own private key, then encrypts the message with a session key, and then encrypts the session key with the recipient's public key.

Compression

PGP compresses the message after applying the signature but before encryption. This has the benefit of saving space both for e-mail transmission and for file storage.

The placement of the compression algorithm, indicated by Z for compression and Z^{-1} for decompression in Figure 1.1.

1) The signature is generated before compression for two reasons:
    - It is preferable to sign an uncompressed message so that one can store only the uncompressed message together with the signature for future verification. If one signed a compressed document, then it would be necessary either to store a compressed version of the message for later verification or to recompress the message when verification is required.
    - Even if one were willing to generate dynamically a recompressed message for verification, PGP's compression algorithm presents a difficulty. The algorithm is not deterministic; various implementations of the algorithm achieve different tradeoffs in running speed versus compression ratio and, as a result, produce different compressed forms. However, these different compression algorithms are interoperable because any version of the algorithm can correctly decompress the output of any other version. Applying the hash function and signature after compression would constrain all PGP implementations to the same version of the compression algorithm.

2) Message encryption is applied after compression to strengthen cryptographic security. Because the compressed message has less redundancy than the original plaintext, and cryptanalysis is more difficult

E-mail Compatibility

When PGP is used, at least part of the block to be transmitted is encrypted. If only the signature service is used, then the message digest is encrypted (with the sender's private key). If the confidentiality service is used, the message plus signature (if present) are encrypted (With a one-time symmetric key). Thus, part or the entire resulting block consists of a stream of arbitrary 8-bit octets. However, many electronic mail systems only permit the use of blocks consisting of ASCII text. To accommodate this restriction, PGP provides the service of converting the raw 8-bit binary stream to a stream of printable ASCII characters.

The scheme used for this purpose is radix-64 conversion. Each group of three octets of binary data is mapped into four ASCII characters. This format also appends a CRC to detect transmission errors

The use of radix 64 expands a message by 33%. Fortunately, the session key and signature portions of the message are relatively compact, and the plaintext message has been compressed. In fact, the compression should be more than enough to compensate for the radix-64 expansion. For example, reports an average compression ratio of about 2.0 using ZIP. If we ignore the relatively small signature and key components, the typical overall effect of compression and expansion of a file of length X would be $1.33 \times 0.5 \times X = 0.665 \times X$. Thus, there is still an overall compression of about one-third.

One noteworthy aspect of the radix-64 algorithm is that it blindly converts the input stream to radix-64 format regardless of content, even if the input happens to be ASCII text. Thus, if a message is signed but not encrypted and the conversion is applied to the entire block, the output will be unreadable to the casual observer, which provides a certain level of confidentiality.

Figure 1.2 shows the relationship among the four services so far discussed. On transmission, if it is required, a signature is generated using a hash code of the uncompressed plaintext. Then the plaintext, plus signature if present, is compressed. Next, if confidentiality is required, the block (compressed plaintext or compressed signature plus plaintext) is encrypted and prepended with the public-key-encrypted symmetric encryption key. Finally, the entire block is converted to radix-64 format.

On reception, the incoming block is first converted back from radix-64 format to binary. Then, if the message is encrypted, the recipient recovers the session key and decrypts the message. The resulting block is then decompressed. If the message is signed, the recipient recovers the transmitted hash code and compares it to its own calculation of the hash code.

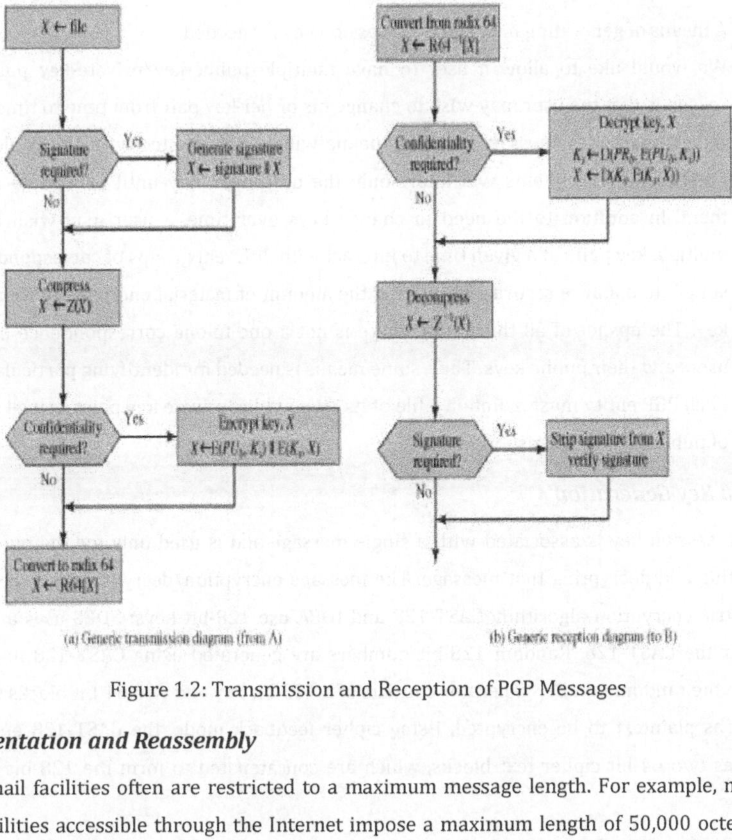

Figure 1.2: Transmission and Reception of PGP Messages

Segmentation and Reassembly

E-mail facilities often are restricted to a maximum message length. For example, many of the facilities accessible through the Internet impose a maximum length of 50,000 octets. Any message longer than that must be broken up into smaller segments, each of which is mailed separately.

To accommodate this restriction, PGP automatically subdivides a message that is too large into segments that are small enough to send via e-mail. The segmentation is done after all of the other processing, including the radix-64 conversion. Thus, the session key component and signature component appear only once, at the beginning of the first segment. At the receiving end, PGP must strip off all e-mail headers and reassemble the entire original block.

Cryptographic Keys and Key Rings

PGP makes use of four types of keys: one-time session symmetric keys, public keys, private keys, and passphrase-based symmetric keys.

Three separate requirements can be identified with respect to these keys:

1) A means of generating unpredictable session keys is needed.
2) We would like to allow a user to have multiple public-key/private-key pairs. One reason is that the user may wish to change his or her key pair from time to time. When this happens, any messages in the pipeline will be constructed with an obsolete key. Furthermore, recipients will know only the old public key until an update reaches them. In addition to the need to change keys over time, a user may wish to have multiple key pairs at a given time to interact with different groups of correspondents or simply to enhance security by limiting the amount of material encrypted with any one key. The upshot of all this is that there is not a one-to-one correspondence between users and their public keys. Thus, some means is needed for identifying particular keys.
3) Each PGP entity must maintain a file of its own public/private key pairs as well as a file of public keys of correspondents.

Session Key Generation

Each session key is associated with a single message and is used only for the purpose of encrypting and decrypting that message. The message encryption/decryption is done with a symmetric encryption algorithm. CAST-128 and IDEA use 128-bit keys; 3DES uses a 168-bit key. For the CAST-128, Random 128-bit numbers are generated using CAST-128 itself. The input to the random number generator consists of a 128-bit key and two 64-bit blocks that are treated as plaintext to be encrypted. Using cipher feedback mode, the CAST-128 encryptor produces two 64-bit cipher text blocks, which are concatenated to form the 128-bit session key.

The "plaintext" input to the random number generator, consisting of two 64-bit blocks, is itself derived from a stream of 128-bit randomized numbers. These numbers are based on keystroke input from the user. Both the keystroke timing and the actual keys struck are used to generate the randomized stream. Thus, if the user hits arbitrary keys at his or her normal pace, a reasonably "random" input will be generated. This random input is also combined with previous session key output from CAST-128 to form the key input to the generator. The result, given the effective scrambling of CAST-128, is to produce a sequence of session keys that is effectively unpredictable.

Key Identifiers

An encrypted message is accompanied by an encrypted form of the session key that was used for message encryption. The session key itself is encrypted with the recipient's public key. Hence, only the recipient will be able to recover the session key and therefore recover the message. If each user employed a single public/private key pair, then the recipient would automatically know which key to use to decrypt the session key: the recipient's unique private key. However, we have stated a requirement that any given user may have multiple public/private key pairs.

How does the recipient know which of its public keys was used to encrypt the session key? One simple solution would be to transmit the public key with the message. The recipient could then verify that this is indeed one of its public keys, and proceed. This scheme would work, but it is unnecessarily wasteful of space. An RSA public key may be hundreds of decimal digits in length.

Another solution would be to associate an identifier with each public key that is unique at least within one user. That is, the combination of user ID and key ID would be sufficient to identify a key uniquely. Then only the much shorter key ID would need to be transmitted. This solution, however, raises a management and overhead problem:

Key IDs must be assigned and stored so that both sender and recipient could map from key ID to public key.

The solution adopted by PGP is to assign a key ID to each public key that is, with very high probability, unique within a user ID. The key ID associated with each public key consists of its least significant 64 bits. That is, the key ID of public *PUa* is (*PUa* mod 2^{64}). This is a sufficient length that the probability of duplicate key IDs is very small.

A key ID is also required for the PGP digital signature. Because a sender may use one of a number of private keys to encrypt the message digest, the recipient must know which public key is intended for use. Accordingly, the digital signature component of a message includes the 64-bit key ID of the required public key. When the message is received, the recipient verifies that the key ID is for a public key that it knows for that sender and then proceeds to verify the signature. With the concept of key ID, we can take a more detailed look at the format of a transmitted message, which is shown in Figure 1.3. A message consists of three components: the message component, a signature (optional), and a session key component (optional). The message component includes the actual data to be stored or transmitted, as well as a filename and a timestamp that specifies the time of creation.

The **signature component** includes the following:

Timestamp: The time at which the signature was made.

Message digest: The 160-bit SHA-1 digest, encrypted with the sender's private signature key. The digest is calculated over the signature timestamp concatenated with the data portion of the message component. The inclusion of the signature timestamp in the digest assures against replay types of attacks. The exclusion of the filename and timestamp portions of the message component ensures that detached signatures are exactly the same as attached signatures prefixed to the message. Detached signatures are calculated on a separate file that has none of the message component header fields.

Leading two octets of message digest: To enable the recipient to determine if the correct public key was used to decrypt the message digest for authentication, by comparing this plaintext copy of the first two octets with the first two octets of the decrypted digest. These octets also serve as a 16-bit frame check sequence for the message.

Key ID of sender's public key: Identifies the public key that should be used to decrypt the message digest and, hence, identifies the private key that was used to encrypt the message digest.

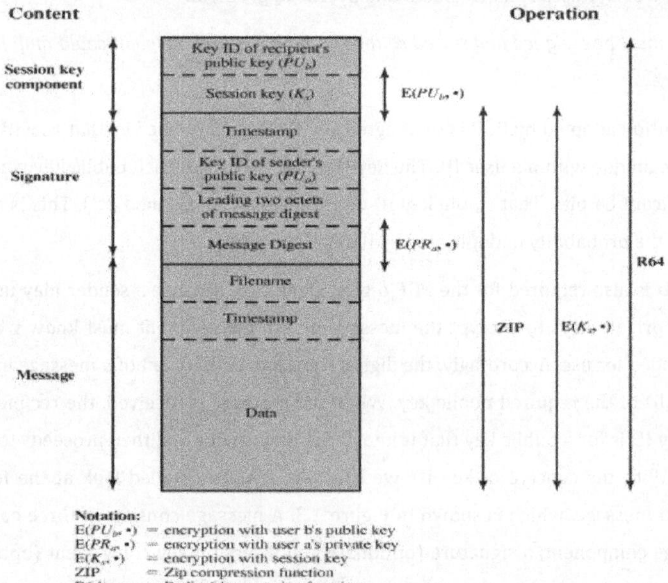

Figure 1.3: General Format of PGP Message (from A to B)

The message component and optional signature component may be compressed using ZIP and may be encrypted using a session key.

The **session key component** includes the session key and the identifier of the recipient's public key that was used by the sender to encrypt the session key.

The entire block is usually encoded with radix-64 encoding.

Key Rings

The key IDs are critical to the operation of PGP and two key IDs are included in any PGP message that provides both confidentiality and authentication. These keys need to be stored and organized in a systematic way for efficient and effective use by all parties. *The scheme used in PGP is to provide a pair of data structures at each node, one to store the public/ private key pairs owned by that node and one to store the public keys of other users known at this node. These data structures are referred to, respectively, as the private-key ring and the public-key ring.*

Figure 1.4 shows the general structure of a private-key ring. We can view the ring as a table, in which each row represents one of the public/private key pairs owned by this user. Each row contains the following entries:

Private-Key Ring

Timestamp	Key ID*	Public Key	Encrypted Private Key	User ID*
⋮	⋮	⋮	⋮	⋮
T_i	$PU_i \bmod 2^{64}$	PU_i	$E(H(P_i), PR_i)$	User i
⋮	⋮	⋮	⋮	⋮

Public-Key Ring

Timestamp	Key ID*	Public Key	Owner Trust	User ID*	Key Legitimacy	Signature(s)	Signature Trust(s)
⋮	⋮	⋮	⋮	⋮	⋮	⋮	⋮
T_i	$PU_i \bmod 2^{64}$	PU_i	$trust\_flag_i$	User i	$trust\_flag_i$		
⋮	⋮	⋮	⋮	⋮	⋮	⋮	⋮

* = field used to index table

Figure 1.4: General Structure of Private- and Public-Key Rings

Timestamp: The date/time when this key pair was generated.

Key ID: The least significant 64 bits of the public key for this entry.

Public key: The public-key portion of the pair.

Private key: The private-key portion of the pair; this field is encrypted.

User ID: Typically, this will be the user's e-mail address (e.g.suresha@revainstitution.org). However, the user may choose to associate a different name with each pair or to reuse the same User ID more than once.

The private-key ring can be indexed by either User ID or Key ID.

Although it is intended that the private-key ring be stored only on the machine of the user that created and owns the key pairs, and that it be accessible only to that user, it makes sense to make the value of the private key as secure as possible. Accordingly, the private key itself is not stored in the key ring. Rather, this key is encrypted using CAST-128.

The procedure is as follows:

1) The user selects a passphrase to be used for encrypting private keys.
2) When the system generates a new public/private key pair using RSA, it asks the user for the passphrase. Using SHA-1, a 160-bit hash code is generated from the passphrase, and the passphrase is discarded.
3) The system encrypts the private key using CAST-128 with the 128 bits of the hash code as the key. The hash code is then discarded, and the encrypted private key is stored in the private-key ring.

Subsequently, when a user accesses the private-key ring to retrieve a private key, he or she must supply the passphrase. PGP will retrieve the encrypted private key, generate the hash code of the passphrase, and decrypt the encrypted private key using CAST-128 with the hash code.

This is a very compact and effective scheme. As in any system based on passwords, the security of this system depends on the security of the password. To avoid the temptation to write it down, the user should use a passphrase that is not easily guessed but that is easily remembered. Figure 1.4 also shows the general structure of a **public-key ring**. This data structure is used to store public keys of other users that are known to this user.

Timestamp: The date/time when this entry was generated.

Key ID: The least significant 64 bits of the public key for this entry.

Public Key: The public key for this entry.

User ID: Identifies the owner of this key. Multiple user IDs may be associated with a single public key.

The public-key ring can be indexed by either User ID or Key ID

Now consider message transmission and reception using key rings. For simplicity, we ignore compression and radix-64 conversion in the following discussion.

First consider message transmission (Figure 1.5) and assume that the message is to be both signed and encrypted. The sending PGP entity performs the following steps

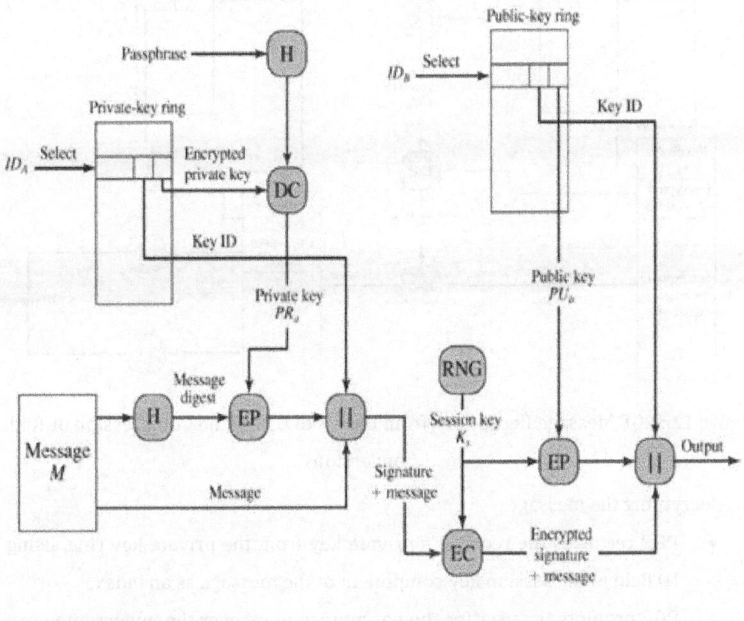

Figure 1.5: PGP Message Generation (from User A to User B, no compression or radix 64 conversion)

1) Signing the message
   - PGP retrieves the sender's private key from the private-key ring using your_userid as an index. If your_userid was not provided in the command, the first private key on the ring is retrieved.
   - PGP prompts the user for the passphrase to recover the unencrypted private key. The signature component of the message is constructed.

2) Encrypting the message

- PGP generates a session key and encrypts the message.
- PGP retrieves the recipient's public key from the public-key ring using her_userid as an index.
- The session key component of the message is constructed.

The receiving PGP entity performs the following steps (Figure 1.6),

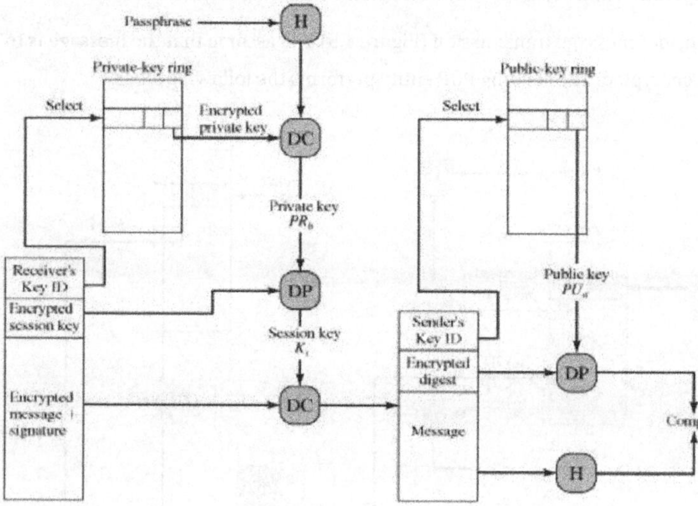

Figure 1.6: PGP Message Reception (from User A to User B, no Compression or Radix 64 Conversion)

1) Decrypting the message

- PGP retrieves the receiver's private key from the private-key ring, using the Key ID field in the session key component of the message as an index.
- PGP prompts the user for the passphrase to recover the unencrypted private key. PGP then recovers the session key and decrypts the message.

2) Authenticating the message

- PGP retrieves the sender's public key from the public-key ring, using the Key ID field in the signature key component of the message as an index.
- PGP recovers the transmitted message digest.
- PGP computes the message digest for the received message and compares it to the transmitted message digest to authenticate.

Public-Key Management

PGP has a clever, efficient, interlocking set of functions and formats to provide an effective confidentiality and authentication service. To complete the system, one final area needs to be addressed, that of public-key management. The PGP documentation captures the importance of this area:

- This whole business of protecting public keys from tampering is the single most difficult problem in practical public key applications. It is the "Achilles heel" of public key cryptography, and a lot of software complexity is tied up in solving this one problem.

PGP provides a structure for solving this problem, with several suggested options that may be used. Because PGP is intended for use in a variety of formal and informal environments with no rigid public-key management scheme is set up. The following methods are used for public key Management are The Use of Trust and Revoking Public Keys.

The Use of Trust

PGP provide a convenient means of using trust, associating trust with public keys, and exploiting trust information.

Each entry in the public-key ring is a public-key certificate, associated with each entry is a **key legitimacy field** that indicates the extent to which PGP will trust that this is a valid public key for this user; the higher the level of trust, the stronger is the binding of this user ID to this key. This field is computed by PGP. Also associated with the entry are zero or more signatures that the key ring owner has collected that sign this certificate. In turn, each signature has associated with it a **signature trust field** that indicates the degree to which this PGP user trusts the signer to certify public keys. The key legitimacy field is derived from the collection of signature trust fields in the entry. Finally, each entry defines a public key associated with a particular owner, and an **owner trust field** is included that indicates the degree to which this public key is trusted to sign other public-key certificates; this level of trust is assigned by the user.

The above three fields are each contained in a structure referred to as a trust flag byte. The content of this trust flag for each of these three uses is shown in Table 1.2

Figure 1.7 provides an example of the way in which signature trust and key legitimacy are related. It shows the structure of a public-key ring. The user has acquired a number of public keys, some directly from their owners and some from a third party such as a key server.

Revoking Public Keys

A user may wish to revoke his or her current public key either because compromise is suspected or simply to avoid the use of the same key for an extended period. Note that a compromise would require that an opponent somehow had obtained a copy of your unencrypted. private key or that the opponent had obtained both the private key from your private-key ring and your passphrase.

The convention for revoking a public key is for the owner to issue a key revocation certificate, signed by the owner. This certificate has the same form as a normal signature certificate but includes an indicator that the purpose of this certificate is to revoke the use of this public key. Note that the corresponding private key must be used to sign a certificate that revokes a public key. The owner should then attempt to disseminate this certificate as widely and as quickly as possible to enable potential correspondents to update their public-key rings.

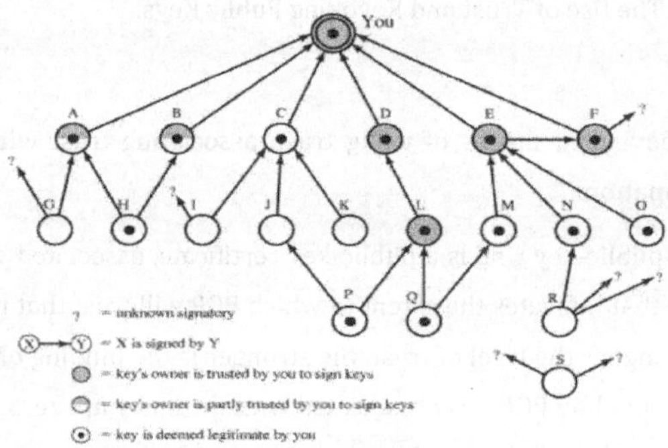

Figure 1.7: PGP Trust Model Example

6.2. S/MIME (Secure/ Multipurpose Internet Mail Extension)

S/MIME is a security enhancement to the MIME Internet e-mail format standard, based on technology from RSA Data Security. Both PGP and S/MIME are on an IETF standards track. S/MIME is the industry standard for commercial and organizational use, while PGP is the choice for personal e-mail security for many users. S/MIME is defined in a number of documents, most importantly RFCs 3369, 3370, 3850 and 3851. To understand S/MIME, we need first to have a general understanding of the underlying e-mail format that it uses, namely MIME. But to understand the significance of MIME, we need to go back to the traditional e-mail format standard, RFC 822, which is still in common use. Accordingly, we discuss RFC822, MIME and S/MIME.

RFC822

RFC 822 defines a format for text messages that are sent using electronic mail.

- It is the standard for Internet-based text mail message
- In the RFC 822 context, messages are viewed as having an envelope and contents.
- The envelope contains whatever information is needed to accomplish transmission and delivery.
- The contents compose the object to be delivered to the recipient.
- The RFC 822 standard applies only to the contents. However, the content standard includes a set of header fields that may be used by the mail system to create the envelope, and the standard is intended to facilitate the acquisition of such information by programs.

The overall structure of a message that conforms to RFC 822 consists of some number of header lines (*the header*) followed by unrestricted text (*the body*). The header is separated from the body by a blank line. A header line usually consists of a keyword, followed by a colon, followed by the keyword's arguments; the format allows a long line to be broken up into several lines. The most frequently used keywords are From, To, Subject, and Date. Here is an example message:

Date: Tue, 16 Jan 1998 10:37:17 (EST)

From: "Suresha" <suresha@revainstitution.org>

Subject: The Syntax in RFC 822

To: edusatvtu@gmail.com

Cc: nalinaniranjan@hotmail.com

Hello. This section begins the actual message body, which is delimited from the message heading by a blank line. Another field that is commonly found in RFC 822 headers is *Message-ID.* This field contains a unique identifier associated with this message.

Multipurpose Internet Mail Extensions(MIME)

MIME is an extension to the RFC 822 framework that is intended to address some of the problems and limitations of the use of SMTP (Simple Mail Transfer Protocol) or some other mail transfer protocol and RFC 822 for electronic mail. The following are the limitations of the SMTP/822 scheme:

1) SMTP cannot transmit executable files or other binary objects. A number of schemes are in use for converting binary files into a text form that can be used by SMTP mail

systems, including the popular UNIX UUencode/UUdecode scheme. However, none of these is a standard or even a de facto standard.

2) SMTP cannot transmit text data that includes national language characters because these are represented by 8-bit codes with values of 128 decimal or higher, and SMTP is limited to 7-bit ASCII.
3) SMTP servers may reject mail message over a certain size.
4) SMTP gateways that translate between ASCII and the character code EBCDIC do not use a consistent set of mappings, resulting in translation problems.
5) SMTP gateways to X.400 electronic mail networks cannot handle nontextual data includedin X.400 messages.
6) Some SMTP implementations do not adhere completely to the SMTP standards defined in RFC 821. Common problems include:

- Deletion, addition, or reordering of carriage return and linefeed
- Truncating or wrapping lines longer than 76 characters
- Removal of trailing white space (tab and space characters)
- Padding of lines in a message to the same length
- Conversion of tab characters into multiple space characters

MIME is intended to resolve these problems in a manner that is compatible with existing RFC 822 implementations. The specification is provided in RFCs 2045 through 2049. The MIME specification includes the following elements

1. Five new message header fields are defined, which may be included in an RFC 822 header. These fields provide information about the body of the message.
2. A number of content formats are defined, thus standardizing representations that support multimedia electronic mail.
3. Transfer encodings are defined that enable the conversion of any content format into a form that is protected from alteration by the mail system.

In this subsection, we introduce the five message header fields. The next two subsections deal with content formats and transfer encodings. The five header fields defined in MIME are as follows:

MIME-Version: Must have the parameter value 1.0. This field indicates that the message conforms to RFCs 2045 and 2046.

Content-Type: Describes the data contained in the body with sufficient detail that the receiving user agent can pick an appropriate agent or mechanism to represent the data to the user or otherwise deal with the data in an appropriate manner.

Content-Transfer-Encoding: Indicates the type of transformation that has been used to represent the body of the message in a way that is acceptable for mail transport.

Content-ID: Used to identify MIME entities uniquely in multiple contexts.

Content-Description: A text description of the object with the body; this is useful when the object is not readable (e.g., audio data).

MIME Content Types

The bulk of the MIME specification is concerned with the definition of a variety of content types. This reflects the need to provide standardized ways of dealing with a wide variety of information representations in a multimedia environment. Table 1.3 lists the content types specified in RFC 2046. There are seven different major types of content and a total of 15 subtypes. In general, a content type declares the general type of data, and the subtype specifies a particular format for that type of data.

Table 1.3: MIME Content Types

Type	Subtype	Description
Text	Plain	Unformatted text; may be ASCII or ISO 8859.
	Enriched	Provides greater format flexibility
Multipart	Mixed	The different parts are independent but are to be transmitted together.
		They should be presented to the receiver in the order that they appear in the mail message.
	Parallel	Differs from Mixed only in that no order is defined for delivering the parts to the receiver.
	Alternative	The different parts are alternative versions of the same information.
		They are ordered in increasing faithfulness to the original, and the recipient's mail system should display the "best" version to the user.
	Digest	Similar to Mixed, but the default type/subtype of each part is message/rfc822.
Message	rfc822	The body is itself an encapsulated message that conforms to RFC 822.
	Partial	Used to allow fragmentation of large mail items, in a way that is transparent to the recipient.
	External-body	Contains a pointer to an object that exists elsewhere.
Image	jpeg	The image is in JPEG format, JFIF encoding
	gif	The image is in GIF format.
Video	Mpeg	MPEG format.
Audio	Basic	Single-channel 8-bit ISDN mu-law encoding at a sample rate of 8 kHz.
Application	PostScript	Adobe Postscript.
	octet-stream	General binary data consisting of 8-bit bytes.

MIME Transfer Encodings

The other major component of the MIME specification is a definition of transfer encodings for message bodies. The objective is to provide reliable delivery across the largest range of environments. The MIME standard defines two methods of encoding data. The Content-Transfer-Encoding field can actually take on six values, as listed in Table 1.4. However, three of these values (7bit, 8bit, and binary) indicate that no encoding has been done but provide some information about the nature of the data. For SMTP transfer, it is safe to use the 7bit form. The 8bit and binary forms may be usable in other mail transport contexts. Another Content-Transfer-Encoding value is x-token, which indicates that some other encoding scheme is used, for which a name is to be supplied. This could be a vendor-specific or application-specific scheme. The two actual encoding schemes defined are quoted-printable and base64. Two schemes are defined to provide a choice between a transfer technique that is essentially human readable and one that is safe for all types of data in a way that is reasonably compact.

Table 1.4: MIME Transfer Encodings

7bit	The data are all represented by short lines of ASCII characters.
8bit	The lines are short, but there may be non-ASCII characters (octets with the high-order bit set).
binary	Not only may non-ASCII characters be present but the lines are not necessarily short enough for SMTP transport.
quoted-printable	Encodes the data in such a way that if the data being encoded are mostly ASCII text, the encoded form of the data remains largely recognizable by humans.
base64	Encodes data by mapping 6-bit blocks of input to 8-bit blocks of output, all of which are printable ASCII characters.
x-token	A named nonstandard encoding.

The **quoted-printable** transfer encoding is useful when the data consists largely of octets that correspond to printable ASCII characters. In essence, it represents nonsafe characters by the hexadecimal representation of their code and introduces reversible (soft) line breaks to limit message lines to 76 characters. The **base64 transfer encoding**, also known as radix-64 encoding, is a common one for encoding arbitrary binary data in such a way as to be invulnerable to the processing by mail transport programs.

Canonical Form

An important concept in MIME and S/MIME is that of canonical form. Canonical form is a format, appropriate to the content type that is standardized for use between systems. This is in contrast to native form, which is a format that may be peculiar to a particular system. Table 1.5, from RFC 2049, should help clarify this matter.

Table 1.5: Native and Canonical Form

Native Form	The body to be transmitted is created in the system's native format. The native character set is used and, where appropriate, local end-of-line conventions are used as well. The body may be a UNIX-style text file, or a Sun raster image, or a VMS indexed file, or audio data in a system-dependent format stored only in memory, or anything else that corresponds to the local model for the representation of some form of information. Fundamentally, the data is created in the "native" form that corresponds to the type specified by the media type.
Canonical Form	The entire body, including "out-of-band" information such as record lengths and possibly file attribute information, is converted to a universal canonical form. The specific media type of the body as well as its associated attributes dictate the nature of the canonical form that is used. Conversion to the proper canonical form may involve character set conversion, transformation of audio data, compression, or various other operations specific to the various media types. If character set conversion is involved, however, care must be taken to understand the semanties of the media type, which may have strong implications for any character set conversion.

S/MIME Functionality

In terms of general functionality, S/MIME is very similar to PGP. Both offer the ability to sign and/or encrypt messages. In this subsection, we briefly summarize S/MIME capability. We then look in more detail at this capability by examining message formats and message preparation.

Functions

S/MIME provides the following functions:

Enveloped data: This consists of encrypted content of any type and encrypted-content encryption keys for one or more recipients.

Signed data: A digital signature is formed by taking the message digest of the content to be signed and then encrypting that with the private key of the signer. The content plus signature are then encoded using base64 encoding. A signed data message can only be viewed by a recipient with S/MIME capability.

Clear-signed data: As with signed data, a digital signature of the content is formed. However, in this case, only the digital signature is encoded using base64. As a result, recipients without S/MIME capability can view the message content, although they cannot verify the signature.

Signed and enveloped data: Signed-only and encrypted-only entities may be nested, so that encrypted data may be signed and signed data or clear-signed data may be encrypted.

Cryptographic Algorithms

Table 1.6 summarizes the cryptographic algorithms used in S/MIME. S/MIME uses the following terminology, taken from RFC 2119 to specify the requirement level:

Must: The definition is an absolute requirement of the specification. An implementation must include this feature or function to be in conformance with the specification.

Should: There may exist valid reasons in particular circumstances to ignore this feature or function, but it is recommended that an implementation include the feature or function.

Table 1.6: Cryptographic Algorithms Used in S/MIME

Function	Requirement
Create a message digest to be used in forming a digital signature. Encrypt message digest to form digital signature. Encrypt session key for transmission with message. Encrypt message for transmission with one-time session key. Create a message authentication code SHA-1.	MUST support SHA-1. Receiver SHOULD support MD5 for backward compatibility. Sending and receiving agents MUST support DSS. Sending agents SHOULD support RSA encryption. Receiving agents SHOULD support verification. RSA signatures with key sizes 512 bits to 1024 bits. Sending and receiving agents SHOULD support Diffie-Hellman. Sending and receiving agents MUST support RSA encryption with key sizes 512 bits to 1024 bits. Sending and receiving agents MUST support encryption with triple DES. Sending agents SHOULD support encryption with AES. Sending agents SHOULD support encryption with RC2/40. Receiving agents MUST support HMAC. Receiving agents SHOULD support HMAC with SHA-1.

S/MIME Incorporates three Public-key Algorithms

The Digital Signature Standard (DSS) is the preferred algorithm for digital signature. S/MIME lists Diffie-Hellman as the preferred algorithm for encrypting session keys. RSA, can be used for both signatures and session key encryption. For message encryption, three-key triple DES (tripleDES) is recommended. The S/MIME specification includes a discussion of the procedure for deciding which content encryption algorithm to use. In essence, a sending agent has two decisions to make. First, the sending agent must determine if the receiving agent is capable of decrypting using a given encryption algorithm. Second, if the receiving agent is only capable of accepting weakly encrypted content, the sending agent must decide if it is acceptable to send using weak encryption.

The following rules, in the following order, should be followed by a sending agent:

1) If the sending agent has a list of preferred decrypting capabilities from an intended recipient, it SHOULD choose the first (highest preference) capability on the list that it is capable of using.

- If the sending agent has no such list of capabilities from an intended recipient but has received one or more messages from the recipient, then the outgoing message SHOULD use the same encryption algorithm as was used on the last signed and encrypted message received from that intended recipient.
- If the sending agent has no knowledge about the decryption capabilities of the intended recipient and is willing to risk that the recipient may not be able to decrypt the message, then the sending agent SHOULD use tripleDES.
- If the sending agent has no knowledge about the decryption capabilities of the intended recipient and is not willing to risk that the recipient may not be able to decrypt the message, then the sending agent MUST use RC2/40.

If a message is to be sent to multiple recipients and a common encryption algorithm cannot be selected for all, then the sending agent will need to send two messages. However, in that case, it is important to note that the security of the message is made vulnerable by the transmission of one copy with lower security.

S/MIME Messages

S/MIME makes use of a number of new MIME content types, which are shown in Table 1.7. All of the new application types use the designation PKCS. This refers to a set of public-key cryptography specifications issued by RSA Laboratories and made available for the S/MIME effort.

Table 1.7: S/MIME Content Types

Type	Subtype	s/mime Parameter	Description
Multipart	Signed		A clear-signed message in two parts: one is the message and the other is the signature.
Application	pkcs 7-mime	signedData	A signed S/MIME entity.
	pkcs 7-mime	envelopedData	An encrypted S/MIME entity.
	pkcs 7-mime	degenerate signedData	CompressedData.
	pkcs 7-mime	CompressedData.	A compressed S/MIME
	pkcs 7-signature	signedData	The content type of the signature of a subpart
			multipart/signed message

Securing a MIME Entity

S/MIME secures a MIME entity with a signature, encryption, or both. A MIME entity may be an entire message (except for the RFC 822 headers), or if the MIME content type is multipart, then a MIME entity is one or more of the subparts of the message. The MIME entity is prepared according to the normal rules for MIME message preparation. Then the MIME entity plus some security-related data, such as algorithm identifiers and certificates, are processed by S/MIME to produce what is known as a PKCS object. A PKCS object is then treated as message content and wrapped in MIME.

Enveloped Data

An application/pkcs7-mime subtype is used for one of four categories of S/MIME processing, each with a unique S/MIME-type parameter. In all cases, the resulting entity, referred to as an object, is represented in a form known as Basic Encoding Rules (BER), which is defined in ITU-T Recommendation X.209. The BER format consists of arbitrary octet strings and is therefore binary data. Such an object should be transfer encoded with base 64 in the outer MIME message. We first look at enveloped Data.

The steps for preparing an enveloped Data MIME entity are as follows:

- Generate a pseudorandom session key for a particular symmetric encryption algorithm (RC2/40 or tripleDES).
- For each recipient, encrypt the session key with the recipient's public RSA key.
- For each recipient, prepare a block known as RecipientInfo that contains an identifier of the recipient's public-key certificate, an identifier of the algorithm used to encrypt the session key, and the encrypted session key.
- Encrypt the message content with the session key.

The RecipientInfo blocks followed by the encrypted content constitute the envelopedData. This information is then encoded into base64.

A sample message (excluding the RFC 822 headers) is the following: Content-Type: application/pkcs7-mime; smime-type=envelopeddata; name=smime.p7m

Content-Transfer-Encoding: base64 Content-Disposition: attachment; filename=smime.p7m

rfvbnj75.6tbBghyHhHUujhJhjH77n8HHGT9HG4VQpfyF467GhIGfHfYT6
7n8HHGghyHhHUujhJh4VQpfyF467GhIGfHfYGTrfvbnjT6jH7756tbB9H
f8HHGTrfvhJhjH776tbB9HG4VQbnj7567GhIGfHfYT6ghyHhHUujpfyF4
0GhIGfHfQbnj756YT64V

To recover the encrypted message, the recipient first strips off the base64 encoding. Then the recipient's private key is used to recover the session key. Finally, the message content is decrypted with the session key.

Signed Data

The signedData smime-type can actually be used with one or more signers. For clarity, we confine our description to the case of a single digital signature. The steps for preparing a signedData MIME entity are as follows:

- Select a message digest algorithm (SHA or MD5).
- Compute the message digest, or hash function, of the content to be signed.
- Encrypt the message digest with the signer's private key.
- Prepare a block known as Signer Info that contains the signer's public-key certificate, an identifier of the message digest algorithm, an identifier of the algorithm used to encrypt the message digest, and the encrypted message digest.

The signedData entity consists of a series of blocks, including a message digest algorithm identifier, the message being signed, and SignerInfo. The signedData entity may also include a set of public-key certificates sufficient to constitute a chain from a recognized root or top-level certification authority to the signer. This information is then encoded into base64.

A sample message (excluding the RFC 822 headers) is the following:

Content-Type:application/pkcs7-mime;smime-type=signed-data; name=smime.p7m
Content-Transfer-Encoding: base64
Content-Disposition: attachment; filename=smime.p7m

567GhIGfHfYT6ghyHhHUujpfyF4f8HHGTrfvhJhjH776tbB9HG4VQbnj7

77n8HHGT9HG4VQpfyF467GhIGfHfYT6rfvbnj756tbBghyHhHUujhJhjH
HUujhJh4VQpfyF467GhIGfHfYGTrfvbnjT6jH7756tbB9H7n8HHGghyHh
6YT64V0GhIGfHfQbnj75

To recover the signed message and verify the signature, the recipient first strips off the base64 encoding. Then the signer's public key is used to decrypt the message digest. The recipient independently computes the message digest and compares it to the decrypted message digest to verify the signature.

Clear Signing

Clear signing is achieved using the multipart content type with a signed subtype. This signing process does not involve transforming the message to be signed, so that the message is sent "in the clear." Thus, recipients with MIME capability but not S/MIME capability are able to read the incoming message.

A multipart/signed message has two parts. The first part can be any MIME type but must be prepared so that it will not be altered during transfer from source to destination. This means that if the first part is not 7bit, then it needs to be encoded using base64 or quoted-printable. Then this part is processed in the same manner as signed Data, but in this case an object with signed Data format is created that has an empty message content field. This object is a detached signature. It is then transfer encoded using base64 to become the second part of the multipart/signed message. This second part has a MIME content type of application and a subtype of pkcs7-signature.

Here is a sample message:

Content-Type: multipart/signed;

protocol="application/pkcs7-signature";

micalg=sha1; boundary=boundary42 boundary42

Content-Type: text/plain

This is a clear-signed message. boundary42

Content-Type: application/pkcs7-signature;

name=smime.p7s Content-Transfer-Encoding: base64

Content-Disposition: attachment; filename=smime.p7s

ghyHhHUujhJhjH77n8HHGTrfvbnj756tbB9HG4VQpfyF467GhIGfHfYT6

4VQpfyF467GhIGfHfYT6jH77n8HHGghyHhHUujhJh756tbB9HGTrfvbnj

n8HHGTrfvhJhjH776tbB9HG4VQbnj7567GhIGfHfYT6ghyHhHUujpfyF4

7GhIGfHfYT64VQbnj756

boundary42

The protocol parameter indicates that this is a two-part clear-signed entity. The micalg parameter indicates the type of message digest used. The receiver can verify the signature by taking the message digest of the first part and comparing this to the message digest recovered from the signature in the second part.

Registration Request

Typically, an application or user will apply to a certification authority for a public-key certificate. The application/pkcs10 S/MIME entity is used to transfer a certification request. The certification request includes certification Request Info block, followed by an identifier of the public-key encryption algorithm, followed by the signature of the certification Request Info block, made using the sender's private key. The certification Request Info block includes a name of the certificate subject (the entity whose public key is to be certified) and a bit-string representation of the user's public key.

Certificates-Only Message

A message containing only certificates or a certificate revocation list (CRL) can be sent in response to a registration request. The message is an application/pkcs7-mime type/subtype with an smime-type parameter of degenerate. The steps involved are the same as those for creating a signed Data message, except that there is no message content and the signer Info field is empty.

S/MIME Certificate Processing

S/MIME uses public-key certificates that conform to version 3 of X.509. The key-management scheme used by S/MIME is in some ways a hybrid between a strict X.509 certification hierarchy and PGP's web of trust. As with the PGP model, S/MIME managers and/or users must configure each client with a list of trusted keys and with certificate revocation lists. That is, the responsibility is local for maintaining the certificates needed to verify incoming signatures and to encrypt outgoing messages. On the other hand, the certificates are signed by certification authorities.

User Agent Role

An S/MIME user has several key-management functions to perform:

Key generation: The user of some related administrative utility (e.g., one associated with LAN management) MUST be capable of generating separate Diffie-Hellman and DSS key pairs and SHOULD be capable of generating RSA key pairs. Each key pair MUST be generated from a good source of nondeterministic random input and be protected in a secure fashion. A user agent SHOULD generate RSA key pairs with a length in the range of 768 to 1024 bits and MUST NOT generate a length of less than 512 bits.

Registration: A user's public key must be registered with a certification authority in order to receive an X.509 public-key certificate.

Certificate storage and retrieval: A user requires access to a local list of certificates in order to verify incoming signatures and to encrypt outgoing messages. Such a list could be maintained by the user or by some local administrative entity on behalf of a number of users.

VeriSign Certificates

There are several companies that provide certification authority (CA) services. For example, Nortel has designed an enterprise CA solution and can provide S/MIME support within an organization. There are a number of Internet-based CAs, including VeriSign, GTE, and the U.S. Postal Service. Of these, the most widely used is the VeriSign CA service, a brief description of which we now provide. VeriSign provides a CA service that is intended to be compatible with S/MIME and a variety of other applications. VeriSign issues X.509 certificates with the product name VeriSign Digital ID. As of early 1998, over 35,000 commercial Web sites were using VeriSign Server Digital IDs, and over a million consumer Digital IDs had been issued to users of Netscape and Microsoft browsers.

The information contained in a Digital ID depends on the type of Digital ID and its use. At a minimum, each Digital ID contains

1. Owner's public key
2. Owner's name or alias
3. Expiration date of the Digital ID
4. Serial number of the Digital ID
5. Name of the certification authority that issued the Digital ID
6. Digital signature of the certification authority that issued the Digital ID Digital IDs can also contain other user-supplied information, including
7. Address
8. E-mail address
9. Basic registration information (country, zip code, age, and gender)

VeriSign provides three levels, or classes, of security for public-key certificates, as summarized in Table 1.8. A user requests a certificate online at VeriSign's Web site or other participating Web sites. Class 1 and Class 2 requests are processed on line, and in most cases take only a few seconds to approve. Briefly, the following procedures are used:

1. For Class 1 Digital IDs, VeriSign confirms the user's e-mail address by sending a PIN and Digital ID pick-up information to the e-mail address provided in the application.
2. For Class 2 Digital IDs, VeriSign verifies the information in the application through an automated comparison with a consumer database in addition to performing all of the checking associated with a Class 1 Digital ID. Finally, confirmation is sent to the specified postal address alerting the user that a Digital ID has been issued in his or her name.
3. For Class 3 Digital IDs, VeriSign requires a higher level of identity assurance. An individual must prove his or her identity by providing notarized credentials or applying in person.

Table 1.8: VeriSign Public-Key Certificate Classes

	Summary of Confirmation of Identity	IA Private Key Protection	Certificate Applicant and Subscriber Private or Key Protection	Applications implemented contemplated by Users
Class 1	Automated unambiguous name and e-mail address search	PCA: trustworthy hardware; CA: trust-worthy software or trustworthy hardware	Encryption software (PIN protected) recommended but not required	Web-browsing and certain e-mail usage
Class 2	Same as Class 1, plus automated enrollment information check plus automated address check	PCA and CA: trustworthy hardware	Encryption software (PIN protected) required	Individual and intra and protected) required inter-company E-mail, online subscriptions, password replacement, and software validation
Class 3	Same as Class 1, plus personal presence and ID documents plus Class 2 automated ID check for individuals; business records (or filings) for organizations	PCA and CA: trustworthy hardware	Encryption software (PIN protected) required;hardware token recommended but not required	E-banking, corp,database access, personal banking, membership-based online services, content integrity services, e-commerce server, software validation; authentication of LRAAs; and strong encryption for certain servers

Enhanced Security Services

Three enhanced security services have been proposed in an Internet draft. The details of these may change, and additional services may be added. The three services are as follows:

1. **Signed receipts:** A signed receipt may be requested in a SignedData object. Returning a signed receipt provides proof of delivery to the originator of a message and allows the originator to demonstrate to a third party that the recipient received the message. In essence, the recipient signs the entire original message plus original (sender's) signature and appends the new signature to form a new S/MIME message.
2. **Security labels:** A security label may be included in the authenticated attributes of a SignedData object. A security label is a set of security information regarding the sensitivity of the content that is protected by S/MIME encapsulation. The labels may be

used for access control, by indicating which users are permitted access to an object. Other uses include priority (secret, confidential, restricted, and so on) or role based, describing which kind of people can see the information (e.g.patient's health-care team, medical billing agents, etc.).

3. **Secure mailing lists:** When a user sends a message to multiple recipients, a certain amount of per-recipient processing is required, including the use of each recipient's public key. The user can be relieved of this work by employing the services of an S/MIME Mail List Agent (MLA). An MLA can take a single incoming message, perform the recipient-specific encryption for each recipient, and forward the message. The originator of a message need only send the message to the MLA, with encryption performed using the MLA's public key.

References

1) Cryptography and Network Security, Principles and Practices, William Stallings, Eastern Economy Edition, Fourth edition.
2) Cryptography & Network Security, Behrouz A. forouzan, The McGraw-Hill Companies, Edition 2007.
3) http://williamstallings.com/Security2e.html

Questions

6a). With a systematic diagram explain Kerberos Ver-4 authentication dialogue clearly mention different steps.

(December 2010)(10 marks)

6b). With a flowchart explain the process of transmission and reception of PGP message.

(December 2010) (10 marks)

6a). Explain the PGP message generation and reception process.

(June 2012) (10 marks)

6b). Explain the different MIME Content types.

(June 2012). (10 marks)

6a). With a neat diagram, explain the digital signature service provided by PGP

(June 2010) (10 Marks)

6b). Explain the different MIME content types.

(June 2010) (10Marks)

6a). Explain PGP message generation and PGP message reception techniques.

(July 2011) (10 Marks)

6b).Describe S/MIME Functionality.

(July 2011) (5 Marks)

6c).Explain S/MIME certificate processing method.

(July 2011)(5 Marks)

6a). Describe the steps involved in providing authentication and confidentiality by PGP, with suitable illusions.

(Dec 2011) (10 Marks)

6b).Discuss the limitations of SMTP and how MIME overcomes these Limitation

(Dec 2011) (10 Marks)

UNIT-7

IP SECURITY

IP-level security encompasses three functional areas: authentication, confidentiality, and key management. The authentication mechanism assures that a received packet was, in fact, transmitted by the party identified as the source in the packet header. In addition, this mechanism assures that the packet has not been altered in transit. The confidentiality facility enables communicating nodes to encrypt messages to prevent eavesdropping by third parties. The key management facility is concerned with the secure exchange of keys.

7.1. IP Security Overview

The IP security capabilities were designed to be used for both with the current IPv4 and the future IPv6 protocols.

Applications of IPSec

IPSec provides the capability to secure communications across a LAN, across private and public WANs, and across the Internet. Examples of its use include the following:

- **Secure branch office connectivity over the Internet:** A company can build a secure virtual private network over the Internet or over a public WAN. This enables a business to rely heavily on the Internet and reduce its need for private networks, saving costs and network management overhead.
- **Secure remote access over the Internet:** An end user whose system is equipped with IP security protocols can make a local call to an Internet service provider (ISP) and gain secure access to a company network. This reduces the cost of toll charges for traveling employees and telecommuters.
- **Establishing extranet and intranet connectivity with partners:** IPSec can be used to secure communication with other organizations, ensuring authentication and confidentiality and providing a key exchange mechanism.
- **Enhancing electronic commerce security:** Even though some Web and electronic commerce applications have built-in security protocols, the use of IPSec enhances that security.

The principal feature of IPSec that enables it to support these varied applications is that it can encrypt and/or authenticate *all* traffic at the IP level. Thus, all distributed applications, including remote logon, client/server, e-mail, file transfer, Web access, and so on, can be secured.

Figure 1.1 is a typical scenario of IPSec usage. An organization maintains LANs at dispersed locations. Nonsecure IP traffic is conducted on each LAN. For traffic offsite, through some sort of private or public WAN, IPSec protocols are used. These protocols operate in networking devices, such as a router or firewall, that connect each LAN to the outside world. The IPSec networking device will typically encrypt and compress all traffic going into the WAN, and decrypt and decompress traffic coming from the WAN; these operations are transparent to workstations and servers on the LAN. Secure transmission is also possible with individual users who dial into the WAN. Such user workstations must implement the IPSec protocols to provide security.

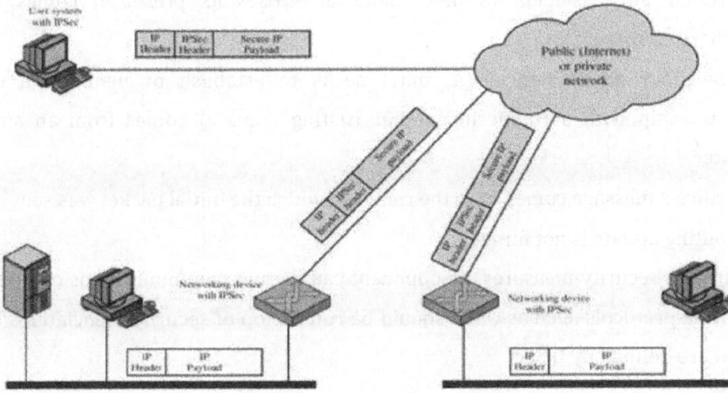

Figure 1.1: An IP Security Scenario

Benefits of IPSec

The following are the benefits of IPSec:

- When IPSec is implemented in a firewall or router, it provides strong security that can be applied to all traffic crossing the perimeter. Traffic within a company or workgroup does not incur the overhead of security-related processing.
- IPSec in a firewall is resistant to bypass if all traffic from the outside must use IP, and the firewall is the only means of entrance from the Internet into the organization.
- IPSec is below the transport layer (TCP, UDP) and so is transparent to applications. There is no need to change software on a user or server system when IPSec is implemented in the firewall or router. Even if IPSec is implemented in end systems, upper-layer software, including applications, is not affected.
- IPSec can be transparent to end users. There is no need to train users on security mechanisms, issue keying material on a per-user basis, or revoke keying material when

users leave the organization.

- IPSec can provide security for individual users if needed. This is useful for offsite workers and for setting up a secure virtual sub network within an organization for sensitive applications.

Routing Applications

In addition to supporting end users and protecting premises systems and networks, IPSec can play a vital role in the routing architecture required for internetworking. [HUIT98] lists the following examples of the use of IPSec. IPSec can assure that

- A router advertisement (a new router advertises its presence) comes from an authorized router
- A neighbor advertisement (a router seeks to establish or maintain a neighbor relationship with a router in another routing domain) comes from an authorized router.
- A redirect message comes from the router to which the initial packet was sent.
- A routing update is not forged.

Without such security measures, an opponent can disrupt communications or divert some traffic. Routing protocols such as OSPF should be run on top of security associations between routers that are defined by IPSec.

7.2. IP Security Architecture

The IPSec specification has become quite complex. To get a feel for the overall architecture, we begin with a look at the documents that define IPSec. Then we discuss IPSec services and introduce the concept of security association.

IPSec Documents

The IPSec specification consists of numerous documents. The most important of these, issued in November of 1998, are RFCs 2401, 2402, 2406, and 2408:

- RFC 2401: An overview of a security architecture
- RFC 2402: Description of a packet authentication extension to IPv4 and IPv6
- RFC 2406: Description of a packet encryption extension to IPv4 and IPv6
- RFC 2408: Specification of key management capabilities

Support for these features is mandatory for IPv6 and optional for IPv4. In both cases, the security features are implemented as extension headers that follow the main IP header.

The extension header for authentication is known as the Authentication header; that for encryption is known as the Encapsulating Security Payload (ESP) header.

In addition to these four RFCs, a number of additional drafts have been published by the IP Security Protocol Working Group set up by the IETF. The documents are divided into seven groups, as depicted in Figure 1.2 (RFC 2401).

- **Architecture:** Covers the general concepts, security requirements, definitions, and mechanisms defining IPSec technology.
- **Encapsulating Security Payload (ESP):** Covers the packet format and general issues related to the use of the ESP for packet encryption and, optionally, authentication.
- **Authentication Header (AH):** Covers the packet format and general issues related to the use of AH for packet authentication.
- **Encryption Algorithm:** A set of documents that describe how various encryption algorithms are used for ESP.

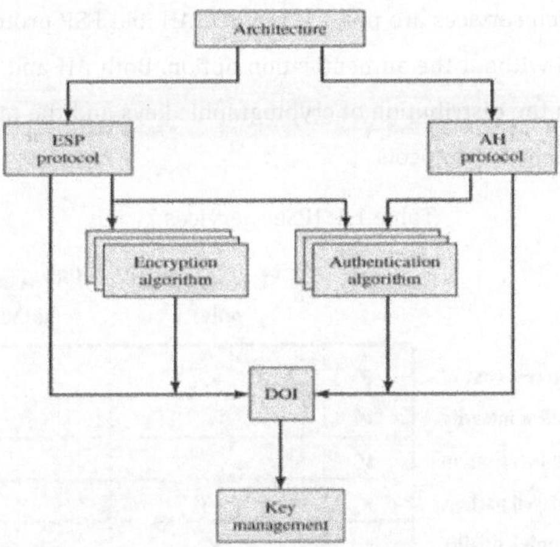

Figure 1.2: IPSec Document Overview

- **Authentication Algorithm:** A set of documents that describe how various authentication algorithms are used for AH and for the authentication option of ESP.
- **Key Management:** Documents that describe key management schemes.

Domain of Interpretation (DOI): Contains values needed for the other documents to relate to each other. These include identifiers for approved encryption and authentication algorithms, as well as operational parameters such as key lifetime.

IPSec Services

IPSec provides security services at the IP layer by enabling a system to select required security protocols, determine the algorithm(s) to use for the service(s), and put in place any cryptographic keys required to provide the requested services. Two protocols are used to provide security: an authentication protocol designated by the header of the protocol, Authentication Header (AH); and a combined encryption/authentication protocol designated by the format of the packet for that protocol, Encapsulating Security Payload (ESP). The services are

- Access control
- Connectionless integrity
- Data origin authentication
- Rejection of replayed packets (a form of partial sequence integrity)
- Confidentiality (encryption)
- Limited traffic flow confidentiality

Table 1.1 shows which services are provided by the AH and ESP protocols. For ESP, there are two cases: with and without the authentication option. Both AH and ESP are vehicles for access control, based on the distribution of cryptographic keys and the management of traffic flows relative to these security protocols.

Table 1.1: IPSec Services

	AH	ESP (encryption only)	ESP (encryption plus authentication)
Access control	✔	✔	✔
Connectionless integrity	✔		✔
Data origin authentication	✔		✔
Rejection of replayed packets	✔	✔	✔
Confidentiality		✔	✔
Limited traffic flow confidentiality		✔	✔

A key concept that appears in both the authentication and confidentiality mechanisms for IP is the security association (SA). **An association is a one-way relationship between a sender and a receiver that affords security services to the traffic carried on it**. If a peer relationship is needed, for two-way secure exchange, then two security associations are required. Security services are afforded to an SA for the use of AH or ESP, but not both.

A security association is uniquely identified by three parameters:

Security Parameters Index (SPI): A bit string assigned to this SA and having local significance only. The SPI is carried in AH and ESP headers to enable the receiving system to select the SA under which a received packet will be processed.

IP Destination Address: Currently, only unicast addresses are allowed; this is the address of the destination endpoint of the SA, which may be an end user system or a network system such as a firewall or router.

Security Protocol Identifier: This indicates whether the association is an AH or ESP security association.

Hence, in any IP packet, the security association is uniquely identified by the Destination Address in the IPv4 or IPv6 header and the SPI in the enclosed extension header (AH or ESP).

SA Parameters

In each IPSec implementation, there is a nominal Security Association Database that defines the parameters associated with each SA. A security association is normally defined by the following parameters:

1) **Sequence Number Counter:** A 32-bit value used to generate the Sequence Number field in AH or ESP headers.
2) **Sequence Counter Overflow:** A flag indicating whether overflow of the Sequence Number Counter should generate an auditable event and prevent further transmission of packets on this SA (required for all implementations).
3) **Anti-Replay Window:** Used to determine whether an inbound AH or ESP packet is a replay.
4) **AH Information:** Authentication algorithm, keys, key lifetimes, and related parameters being used with AH (required for AH implementations).
5) **ESP Information:** Encryption and authentication algorithm, keys, initialization values, key lifetimes, and related parameters being used with ESP (required for ESP implementations).
6) **Lifetime of This Security Association:** A time interval or byte count after which an SA must be replaced with a new SA (and new SPI) or terminated, plus an indication of which of these actions should occur (required for all implementations).
7) **IPSec Protocol Mode:** Tunnel, transport, or wildcard (required for all implementations).

8) **Path MTU:** Any observed path maximum transmission unit (maximum size of a packet that can be transmitted without fragmentation) and aging variables (required for all implementations).

The key management mechanism that is used to distribute keys is coupled to the authentication and privacy mechanisms only by way of the Security Parameters Index. Hence, authentication and privacy have been specified independent of any specific key management mechanism.

SA Selectors

IPSec provides the user with considerable flexibility in the way in which IPSec services are applied to IP traffic. SAs can be combined in a number of ways to yield the desired user configuration. Furthermore, IPSec provides a high degree of granularity in discriminating between traffic that is afforded IPSec protection and traffic that is allowed to bypass IPSec, in the former case relating IP traffic to specific SAs.

The means by which IP traffic is related to specific SAs (or no SA in the case of traffic allowed to bypass IPSec) is the nominal Security Policy Database (SPD). In its simplest form, an SPD contains entries, each of which defines a subset of IP traffic and points to an SA for that traffic. In more complex environments, there may be multiple entries that potentially relate to a single SA or multiple SAs associated with a single SPD entry. The reader is referred to the relevant IPSec documents for a full discussion.

Each SPD entry is defined by a set of IP and upper-layer protocol field values, called *selectors*. In effect, these selectors are used to filter outgoing traffic in order to map it into a particular SA. Outbound processing obeys the following general sequence for each IP packet:

- Compare the values of the appropriate fields in the packet (the selector fields) against the SPD to find a matching SPD entry, which will point to zero or more SAs.
- Determine the SA if any for this packet and its associated SPI.
- Do the required IPSec processing (i.e., AH or ESP processing).

The following selectors determine an SPD entry:

- **Destination IP Address:** This may be a single IP address, an enumerated list or range of addresses, or a wildcard (mask) address. The latter two are required to support more than one destination system sharing the same SA (e.g., behind a firewall).
- **Source IP Address:** This may be a single IP address, an enumerated list or range of addressee, or a wildcard (mask) address. The latter two are required to support more

than one source system sharing the same SA (e.g., behind a firewall).

- **User ID:** A user identifier from the operating system. This is not a field in the IP or upper-layer headers but is available if IPSec is running on the same operating system as the user.
- **Data Sensitivity Level:** Used for systems providing information flow security (e.g., Secret or Unclassified).
- **Transport Layer Protocol:** Obtained from the IPv4 Protocol or IPv6 Next Header field. This may be an individual protocol number, a list of protocol numbers, or a range of protocol numbers.
- **Source and Destination Ports:** These may be individual TCP or UDP port values, an enumerated list of ports, or a wildcard port.

7.3. Authentication Header

The Authentication Header provides support for data integrity and authentication of IP packets. The data integrity feature ensures that undetected modification to a packet's content in transit is not possible. The authentication feature enables an end system or network device to authenticate the user or application and filter traffic accordingly; it also prevents the address spoofing attacks observed in today's Internet. The AH also guards against the replay attack. Authentication is based on the use of a message authentication code (MAC), hence the two parties must share a secret key.

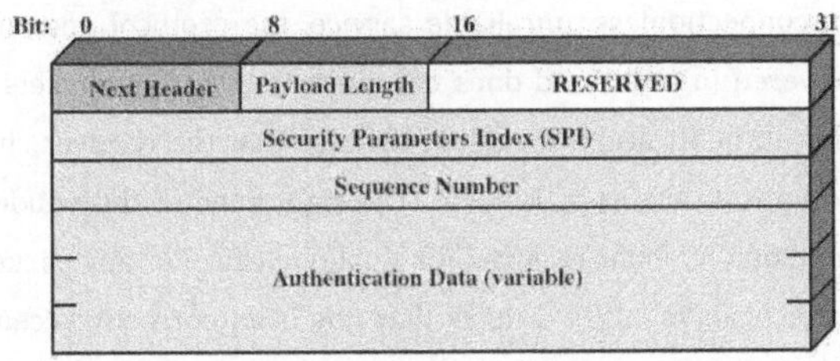

Figure 1.3: IPSec Authentication Header

The Authentication Header consists of the following fields (Figure 1.3):

- **Next Header (8 bits):** Identifies the type of header immediately following this header.
- **Payload Length (8 bits):** Length of Authentication Header in 32-bit words, minus 2. For example, the default length of the authentication data field is 96 bits, or three 32-bit words. With a three-word fixed header, there are a total of six words in the header, and the Payload Length field has a value of 4.

- **Reserved (16 bits):** For future use.
- **Security Parameters Index (32 bits):** Identifies a security association.
- **Sequence Number (32 bits):** A monotonically increasing counter value, discussed later.
- **Authentication Data (variable):** A variable-length field (must be an integral number of 32-bit words) that contains the Integrity Check Value (ICV), or MAC, for this packet, discussed later.

Anti-Replay Service

A replay attack is one in which an attacker obtains a copy of an authenticated packet and later transmits it to the intended destination. The receipt of duplicate, authenticated IP packets may disrupt service in some way or may have some other undesired consequence. The Sequence Number field is designed to thwart such attacks

When a new SA is established, the **sender** initializes a sequence number counter to 0. Each time that a packet is sent on this SA, the sender increments the counter and places the value in the Sequence Number field. Thus, the first value to be used is 1. If anti-replay is enabled (the default), the sender must not allow the sequence number to cycle past $2^{32} - 1$ back to zero. Otherwise, there would be multiple valid packets with the same sequence number. If the limit of $2^{32} -1$ is reached, the sender should terminate this SA and negotiate a new SA with a new key.

Because IP is a connectionless, unreliable service, the protocol does not guarantee that packets will be delivered in order and does not guarantee that all packets will be delivered. Therefore, the IPSec authentication document dictates that the receiver should implement a window of size W, with a default of $W = 64$. The right edge of the window represents the highest sequence number, N, so far received for a valid packet. For any packet with a sequence number in the range from $N - W + 1$ to N that has been correctly received (i.e., properly authenticated), the corresponding slot in the window is marked (Figure 1.4). Inbound processing proceeds as follows when a packet is received:

- If the received packet falls within the window and is new, the MAC is checked. If the packet is authenticated, the corresponding slot in the window is marked.
- If the received packet is to the right of the window and is new, the MAC is checked. If the packet is authenticated, the window is advanced so that this sequence number is the right edge of the window, and the corresponding slot in the window is marked.
- If the received packet is to the left of the window, or if authentication fails, the packet is

discarded; this is an auditable event.

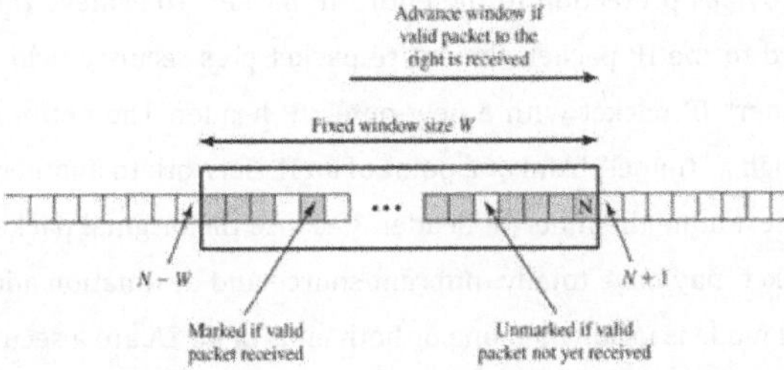

Figure 1.4: Antireplay Mechanism

Integrity Check Value

The Authentication Data field holds a value referred to as the Integrity Check Value. The ICV is a message authentication code or a truncated version of a code produced by a MAC algorithm. The current specification dictates that a compliant implementation must support

- HMAC-MD5-96
- HMAC-SHA-1-96

Both of these use the HMAC algorithm, the first with the MD5 hash code and the second with the SHA-1 hash code. In both cases, the full HMAC value is calculated but then truncated by using the first 96 bits, which is the default length for the Authentication Data field.

The MAC is calculated over:

1) IP header fields that either do not change in transit (immutable) or that are predictable in value upon arrival at the endpoint for the AH SA. Fields that may change in transit and whose value on arrival is unpredictable are set to zero for purposes of calculation at both source and destination.
2) The AH header other than the Authentication Data field. The Authentication Data field is set to zero for purposes of calculation at both source and destination.
3) The entire upper-level protocol data, which is assumed to be immutable in transit (e.g., a TCP segment or an inner IP packet in tunnel mode).

For IPv4, examples of immutable fields are Internet Header Length and Source Address. An example of a mutable but predictable field is the Destination Address (with loose or strict source routing). Examples of mutable fields that are zeroed prior to ICV calculation are the Time to Live and Header Checksum fields. Note that both source and destination address fields are protected, so that address spoofing is prevented.

Transport and Tunnel Modes

Tunnel mode provides protection to the entire IP packet. To achieve this, after the AH or ESP fields are added to the IP packet, the entire packet plus security fields is treated as the payload of new "outer" IP packet with a new outer IP header. The entire original, or inner, packet travels through a "tunnel" from one point of an IP network to another; no routers along the way are able to examine the inner IP header. Because the original packet is encapsulated, the new, larger packet may have totally different source and destination addresses, adding to the security. Tunnel mode is used when one or both ends of an SA are a security gateway, such as a firewall or router that implements IPSec. With tunnel mode, a number of hosts on networks behind firewalls may engage in secure communications without implementing IPSec. The unprotected packets generated by such hosts are tunneled through external networks by tunnel mode SAs set up by the IPSec software in the firewall or secure router at the boundary of the local network.

ESP in tunnel mode encrypts and optionally authenticates the entire inner IP packet, including the inner IP header. AH in tunnel mode authenticates the entire inner IP packet and selected portions of the outer IP header. Table 1.2 summarizes transport and tunnel mode functionality.

Table 1.2: Tunnel Mode and Transport Mode Functionality

	Transport Mode SA	Tunnel Mode SA
AH	Authenticates IP payload and selected portions of IP header and IPv6 extension headers.	Authenticates entire inner IP packet (inner header plus IP payload) plus selected portions of outer IP header and outer IPv6 extension headers.
ESP	Encrypts IP payload and any IPv6 extension headers following the ESP header.	Encrypts entire inner IP packet.
ESP with Authentication	Encrypts IP payload and any IPv6 extension headers following the ESP header. Authenticates IP payload but not IP header.	Encrypts entire inner IP packet. Authenticates inner IP packet.

Figure 1.5 shows two ways in which the IPSec authentication service can be used. In one case, authentication is provided directly between a server and client workstations; the workstation can be either on the same network as the server or on an external network. As long as the workstation and the server share a protected secret key, the authentication process is secure. This case uses a transport mode SA. In the other case, a remote workstation authenticates itself to the corporate firewall, either for access to the entire internal network or

because the requested server does not support the authentication feature. This case uses a tunnel mode SA.

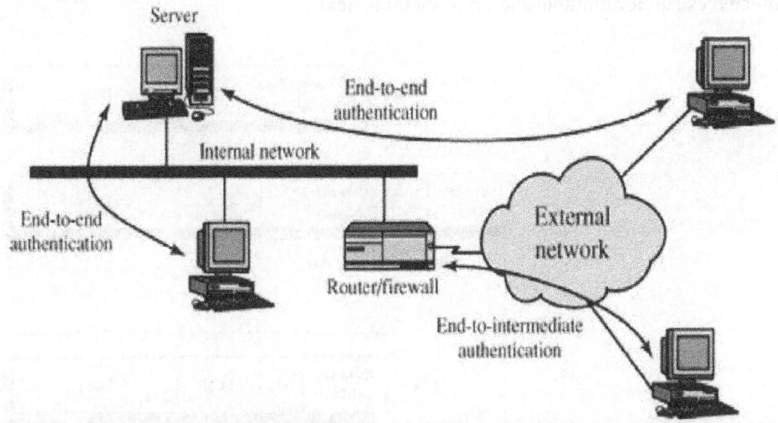

Figure 1.5: End-to-End versus End-to-Intermediate Authentication

Now we look at the scope of authentication provided by AH and the authentication header location for the two modes. The considerations are somewhat different for IPv4 and IPv6. Figure 1.6a shows typical IPv4 and IPv6 packets. In this case, the IP payload is a TCP segment; it could also be a data unit for any other protocol that uses IP, such as UDP or ICMP.

For transport mode AH using IPv4, the AH is inserted after the original IP header and before the IP payload (e.g., a TCP segment); this is shown in the upper part of Figure 1.6b. Authentication covers the entire packet, excluding mutable fields in the IPv4 header that are set to zero for MAC calculation.

In the context of IPv6, AH is viewed as an end-to-end payload; that is, it is not examined or processed by intermediate routers. Therefore, the AH appears after the IPv6 base header and the hop-by-hop, routing, and fragment extension headers. The destination options extension header could appear before or after the AH header, depending on the semantics desired. Again, authentication covers the entire packet, excluding mutable fields that are set to zero for MAC calculation.

For tunnel mode AH, the entire original IP packet is authenticated, and the AH is inserted between the original IP header and a new outer IP header (Figure 1.6c). The inner IP header carries the ultimate source and destination addresses, while an outer IP header may contain different IP addresses (e.g., addresses of firewalls or other security gateways).

With tunnel mode, the entire inner IP packet, including the entire inner IP header is protected by AH. The outer IP header (and in the case of IPv6, the outer IP extension headers) is protected except for mutable and unpredictable fields.

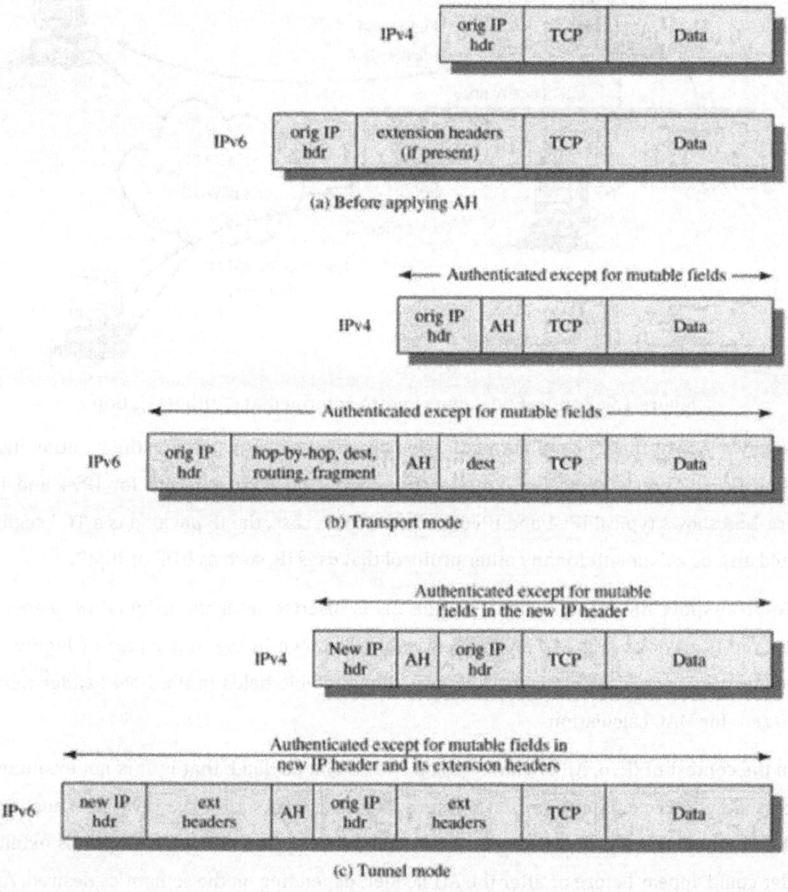

Figure 1.6: Scope of AH Authentication

7.4. Encapsulating Security Payload

The Encapsulating Security Payload provides confidentiality services, including confidentiality of message contents and limited traffic flow confidentiality. As an optional feature, ESP can also provide an authentication service.

ESP Format

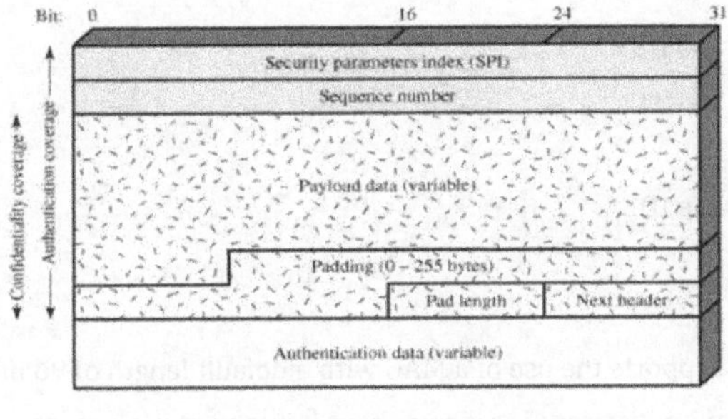

Figure 1.7: IPSec ESP format

Figure 1.7 shows the format of an ESP packet. It contains the following fields:

1) Security Parameters Index (32 bits): Identifies a security association.
2) Sequence Number (32 bits): A monotonically increasing counter value; this provides an anti-replay function, as discussed for AH.
3) Payload Data (variable): This is a transport-level segment (transport mode) or IP packet (tunnel mode) that is protected by encryption.
4) Padding (0255 bytes): The purpose of this field is discussed later.
5) Pad Length (8 bits): Indicates the number of pad bytes immediately preceding this field.
6) Next Header (8 bits): Identifies the type of data contained in the payload data field by identifying the first header in that payload
7) Authentication Data (variable): A variable-length field (must be an integral number of 32-bit words) that contains the Integrity. Check Value computed over the ESP packet minus the Authentication Data field.

Encryption and Authentication Algorithms

The Payload Data, Padding, Pad Length, and Next Header fields are encrypted by the ESP service. If the algorithm used to encrypt the payload requires cryptographic synchronization data, such as an initialization vector (IV), then these data may be carried explicitly at the beginning of the Payload Data field. If included, an IV is usually not encrypted, although it is often referred to as being part of the ciphertext. The current specification dictates that a compliant implementation must support DES in cipher block chaining (CBC) mode. A number of other algorithms have been assigned identifiers in the DOI document and could therefore easily be used for encryption; these include:

1) Three-key triple DES.
2) RC5.
3) IDEA.
4) Three-key triple IDEA.
5) CAST.
6) Blowfish.

As with AH, ESP supports the use of a MAC with a default length of 96 bits. Also as with AH, the current specification dictates that a compliant implementation must support HMAC-MD5-96 and HMAC-SHA-1-96.

Padding

The Padding field serves several purposes:

1) If an encryption algorithm requires the plaintext to be a multiple of some number of bytes (e.g., the multiple of a single block for a block cipher), the Padding field is used to expand the plaintext (consisting of the Payload Data, Padding, Pad Length, and Next Header fields) to the required length.
2) The ESP format requires that the Pad Length and Next Header fields be right aligned within a 32-bit word. Equivalently, the ciphertext must be an integer multiple of 32 bits. The Padding field is used to assure this alignment.
3) Additional padding may be added to provide partial traffic flow confidentiality by concealing the actual length of the payload.

Transport and Tunnel Modes

Figure 1.8 shows two ways in which the IPSec ESP service can be used. In the upper part of the figure, encryption (and optionally authentication) is provided directly between two hosts. Figure 1.8b shows how tunnel mode operation can be used to set up a *virtual private network*. In this example, an organization has four private networks interconnected across the Internet. Hosts on the internal networks use the Internet for transport of data but do not interact with other Internet-based hosts. By terminating the tunnels at the security gateway to each internal network, the configuration allows the hosts to avoid implementing the security capability. The former technique is support by a transport mode SA, while the latter technique uses a tunnel mode SA.

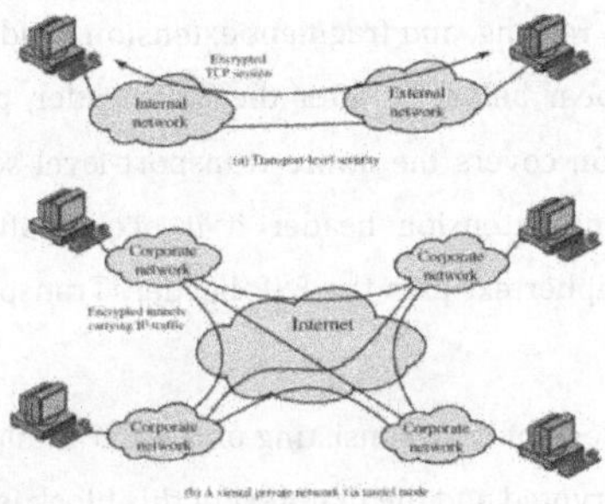

Figure 1.8: Transport-Mode vs. Tunnel-Mode Encryption

Transport Mode ESP

Transport mode ESP is used to encrypt and optionally authenticate the data carried by IP (e.g., a TCP segment), as shown in Figure 1.9a. For this mode using IPv4, the ESP header is inserted into the IP packet immediately prior to the transport-layer header (e.g., TCP, UDP, ICMP) and an ESP trailer (Padding, Pad Length, and Next Header fields) is placed after the IP packet; if authentication is selected, the ESP Authentication Data field is added after the ESP trailer. The entire transport-level segment plus the ESP trailer are encrypted. Authentication covers all of the ciphertext plus the ESP header.

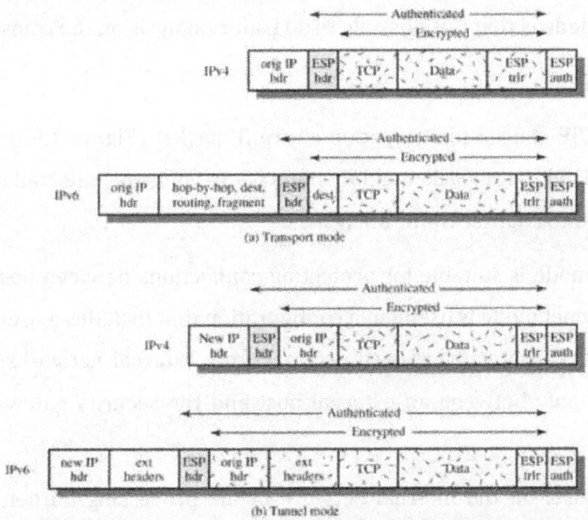

Figure 1.9: Scope of ESP Encryption and Authentication

In the context of IPv6, ESP is viewed as an end-to-end payload; that is, it is not examined or processed by intermediate routers. Therefore, the ESP header appears after the IPv6 base header and the hop-by-hop, routing, and fragment extension headers. The destination options extension header could appear before or after the ESP header, depending on the semantics desired. For IPv6, encryption covers the entire transport-level segment plus the ESP trailer plus the destination options extension header if it occurs after the ESP header. Again, authentication covers the ciphertext plus the ESP header. Transport mode operation may be summarized as follows:

1) At the source, the block of data consisting of the ESP trailer plus the entire transport-layer segment is encrypted and the plaintext of this block is replaced with its ciphertext to form the IP packet for transmission. Authentication is added if this option is selected.
2) The packet is then routed to the destination. Each intermediate router needs to examine and process the IP header plus any plaintext IP extension headers but does not need to examine the ciphertext.
3) The destination node examines and processes the IP header plus any plaintext IP extension headers. Then, on the basis of the SPI in the ESP header, the destination node decrypts the remainder of the packet to recover the plaintext transport-layer segment.

Transport mode operation provides confidentiality for any application that uses it, thus avoiding the need to implement confidentiality in every individual application. This mode of operation is also reasonably efficient, adding little to the total length of the IP packet. One drawback to this mode is that it is possible to do traffic analysis on the transmitted packets.

Tunnel Mode ESP

Tunnel mode ESP is used to encrypt an entire IP packet (Figure 1.9b). For this mode, the ESP header is prefixed to the packet and then the packet plus the ESP trailer is encrypted. This method can be used to counter traffic analysis.

The transport mode is suitable for protecting connections between hosts that support the ESP feature, the tunnel mode is useful in a configuration that includes a firewall or other sort of security gateway that protects a trusted network from external networks. In this latter case, encryption occurs only between an external host and the security gateway or between two security gateways.

This relieves hosts on the internal network of the processing burden of encryption and simplifies the key distribution task by reducing the number of needed keys. Further, it thwarts traffic analysis based on ultimate destination.

Consider a case in which an external host wishes to communicate with a host on an internal network protected by a firewall, and in which ESP is implemented in the external host and the firewalls. The following steps occur for transfer of a transport-layer segment from the external host to the internal host:

1) The source prepares an inner IP packet with a destination address of the target internal host. This packet is prefixed by an ESP header; then the packet and ESP trailer are encrypted and Authentication Data may be added. The resulting block is encapsulated with a new IP header (base header plus optional extensions such as routing and hop-by-hop options for IPv6) whose destination address is the firewall; this forms the outer IP packet.
2) The outer packet is routed to the destination firewall. Each intermediate router needs to examine and process the outer IP header plus any outer IP extension headers but does not need to examine the ciphertext.
3) The destination firewall examines and processes the outer IP header plus any outer IP extension headers. Then, on the basis of the SPI in the ESP header, the destination node decrypts the remainder of the packet to recover the plaintext inner IP packet. This packet is then transmitted in the internal network.
4) The inner packet is routed through zero or more routers in the internal network to the destination host.

7.5. Combining Security Associations

An individual SA can implement either the AH or ESP protocol but not both. Sometimes a particular traffic flow will call for the services provided by both AH and ESP. Further, a particular traffic flow may require IPSec services between hosts and, for that same flow, separate services between security gateways, such as firewalls. In all of these cases, multiple SAs must be employed for the same traffic flow to achieve the desired IPSec services. The term security association bundle refers to a sequence of SAs through which traffic must be processed to provide a desired set of IPSec services. The SAs in a bundle may terminate at different endpoints or at the same endpoints.

Security associations may be combined into bundles in two ways:

- **Transport adjacency:** Refers to applying more than one security protocol to the same IP packet, without invoking tunneling. This approach to combining AH and ESP allows for only one level of combination; further nesting yields no added benefit since the processing is performed at one IPsec instance: the (ultimate) destination.
- **Iterated tunneling:** Refers to the application of multiple layers of security protocols effected through IP tunneling. This approach allows for multiple levels of nesting, since

each tunnel can originate or terminate at a different IPsec site along the path.

The two approaches can be combined, for example, by having a transport SA between hosts travel part of the way through a tunnel SA between security gateways.

One interesting issue that arises when considering SA bundles is the order in which authentication and encryption may be applied between a given pair of endpoints and the ways of doing so. We examine that issue next. Then we look at combinations of SAs that involve at least one tunnel.

Authentication Plus Confidentiality

Encryption and authentication can be combined in order to transmit an IP packet that has both confidentiality and authentication between hosts. We look at several approaches.

ESP with Authentication Option

This approach is illustrated in Figure 1.9. In this approach, the user first applies ESP to the data to be protected and then appends the authentication data field. There are actually two subcases:

- Transport **mode ESP:** Authentication and encryption apply to the IP payload delivered to the host, but the IP header is not protected.
- **Tunnel mode ESP:** Authentication applies to the entire IP packet delivered to the outer IP destination address (e.g., a firewall), and authentication is performed at that destination. The entire inner IP packet is protected by the privacy mechanism, for delivery to the inner IP destination.

For both cases, authentication applies to the ciphertext rather than the plaintext.

Transport Adjacency

Another way to apply authentication after encryption is to use two bundled transport SAs, with the inner being an ESP SA and the outer being an AH SA. In this case ESP is used without its authentication option. Because the inner SA is a transport SA, encryption is applied to the IP payload. The resulting packet consists of an IP header (and possibly IPv6 header extensions) followed by an ESP. AH is then applied in transport mode, so that authentication covers the ESP plus the original IP header (and extensions) except for mutable fields. The advantage of this approach over simply using a single ESP SA with the ESP authentication option is that the authentication covers more fields, including the source and destination IP addresses. The disadvantage is the overhead of two SAs versus one SA.

Transport-Tunnel Bundle

The use of authentication prior to encryption might be preferable for several reasons. First, because the authentication data are protected by encryption, it is impossible for anyone to intercept the message and alter the authentication data without detection. Second, it may be desirable to store the authentication information with the message at the destination for later reference. It is more convenient to do this if the authentication information applies to the unencrypted message; otherwise the message would have to be reencrypted to verify the authentication information.

One approach to applying authentication before encryption between two hosts is to use a bundle consisting of an inner AH transport SA and an outer ESP tunnel SA. In this case, authentication is applied to the IP payload plus the IP header (and extensions) except for mutable fields. The resulting IP packet is then processed in tunnel mode by ESP; the result is that the entire, authenticated inner packet is encrypted and a new outer IP header (and extensions) is added.

7.6. Basic Combinations of Security Associations

The IPSec Architecture document lists four examples of combinations of SAs that must be supported by compliant IPSec hosts (e.g.workstation, server) or security gateways (e.g. firewall, router). These are illustrated in Figure 1.10. The lower part of each case in the figure represents the physical connectivity of the elements; the upper part represents logical connectivity via one or more nested SAs. Each SA can be either AH or ESP. For host-to-host SAs, the mode may be either transport or tunnel; otherwise it must be tunnel mode.

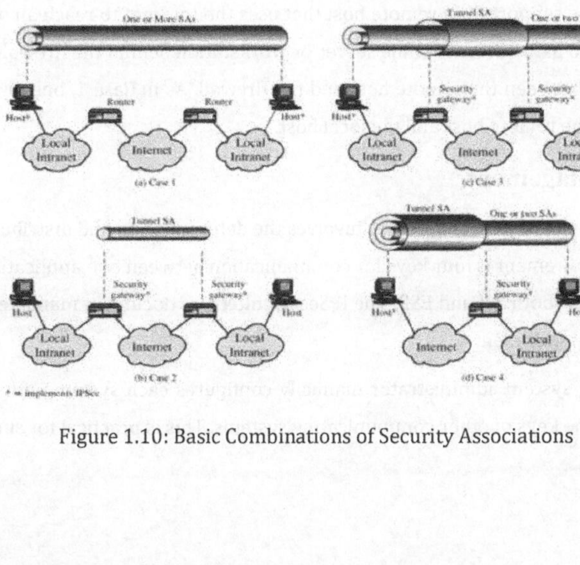

Figure 1.10: Basic Combinations of Security Associations

In **Case 1,** all security is provided between end systems that implement IPSec. For any two end systems to communicate via an SA, they must share the appropriate secret keys. Among the possible combinations:

1) AH in transport mode
2) ESP in transport mode
3) ESP followed by AH in transport mode (an ESP SA inside an AH SA)
4) Any one of a, b, or c inside an AH or ESP in tunnel mode

We have already discussed how these various combinations can be used to support authentication, encryption, authentication before encryption, and authentication after encryption.

For **Case 2,** security is provided only between gateways (routers, firewalls, etc.) and no hosts implement IPSec. This case illustrates simple virtual private network support. The security architecture document specifies that only a single tunnel SA is needed for this case.

The tunnel could support AH, ESP, or ESP with the authentication option. Nested tunnels are not required because the IPSec services apply to the entire inner packet.

Case 3 builds on Case 2 by adding end-to-end security. The same combinations discussed for cases 1 and 2 are allowed here. The gateway-to-gateway tunnel provides either authentication or confidentiality or both for all traffic between end systems. When the gateway-to-gateway tunnel is ESP, it also provides a limited form of traffic confidentiality. Individual hosts can implement any additional. IPSec services required for given applications or given users by means of end-to-end SAs.

Case 4 provides support for a remote host that uses the Internet to reach an organization's firewall and then to gain access to some server or workstation behind the firewall. Only tunnel mode is required between the remote host and the firewall. As in Case 1, one or two SAs may be used between the remote host and the local host.

7.7. Key Management

The key management portion of IPSec involves the determination and distribution of secret keys. A typical requirement is four keys for communication between two applications: transmit and receive pairs for both AH and ESP. The IPSec Architecture document mandates support for two types of key management:

1) **Manual:** A system administrator manually configures each system with its own keys and with the keys of other communicating systems. This is practical for small, relatively

static environments.

2) **Automated:** An automated system enables the on-demand creation of keys for SAs and facilitates the use of keys in a large distributed system with an evolving configuration.

The default automated key management protocol for IPSec is referred to as ISAKMP/Oakley and consists of the following elements:

1) **Oakley Key Determination Protocol**: Oakley is a key exchange protocol based on the Diffie-Hellman algorithm but providing added security. Oakley is generic in that it does not dictate specific formats.

2) **Internet Security Association and Key Management Protocol (ISAKMP):** ISAKMP provides a framework for Internet key management and provides the specific protocol support, including formats, for negotiation of security attributes. ISAKMP by itself does not dictate a specific key exchange algorithm; rather, ISAKMP consists of a set of message types that enable the use of a variety of key exchange algorithms. Oakley is the specific key exchange algorithm mandated for use with the initial version of ISAKMP.

Oakley Key Determination Protocol

Oakley is a refinement of the Diffie-Hellman key exchange algorithm. Recall that Diffie-Hellman involves the following interaction between users A and B. There is prior agreement on two global parameters: *q*, a large prime number; and a a primitive root of *q*. A selects a random integer *XA* as its private key, and transmits to B its public key$Y A = a^{XA}$ mod *q*. Similarly, B selects a random integer *XB* as its private key and transmits to A its public key Y*B* = a ^{XB}mod *q*. Each side can now compute the secret session key:

$$K = (Y_B)^{X_A} \bmod q = (Y_A)^{X_B} \bmod q = \alpha^{X_A X_B} \bmod q$$

The Diffie-Hellman algorithm has two attractive features:

1) Secret keys are created only when needed. There is no need to store secret keys for a long period of time, exposing them to increased vulnerability.

2) The exchange requires no preexisting infrastructure other than an agreement on the global parameters.

However, there are a number of weaknesses to Diffie-Hellman.

1) It does not provide any information about the identities of the parties.

2) It is subject to a man-in-the-middle attack, in which a third party C impersonates B while communicating with A and impersonates A while communicating with B. Both A

and B end up negotiating a key with C, which can then listen to and pass on traffic.

The man-in-the-middle attack proceeds as follows:

1) B sends his public key YB in a message addressed to A. The enemy (E) intercepts this message. E saves B's public key and sends a message to A that has B's User ID but E's public key YE. This message is sent in such a way that it appears as though it was sent from B's host system. A receives E's message and stores E's public key with B's User ID. Similarly, E sends a message to B with E's public key, purporting to come from A.
2) B computes a secret key K1 based on B's private key and YE. A computes a secret key K2 based on A's private key and YE. E computes K1 using E's secret key XE and YB and computer K2 using YE and YB.
3) From now on E is able to relay messages from A to B and from B to A, appropriately changing their encipherment en route in such a way that neither A nor B will know that they share their communication with E.
4) It is computationally intensive. As a result, it is vulnerable to a clogging attack, in which an opponent requests a high number of keys. The victim spends considerable computing resources doing useless modular exponentiation rather than real work.
   - It is computationally intensive. As a result, it is vulnerable to a clogging attack, in which an opponent requests a high number of keys. The victim spends considerable computing resources doing useless modular exponentiation rather than real work.

Oakley is designed to retain the advantages of Diffie-Hellman while countering its weaknesses.

Features of Oakley

The Oakley algorithm is characterized by five important features:

1) It employs a mechanism known as cookies to thwart clogging attacks.
2) It enables the two parties to negotiate a group; this, in essence, specifies the global parameters of the Diffie-Hellman key exchange.
3) It uses nonces to ensure against replay attacks.
4) It enables the exchange of Diffie-Hellman public key values.
5) It authenticates the Diffie-Hellman exchange to thwart man-in-the-middle attacks.

ISAKMP mandates that cookie generation satisfy three basic requirements:

1) The cookie must depend on the specific parties. This prevents an attacker from obtaining a cookie using a real IP address and UDP port and then using it to swamp the

victim with requests from randomly chosen IP addresses or ports.

2) It must not be possible for anyone other than the issuing entity to generate cookies that will be accepted by that entity. This implies that the issuing entity will use local secret information in the generation and subsequent verification of a cookie. It must not be possible to deduce this secret information from any particular cookie. The point of this requirement is that the issuing entity need not save copies of its cookies, which are then more vulnerable to discovery, but can verify an incoming cookie acknowledgment when it needs to.

   - The cookie generation and verification methods must be fast to thwart attacks intended to sabotage processor resources.

The recommended method for creating the cookie is to perform a fast hash (e.g., MD5) over the IP Source and Destination addresses, the UDP Source and Destination ports, and a locally generated secret value.

Three different **authentication** methods can be used with Oakley:

1) **Digital signatures:** The exchange is authenticated by signing a mutually obtainable hash; each party encrypts the hash with its private key. The hash is generated over important parameters, such as user IDs and nonces.
2) **Public-key encryption**: The exchange is authenticated by encrypting parameters such as IDs and nonces with the sender's private key.
3) **Symmetric-key encryption:** A key derived by some out-of-band mechanism can be used to authenticate the exchange by symmetric encryption of exchange parameters.

ISAKMP

ISAKMP defines procedures and packet formats to establish, negotiate, modify, and delete security associations. As part of SA establishment, ISAKMP defines payloads for exchanging key generation and authentication data.

These payload formats provide a consistent framework independent of the specific key exchange protocol, encryption algorithm, and authentication mechanism.

ISAKMP Header Format

An ISAKMP message consists of an ISAKMP header followed by one or more payloads. All of this is carried in a transport protocol. The specification dictates that implementations must support the use of UDP for the transport protocol.

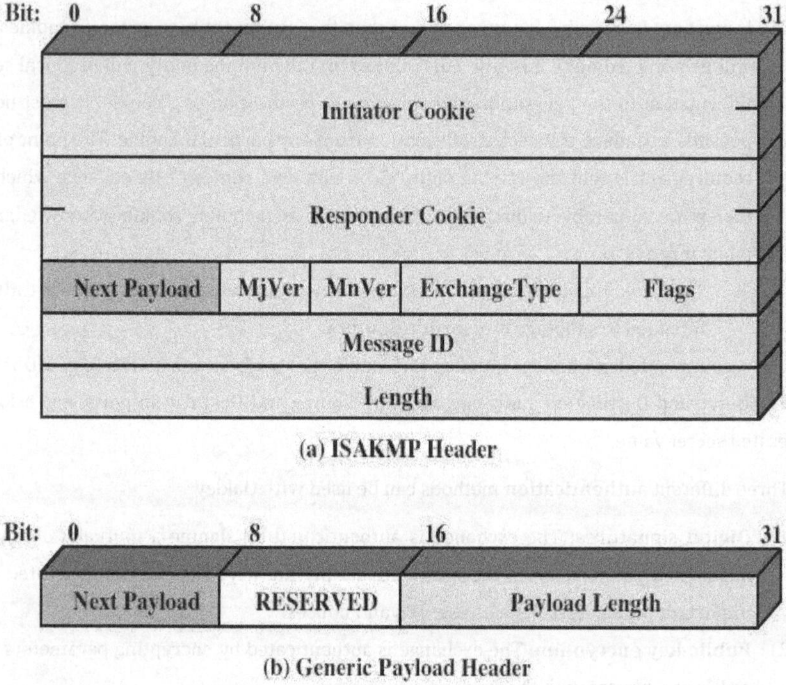

Figure 1.11: ISAKMP Formats

ISAKMP Payload Types

All ISAKMP payloads begin with the same generic payload header shown in Figure 1.11b. The Next Payload field has a value of 0 if this is the last payload in the message; otherwise its value is the type of the next payload. The Payload Length field indicates the length in octets of this payload, including the generic payload header.

Table 1.3 summarizes the payload types defined for ISAKMP, and lists the fields, or parameters, that are part of each payload. The **SA payload** is used to begin the establishment of an SA. In this payload, the Domain of Interpretation parameter identifies the DOI under which negotiation is taking place. The IPSec DOI is one example, but ISAKMP can be used in other contexts. The Situation parameter defines the security policy for this negotiation; in essence, the levels of security required for encryption and confidentiality are specified (e.g., sensitivity level, security compartment).

Table 1.3: ISAKMP Payload Types

Type	Parameters	Description
Security Association (SA)	Domain of Interpretation, Situation	Used to negotiate security attributes and indicate the DOI and Situation under which negotiation is taking place.
Proposal (P)	Proposal #, Protocol-ID, SPI Size, # of Transforms, SPI	Used during SA negotiation; indicates protocol to be used and number of transforms.
Transform (T)	Transform #, Transform-ID, SA	Used during SA negotiation; indicates transform and related SA attributes.
Key Exchange (KE)	Attributes Key Exchange Data	Supports a variety of key exchange techniques.
Identification (ID)	ID Type, ID Data	Used to exchange identification information.
Certificate (CERT)	Cert Encoding, Certificate Data	Used to transport certificates and other certificate related information.
Certificate Request (CR)	# Cert Types, Certificate Types, # Cert Auths.	Used to request certificates; indicates the types of certificates requested and the acceptable certificate authorities.
Hash (HASH)	Certificate Authorities Hash Data	Contains data generated by a hash function
Signature (SIG)	Signature Data	Contains data generated by a digital signature function. Contains a nonce.
Nonce (NONCE) Notification (N)	Nonce Data DOI, Protocol-ID, SPI Size, Notify	Used to transmit notification data, such as an error condition.
Delete (D)	Message Type, SPI, Notification Data DOI, Protocol-ID, SPI Size, #of SPIs, SPI (one or more)	Indicates an SA that is no longer valid.

The **Proposal payload** contains information used during SA negotiation. The payload indicates the protocol for this SA (ESP or AH) for which services and mechanisms are being negotiated. The payload also includes the sending entity's SPI and the number of transforms.

Each transform is contained in a transform payload. The use of multiple transform payloads enables the initiator to offer several possibilities, of which the responder must choose one or reject the offer.

The **Transform payload** defines a security transform to be used to secure the communications channel for the designated protocol. The Transform # parameter serves to identify this particular payload so that the responder may use it to indicate acceptance of this transform. The Transform-ID and Attributes fields identify a specific transform (e.g., 3DES for ESP, HMAC-SHA-1-96 for AH) with its associated attributes (e.g., hash length).

The **Key Exchange payload** can be used for a variety of key exchange techniques, including Oakley, Diffie-Hellman, and the RSA-based key exchange used by PGP.

The Key Exchange data field contains the data required to generate a session key and is dependent on the key exchange algorithm used.

The **Identification payload** is used to determine the identity of communicating peers and may be used for determining authenticity of information. Typically the ID Data field will contain an IPv4 or IPv6 address.

The **Hash payload** contains data generated by a hash function over some part of the message and/or ISAKMP state. This payload may be used to verify the integrity of the data in a message or to authenticate negotiating entities.

The **Signature payload** contains data generated by a digital signature function over some part of the message and/or ISAKMP state. This payload is used to verify the integrity of the data in a message and may be used for non repudiation services.

The **Nonce payload** contains random data used to guarantee liveness during an exchange and protect against replay attacks.

The only ISAKMP status message so far defined is Connected. In addition to these ISAKMP notifications, DOI-specific notifications are used.

For IPSec, the following additional status messages are defined:

1) **Responder-Lifetime:** Communicates the SA lifetime chosen by the responder.
2) **Replay-Status:** Used for positive confirmation of the responder's election of whether or not the responder will perform anti-replay detection.
3) **Initial-Contact:** Informs the other side that this is the first SA being established with the remote system. The receiver of this notification might then delete any existing SA's it has for the sending system under the assumption that the sending system has rebooted and no longer has access to those SAs.

The **Delete payload** indicates one or more SAs that the sender has deleted from its database and that therefore are no longer valid.

ISAKMP Exchanges

ISAKMP provides a framework for message exchange, with the payload types serving as the building blocks. The specification identifies five default exchange types that should be supported.

The Base Exchange allows key exchange and authentication material to be transmitted together. This minimizes the number of exchanges at the expense of not providing identity protection. The first two messages provide cookies and establish an SA with agreed protocol and transforms; both sides use a nonce to ensure against replay attacks. The last two messages exchange the key material and user IDs, with an authentication mechanism used to authenticate keys, identities, and the nonces from the first two messages.

The **Identity Protection Exchange** expands the Base Exchange to protect the users' identities. The first two messages establish the SA. The next two messages perform key exchange, with nonces for replay protection. Once the session key has been computed, the two parties exchange encrypted messages that contain authentication information, such as digital signatures and optionally certificates validating the public keys.

The **Authentication Only Exchange** is used to perform mutual authentication, without a key exchange. The first two messages establish the SA. In addition, the responder uses the second message to convey its ID and uses authentication to protect the message. The initiator sends the third message to transmit its authenticated ID.

The **Aggressive Exchange** minimizes the number of exchanges at the expense of not providing identity protection. In the first message, the initiator proposes an SA with associated offered protocol and transforms options. The initiator also begins the key exchange and provides its ID. In the second message, the responder indicates its acceptance of the SA with a particular protocol and transform, completes the key exchange, and authenticates the transmitted information. In the third message, the initiator transmits an authentication result that covers the previous information, encrypted using the shared secret session key. The **Informational Exchange** is used for one-way transmittal of information for SA management.

References

1) Cryptography and Network Security, Principles and Practices, William Stallings, Eastern Economy Edition, Fourth edition.
2) Cryptography & Network Security, Behrouz A. forouzan, The McGraw-Hill Companies, Edition 2007.
3) http://williamstallings.com/Security2e.html

Questions

7a). Give a general structure of IPSEC Authentication header. Describe how anti reply service is supported.

December 2010 (10 marks)

7b). With a neat diagram explain the basic combination of security association.

December 2010 10 marks

7a). Mention the application of IPSEC.

(June 2012) (4 marks)

7b). Explain the security association selector that determine the security policy database entry.

(June 2012) (6marks)

7c). Draw a neat diagram IPSEC ESP format and explain.

(June 201) (5 marks)

7d). Mention the important features of OAKLEY algorithm.

(June 2012) (6 marks)

7a). Explain the format of an ESP packet in IP security.

(June 2010) (07 Marks)

7b). Why does ESP include a padding field?

(June 2010) (3 Marks)

7c). Give an example of an aggressive Oakley key.

(June 2010) (10 Marks)

7a). Describe SA parameters and SA selectors in detail.

(July 2011) (10 Marks)

7a). Describe the benefits of IPSec.

(Dec 2011) (5 Marks)

7c). Describe the transport and tunnel modes used for IPSec AH authentication bringing out their scope relevant to IPV4.

(Dec 2011) (10 Marks)

UNIT-8

WEB SECURITY

Virtually all businesses, most government agencies, and many individuals now have Web sites. The number of individuals and companies with Internet access is expanding rapidly and all of these have graphical Web browsers. As a result, businesses are enthusiastic about setting up facilities on the Web for electronic commerce. But the reality is that the Internet and the Web are extremely vulnerable to compromises of various sorts. As businesses wake up to this reality, the demand for secure Web services grows.

The topic of Web security is a Very broad one. In this chapter, we begin with a discussion of the general requirements for Web security and then focus on two standardized schemes that are becoming increasingly important as part of Web commerce: SSL/TLS and SET.

8.1. Web Security Considerations

The World Wide Web is fundamentally a client/server application running over the Internet and TCP/IP intranets. As such, the security tools and approaches discussed so far in this book are relevant to the issue of Web security. But, the Web presents new challenges not generally appreciated in the context of computer and network security:

1) The Internet is two way. Unlike traditional publishing environments, even electronic publishing systems involving teletext, voice response, or fax-back, the Web is vulnerable to attacks on the Web servers over the Internet.
2) The Web is increasingly serving as a highly visible outlet for corporate and product information and as the platform for business transactions. Reputations can be damaged and money can be lost if the Web servers are subverted.
3) Although Web browsers are very easy to use, Web servers are relatively easy to configure and manage, and Web content is increasingly easy to develop, the underlying software is extraordinarily complex. This complex software may hide many potential security flaws. The short history of the Web is filled with examples of new and upgraded systems, properly installed, that are vulnerable to a variety of security attacks.
4) A Web server can be exploited as a launching pad into the corporation's or agency's entire computer complex. Once the Web server is subverted, an attacker may be able to gain access to data and systems not part of the Web itself but connected to the server at the local site.

5) Casual and untrained (in security matters) users are common clients for Web-based services. Such users are not necessarily aware of the security risks that exist and do not have the tools or knowledge to take effective countermeasures.

Web Security Threats

Table 1.1 provides a summary of the types of security threats faced in using the Web. One way to group these threats is in terms of passive and active attacks. Passive attacks include eavesdropping on network traffic between browser and server and gaining access to information on a Web site that is supposed to be restricted. Active attacks include impersonating another user, altering messages in transit between client and server, and altering information on a Web site.

Table 1.1: A Comparison of Threats on the Web

	Threats	Consequences	Countermeasures
Integrity	Modification of user data Trojan horse browser Modification of memory Modification of message traffic in transit	Loss of information Compromise of machine Vulnerability to all other threats	Cryptographic checksums
Confidentiality	Eavesdropping on the Net Theft of info from server Theft of data from client Info about network configuration Info about which client talks to server	Loss of information Loss of privacy	Encryption, web proxies
Denial of Service	Killing of user threads Flooding machine with bogus requests Filling up disk or memory Isolating machine by DNS attacks	Disruptive Annoying Prevent user from getting work done	Difficult to prevent
Authentication	Impersonation of legitimate users Data forgery	Misrepresentation of user Belief that false information is valid	Cryptographic techniques

Web Traffic Security Approaches

A number of approaches to providing Web security are possible. The various approaches that have been considered are similar in the services they provide and, to some extent, in the mechanisms that they use, but they differ with respect to their scope of applicability and their relative location within the TCP/IP protocol stack.

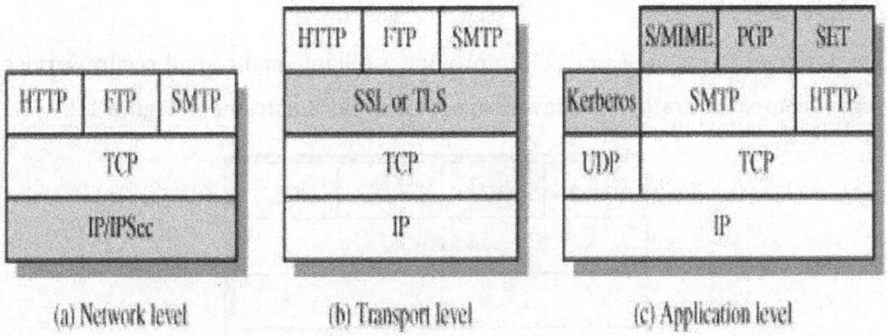

Figure 1.1: Relative Location of Security Facilities in the TCP/IP Protocol Stack

Figure 1.1 illustrates this difference. One way to provide Web security is to use IP Security (Figure 1.1a). The advantage of using IPSec is that it is transparent to end users and applications and provides a general-purpose solution. Further, IPSec includes a filtering capability so that only selected traffic need incur the overhead of IPSec processing.

Another relatively general-purpose solution is to implement security just above TCP (Figure 1.1b). The foremost example of this approach is the Secure Sockets Layer (SSL) and the follow-on Internet standard known as Transport Layer Security (TLS). At this level, there are two implementation choices. For full generality, SSL (or TLS) could be provided as part of the underlying protocol suite and therefore be transparent to applications. Alternatively, SSL can be embedded in specific packages. For example, Netscape and Microsoft Explorer browsers come equipped with SSL, and most Web servers have implemented the protocol. Application-specific security services are embedded within the particular application. Figure 1.1c shows examples of this architecture. The advantage of this approach is that the service can be tailored to the specific needs of a given application. In the context of Web security, an important example of this approach is Secure Electronic Transaction (SET). The remainder of this chapter is devoted to a discussion of SSL/TLS and SET.

8.2. Secure Socket Layer and Transport Layer Security

Netscape originated SSL. Version 3 of the protocol was designed with public review and input from industry and was published as an Internet draft document. Subsequently, when a consensus was reached to submit the protocol for Internet standardization, the TLS working group was formed within IETF to develop a common standard. This first published version of TLS can be viewed as essentially an SSLv3.1 and is very close to and backward compatible with SSLv3.

SSL Architecture

SSL is designed to make use of TCP to provide a reliable end-to-end secure service. SSL is not a single protocol but rather two layers of protocols, as illustrated in Figure 1.2.

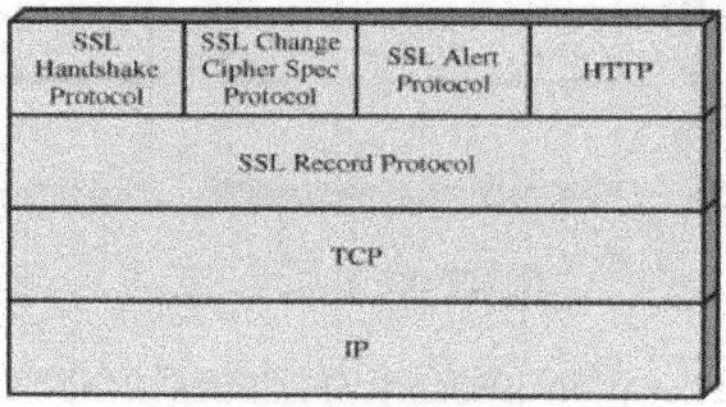

Figure 1.2: SSL Protocol Stack

The SSL Record Protocol provides basic security services to various higher-layer protocols. In particular, the Hypertext Transfer Protocol (HTTP), which provides the transfer service for Web client/server interaction, can operate on top of SSL. Three higher-layer protocols are defined as part of SSL: the Handshake Protocol, The Change Cipher Spec Protocol, and the Alert Protocol. These SSL-specific protocols are used in the management of SSL exchanges and are examined later in this section. Two important SSL concepts are the SSL session and the SSL connection, which are defined in the specification as follows:

1) **Connection:** A connection is a transport (in the OSI layering model definition) that provides a suitable type of service. For SSL, such connections are peer-to-peer relationships. The connections are transient. Every connection is associated with one session.
2) **Session:** An SSL session is an association between a client and a server. Sessions are created by the Handshake Protocol. Sessions define a set of cryptographic security parameters, which can be shared among multiple connections. Sessions are used to avoid the expensive negotiation of new security parameters for each connection. Between any pair of parties (applications such as HTTP on client and server), there may be multiple secure connections. In theory, there may also be multiple simultaneous sessions between parties, but this feature is not used in practice.

There are actually a number of states associated with each session. Once a session is established, there is a current operating state for both read and write (i.e., receive and send). In addition, during the Handshake Protocol, pending read and write states are created. Upon successful conclusion of the Handshake Protocol, the pending states becomes the current states.

A session state is defined by the following parameters (definitions taken from the SSL specification):

1) **Session identifier:** An arbitrary byte sequence chosen by the server to identify an active or resumable session state.
2) **Peer certificate:** An X509.v3 certificate of the peer. This element of the state may be null.
3) **Compression method:** The algorithm used to compress data prior to encryption.
4) **Cipher spec:** Specifies the bulk data encryption algorithm (such as null, AES, etc.) and a hash algorithm (such as MD5 or SHA-1) used for MAC calculation. It also defines cryptographic attributes such as the hash_size.
5) **Master secret:** 48-byte secret shared between the client and server.
6) **Is resumable:** A flag indicating whether the session can be used to initiate new connections.

- **Server write MAC secret:** The secret key used in MAC operations on data sent by the server.
- **Client write MAC secret:** The secret key used in MAC operations on data sent by the client.
- **Server write key:** The conventional encryption key for data encrypted by the server and decrypted by the client.
- **Client write key:** The conventional encryption key for data encrypted by the client and decrypted by the server.
- **Initialization vectors:** When a block cipher in CBC mode is used, an initialization vector (IV) is maintained for each key. This field is first initialized by the SSL Handshake Protocol. Thereafter the final ciphertext block from each record is preserved for use as the IV with the following record.
- **Sequence numbers:** Each party maintains separate sequence numbers for transmitted and received messages for each connection. When a party sends or receives a change cipher spec message, the appropriate sequence number is set to zero. Sequence numbers may not exceed 2^{64}- 1.

SSL Record Protocol

The SSL Record Protocol provides two services for SSL connections:

- **Confidentiality:** The Handshake Protocol defines a shared secret key that is used for conventional encryption of SSL payloads.

- **Message Integrity:** The Handshake Protocol also defines a shared secret key that is used to form a message authentication code (MAC).

Figure 1.3 indicates the overall operation of the SSL Record Protocol. The Record Protocol takes an application message to be transmitted, fragments the data into manageable blocks, optionally compresses the data, applies a MAC, encrypts, adds a header, and transmits the resulting unit in a TCP segment. Received data are decrypted, verified, decompressed, and reassembled and then delivered to higher-level users.

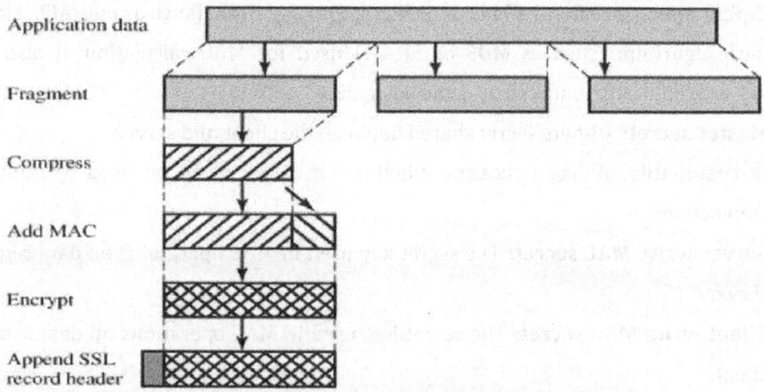

Figure 1.3: SSL Record Protocol Operation

The first step is **fragmentation.** Each upper-layer message is fragmented into blocks of 2^{14} bytes (16384 bytes) or less. Next, **compression** is optionally applied. Compression must be lossless and may not increase the content length by more than 1024 bytes.[2] In SSLv3 (as well as the current version of TLS), no compression algorithm is specified, so the default compression algorithm is null. The next step in processing is to compute a **message authentication code** over the compressed data. For this purpose, a shared secret key is used. The calculation is defined as

hash(MAC_write_secret

|| pad_2 ||

hash(MAC_write_secret

|| pad_1 || seq_num ||

SSLCompressed.type ||

SSLCompressed.length ||

SSLCompressed.fragment))

Where

||	= concatenation
MAC_write_secret	= shared secret key
hash	= cryptographic hash algorithm; either MD5 or SHA-1
pad_1	= the byte 0x36 (0011 0110) repeated 48 times (384

bits) for MD5 and 40 times (320 bits) for SHA-1

pad_2= the byte 0x5C (0101 1100) repeated 48 times for MD5 and 40 times for SHA-1

seq_num= the sequence number for this message

SSLCompressed.type= the higher-level protocol used to process this fragment

SSLCompressed.length= the length of the compressed fragment

SSLCompressed.fragment= the compressed fragment (if compression is not used, the plaintext fragment).

The difference is that the two pads are concatenated in SSLv3 and are XORed in HMAC. The SSLv3 MAC algorithm is based on the original Internet draft for HMAC, which used concatenation. The final version of HMAC, defined in RFC 2104, uses the XOR.

Next, the compressed message plus the MAC are **encrypted** using symmetric encryption. Encryption may not increase the content length by more than 1024 bytes, so that the total length may not exceed 2^{14} + 2048. The following encryption algorithms are permitted:

For block encryption, padding may be added after the MAC prior to encryption. The padding is in the form of a number of padding bytes followed by a one-byte indication of the length of the padding. The total amount of padding is the smallest amount such that the total size of the data to be encrypted (plaintext plus MAC plus padding) is a multiple of the cipher's block length. An example is a plaintext (or compressed text if compression is used) of 58 bytes, with a MAC of 20 bytes (using SHA-1), that is encrypted using a block length of 8 bytes (e.g., DES). With the padding.length byte, this yields a total of 79 bytes. To make the total an integer multiple of 8, one byte of padding is added. The final step of SSL Record Protocol processing is to prepend a header, consisting of the following fields:

- **Content Type (8 bits):** The higher layer protocol used to process the enclosed fragment.
- **Major Version (8 bits):** Indicates major version of SSL in use. For SSLv3, the value is 3.
- **Minor Version (8 bits):** Indicates minor version in use. For SSLv3, the value is 0.
- **Compressed Length (16 bits):** The length in bytes of the plaintext fragment (or compressed fragment if compression is used). The maximum value is 2^{14} + 2048.

Figure 1.4 illustrates the SSL record format.

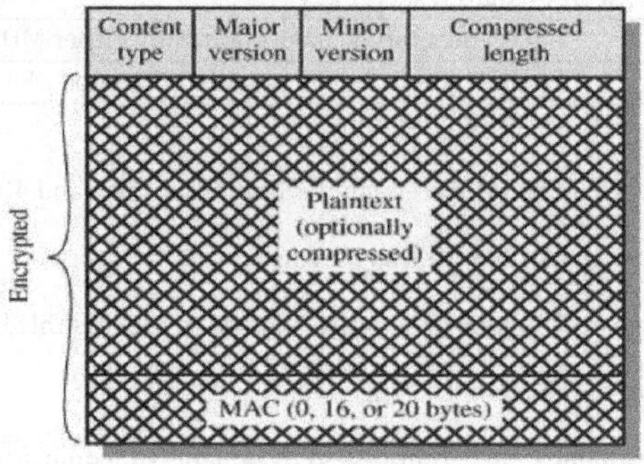

Figure 1.4: SSL Record Format

Change Cipher Spec Protocol

The Change Cipher Spec Protocol is one of the three SSL-specific protocols that use the SSL Record Protocol, and it is the simplest. This protocol consists of a single message (Figure 1.5a), which consists of a single byte with the value 1. The sole purpose of this message is to cause the pending state to be copied into the current state, which updates the cipher suite to be used on this connection.

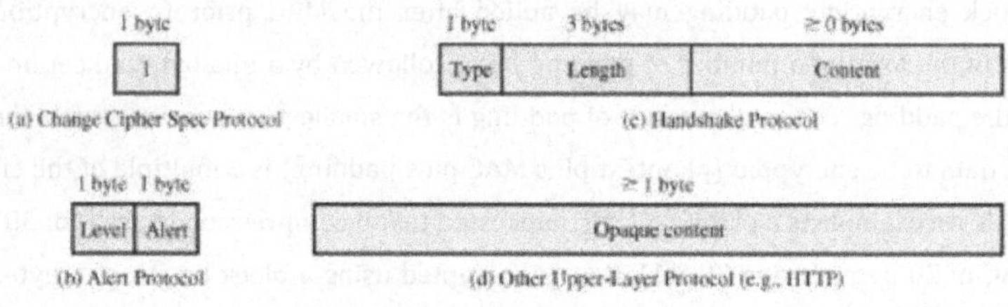

Figure 1.5: SSL Record Protocol Payload

Alert Protocol

The Alert Protocol is used to convey SSL-related alerts to the peer entity. As with other applications that use SSL, alert messages are compressed and encrypted, as specified by the current state. Each message in this protocol consists of two bytes (Figure 17.5b). The first byte takes the value warning(1) or fatal(2) to convey the severity of the message. If the level is fatal, SSL immediately terminates the connection. Other connections on the same session may continue, but no new connections on this session may be established. The second byte contains a code that indicates the specific alert.

First, we list those alerts that are always fatal (definitions from the SSL specification):

- **unexpected_message:** An inappropriate message was received.
- **bad_record_mac:** An incorrect MAC was received.
- **decompression_failure:** The decompression function received improper input (e.g., unable to decompress or decompress to greater than maximum allowable length).
- **handshake_failure:** Sender was unable to negotiate an acceptable set of security parameters given the options available.
- **illegal_parameter:** A field in a handshake message was out of range or inconsistent with other fields. The remainder of the alerts are the following:
- **close_notify:** Notifies the recipient that the sender will not send any more messages on this connection. Each party is required to send a close_notify alert before closing the write side of a connection.
- **no_certificate:** May be sent in response to a certificate request if no appropriate certificate is available.
- **bad_certificate:** A received certificate was corrupt (e.g., contained a signature that did not verify).
- **unsupported_certificate:** The type of the received certificate is not supported.
- **certificate_revoked:** A certificate has been revoked by its signer.
- **certificate_expired:** A certificate has expired.
- **certificate_unknown:** Some other unspecified issue arose in processing the certificate, rendering it unacceptable.

Handshake Protocol

The most complex part of SSL is the Handshake Protocol. This protocol allows the server and client to authenticate each other and to negotiate an encryption and MAC algorithm and cryptographic keys to be used to protect data sent in an SSL record. The Handshake Protocol is used before any application data is transmitted.

The Handshake Protocol consists of a series of messages exchanged by client and server. All of these have the format shown in Figure 1.5c. Each message has three fields:

- **Type (1 byte):** Indicates one of 10 messages.
- **Length (3 bytes):** The length of the message in bytes.
- **Content (≥ 0 bytes):** The parameters associated with this message

Figure 1.6 shows the initial exchange needed to establish a logical connection between client and server. The exchange can be viewed as having four phases.

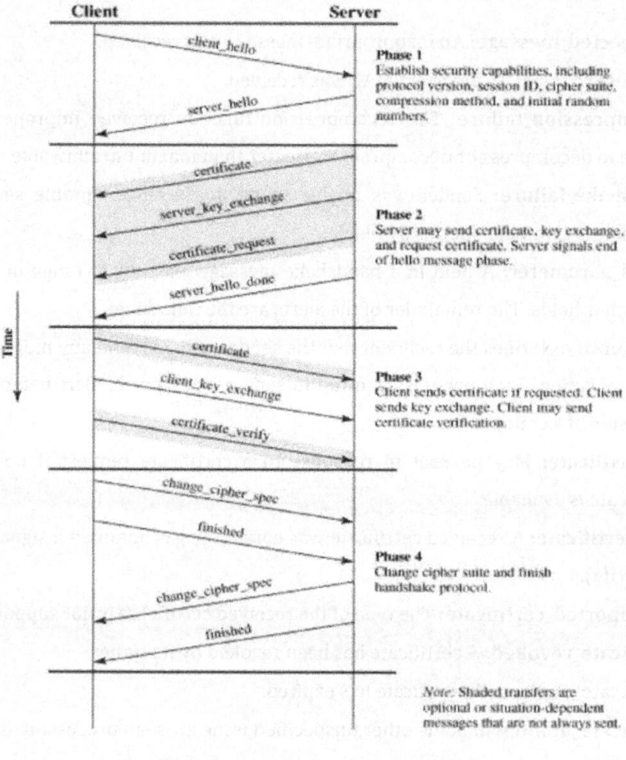

Figure 1.6: Handshake Protocol Action

Phase 1: Establish Security Capabilities

This phase is used to initiate a logical connection and to establish the security capabilities that will be associated with it. The exchange is initiated by the client, which sends a **client_hello message** with the following parameters:

1) **Version:** The highest SSL version understood by the client.
2) **Random:** A client-generated random structure, consisting of a 32-bit timestamp and 28 bytes generated by a secure random number generator. These values serve as nonces and are used during key exchange to prevent replay attacks.
3) **Session ID:** A variable-length session identifier. A nonzero value indicates that the client wishes to update the parameters of an existing connection or create a new connection on this session. A zero value indicates that the client wishes to establish a new connection on a new session.

4) **CipherSuite:** This is a list that contains the combinations of cryptographic algorithms supported by the client, in decreasing order of preference. Each element of the list (each cipher suite) defines both a key exchange algorithm and a CipherSpec; these are discussed subsequently.

5) **Compression Method:** This is a list of the compression methods the client supports.

After sending the client_hello message, the client waits for the **server_hello message**, which contains the same parameters as the client_hello message. For the server_hello message, the following conventions apply. The Version field contains the lower of the version suggested by the client and the highest supported by the server. The Random field is generated by the server and is independent of the client's Random field. If the SessionID field of the client was nonzero, the same value is used by the server; otherwise the server's SessionID field contains the value for a new session. The CipherSuite field contains the single cipher suite selected by the server from those proposed by the client. The Compression field contains the compression method selected by the server from those proposed by the client. The first element of the Cipher Suite parameter is the key exchange method (i.e., the means by which the cryptographic keys for conventional encryption and MAC are exchanged). The following key exchange methods are supported:

RSA: The secret key is encrypted with the receiver's RSA public key. A public-key certificate for the receiver's key must be made available.

- **Fixed Diffie-Hellman:** This is a Diffie-Hellman key exchange in which the server's certificate contains the Diffie-Hellman public parameters signed by the certificate authority (CA). That is, the public-key certificate contains the Diffie-Hellman public-key parameters. The client provides its Diffie-Hellman public key parameters either in a certificate, if client authentication is required, or in a key exchange message. This method results in a fixed secret key between two peers, based on the Diffie-Hellman calculation using the fixed public keys.
- **Ephemeral Diffie-Hellman:** This technique is used to create ephemeral (temporary, one-time) secret keys. In this case, the Diffie-Hellman public keys are exchanged, signed using the sender's private RSA or DSS key. The receiver can use the corresponding public key to verify the signature. Certificates are used to authenticate the public keys. This would appear to be the most secure of the three Diffie-Hellman options because it results in a temporary, authenticated key.
- **Anonymous Diffie-Hellman:** The base Diffie-Hellman algorithm is used, with no authentication. That is, each side sends its public Diffie-Hellman parameters to the

other, with no authentication. This approach is vulnerable to man-in-the-middle attacks, in which the attacker conducts anonymous Diffie-Hellman with both parties.

- **Fortezza:** The technique defined for the Fortezza scheme.

Following the definition of a key exchange method is the CipherSpec, which includes the following fields:

- **CipherAlgorithm:** Any of the algorithms mentioned earlier: RC4, RC2, DES, 3DES, DES40, IDEA, Fortezza
- **MACAlgorithm:** MD5 or SHA-1
- **CipherType:** Stream or Block
- **IsExportable:** True or False
- **HashSize:** 0, 16 (for MD5), or 20 (for SHA-1) bytes
- **Key Material:** A sequence of bytes that contain data used in generating the write keys

IV Size: The size of the Initialization Value for Cipher Block Chaining (CBC) encryption.

Phase 2: Server Authentication and Key Exchange

The server begins this phase by sending its certificate, if it needs to be authenticated; the message contains one or a chain of X.509 certificates. The **certificate message** is required for any agreed-on key exchange method except anonymous Diffie-Hellman. Note that if fixed Diffie-Hellman is used, this certificate message functions as the server's key exchange message because it contains the server's public Diffie-Hellman parameters.

Next, a **server_key**_exchange **message** may be sent if it is required. It is not required in two instances: (1) The server has sent a certificate with fixed Diffie-Hellman parameters, or (2) RSA key exchange is to be used. The server_key_exchange message is needed for the following:

- **Anonymous Diffie-Hellman:** The message content consists of the two global Diffie-Hellman values (a prime number and a primitive root of that number) plus the server's public Diffie-Hellman key.
- **Ephemeral Diffie-Hellman:** The message content includes the three Diffie-Hellman parameters provided for anonymous Diffie-Hellman, plus a signature of those parameters.
- **RSA key exchange, in which the server is using RSA but has a signature-only RSA key:** Accordingly, the client cannot simply send a secret key encrypted with the server's public key. Instead, the server must create a temporary RSA public/private key pair and use the server_key_exchange message to send the public key. The message content includes the two parameters of the temporary RSA public key plus a signature

of those parameters.

- **Fortezza**

Some further details about the signatures are warranted. As usual, a signature is created by taking the hash of a message and encrypting it with the sender's private key.

Phase 3: Client Authentication and Key Exchange

Upon receipt of the server_done message, the client should verify that the server provided a valid certificate if required and check that the server_hello parameters are acceptable. If all is satisfactory, the client sends one or more messages back to the server.

If the server has requested a certificate, the client begins this phase by sending a **certificate message**. If no suitable certificate is available, the client sends a no_certificate alert instead. Next is the **client_key_exchange message**, which must be sent in this phase. The content of the message depends on the type of key exchange, as follows:

- **RSA:** The client generates a 48-byte *pre-master secret* and encrypts with the public key from the server's certificate or temporary RSA key from a server_key_exchange message. Its use to compute a *master secret* is explained later.
- **Ephemeral or Anonymous Diffie-Hellman:** The client's public Diffie-Hellman parameters are sent.
- **Fixed Diffie-Hellman:** The client's public Diffie-Hellman parameters were sent in a certificate message, so the content of this message is null.
- **Fortezza:** The client's Fortezza parameters are sent.

Finally, in this phase, the client may send a **certificate_verify message** to provide explicit verification of a client certificate.

Phase 4: Finish

This phase completes the setting up of a secure connection. The client sends a **change_cipher_spec message** and copies the pending CipherSpec into the current CipherSpec. Note that this message is not considered part of the Handshake Protocol but is sent using the Change Cipher Spec Protocol. The client then immediately sends the **finished message** under the new algorithms, keys, and secrets. The finished message verifies that the key exchange and authentication processes were successful. The content of the finished message is the concatenation of two hash values:

MD5(master_secret || pad2 ||
MD5(handshake_messages || Sender ||
master_secret || pad1))

SHA(master_secret || pad2 ||

SHA(handshake_messages || Sender ||

master_secret || pad1))

Where Sender is a code that identifies that the sender is the client and handshake_messages is all of the data from all handshake messages up to but not including this message. In response to these two messages, the server sends its own change_cipher_spec message, transfers the pending to the current CipherSpec, and sends its finished message. At this point the handshake is complete and the client and server may begin to exchange application layer data.

Master Secret Creation

The shared master secret is a one-time 48-byte value (384 bits) generated for this session by means of secure key exchange. The creation is in two stages. First, a pre_master_secret is exchanged. Second, the master_secret is calculated by both parties. For pre_master_secret exchange, there are two possibilities:

1) **RSA:** A 48-byte pre_master_secret is generated by the client, encrypted with the server's public RSA key, and sent to the server. The server decrypts the ciphertext using its private key to recover the pre_master_secret.
2) **Diffie-Hellman:** Both client and server generate a Diffie-Hellman public key. After these are exchanged, each side performs the Diffie-Hellman calculation to create the shared pre_master_secret.

Both sides now compute the master_secret as follows:

master_secret = MD5(pre_master_secret

|| SHA('A' || pre_master_secret

||ClientHello.random ||

ServerHello.random)) ||

MD5(pre_master_secret ||

SHA('BB' ||

pre_master_secret ||

ClientHello.random ||

ServerHello.random)) ||

MD5(pre_master_secret ||

SHA('CCC' ||

pre_master_secret ||

ClientHello.random ||

ServerHello.random))

where ClientHello.random and ServerHello.random are the two nonce values exchanged in the initial hello messages.

Generation of Cryptographic Parameters

CipherSpecs require a client write MAC secret, a server write MAC secret, a client write key, a server write key, a client write IV, and a server write IV, which are generated from the master secret in that order. These parameters are generated from the master secret by hashing the master secret into a sequence of secure bytes of sufficient length for all needed parameters. The generation of the key material from the master secret uses the same format for generation of the master secret from the pre-master secret:

key_block = MD5(master_secret || SHA('A' ||
master_secret || ServerHello.random ||
ClientHello.random)) || MD5(master_secret ||
SHA('BB' || master_secret || ServerHello.random ||
ClientHello.random)) || MD5(master_secret ||
SHA('CCC' || master_
secret ||
ServerHello.ra
ndom ||
ClientHello.ran
dom)) || . . .

until enough output has been generated. The result of this algorithmic structure is a pseudorandom function. We can view the master_secret as the pseudorandom seed value to the function. The client and server random numbers can be viewed as salt values to complicate cryptanalysis.

Transport Layer Security

TLS is an IETF standardization initiative whose goal is to produce an Internet standard version of SSL. TLS is defined as a Proposed Internet Standard in RFC 2246. RFC 2246 is very similar to SSLv3. In this section, we highlight the differences.

Message Authentication Code

There are two differences between the SSLv3 and TLS MAC schemes: the actual algorithm and the scope of the MAC calculation. TLS makes use of the HMAC algorithm defined in RFC 2104.

HMAC is defined as follows:

$HMAC_K(M) = H[(K^+ \text{ EX-OR opad})||H[(K^+ \text{ EX-OR}$
$\text{ipad})||M]]$ where

H = embedded hash function (for TLS, either MD5 or SHA-1)

M = message input to HMAC

K^+ = secret key padded with zeros on the left so that the result is equal to the block length of the hash code(for MD5 and SHA-1, block length = 512 bits)

ipad = 00110110 (36 in hexadecimal) repeated 64 times (512 bits) opad = 01011100 (5C in hexadecimal) repeated 64 times (512 bits)

SSLv3 uses the same algorithm, except that the padding bytes are concatenated with the secret key rather than being XORed with the secret key padded to the block length. The level of security should be about the same in both cases.

Pseudorandom Function

TLS makes use of a pseudorandom function referred to as PRF to expand secrets into blocks of data for purposes of key generation or validation. The objective is to make use of a relatively small shared secret value but to generate longer blocks of data in a way that is secure from the kinds of attacks made on hash functions and MACs. The PRF is based on the following data expansion function (Figure 1.7):

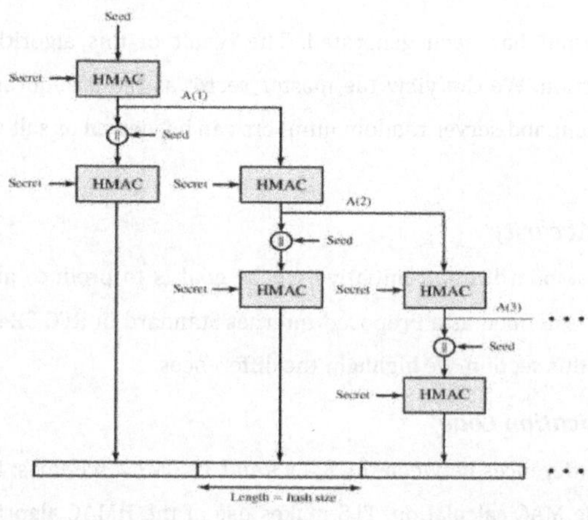

Figure 1.7: TLS Function P_hash (secret, seed)

Alert Codes

TLS supports all of the alert codes defined in SSLv3 with the exception of no certificate. A number of additional codes are defined in TLS; of these, the following are always fatal:

decryption_failed: A ciphertext decrypted in an invalid way; either it was not an even multiple of the block length or its padding values, when checked, were incorrect.

record_overflow: A TLS record was received with a payload (ciphertext) whose length exceeds 214 + 2048 bytes, or the ciphertext decrypted to a length of greater than 214 + 1024 bytes.

unknown_ca: A valid certificate chain or partial chain was received, but the certificate was not accepted because the CA certificate could not be located or could not be matched with a known, trusted CA.

access_denied: A valid certificate was received, but when access control was applied, the sender decided not to proceed with the negotiation.

decode_error: A message could not be decoded because a field was out of its specified range or the length of the message was incorrect.

export_restriction: A negotiation not in compliance with export restrictions on key length was detected.

protocol_version: The protocol version the client attempted to negotiate is recognized but not supported.

insufficient_security: Returned instead of handshake_failure when a negotiation has failed specifically because the server requires ciphers more secure than those supported by the client.

internal_error: An internal error unrelated to the peer or the correctness of the protocol makes it impossible to continue. The remainder of the new alerts include the following: **decrypt_error:** A handshake cryptographic operation failed, including being unable to verify a signature, decrypt a key exchange, or validate a finished message.

user_canceled: This handshake is being canceled for some reason unrelated to a protocol failure.

no_renegotiation: Sent by a client in response to a hello request or by the server in response to a client hello after initial handshaking. Either of these messages would normally result in renegotiation, but this alert indicates that the sender is not able to renegotiate. This message is always a warning.

Cipher Suites

There are several small differences between the cipher suites available under SSLv3 and under TLS:

- **Key Exchange:** TLS supports all of the key exchange techniques of SSLv3 with the exception of Fortezza.
- **Symmetric Encryption Algorithms:** TLS includes all of the symmetric encryption algorithms found in SSLv3, with the exception of Fortezza.

Client Certificate Types

TLS defines the following certificate types to be requested in a certificate_request message: rsa_sign, dss_sign, rsa_fixed_dh, and dss_fixed_dh. These are all defined in SSLv3. In addition, SSLv3 includes rsa_ephemeral_dh, dss_ephemeral_dh, and fortezza_kea.

Ephemeral Diffie-Hellman involves signing the Diffie-Hellman parameters with either RSA or DSS; for TLS, the rsa_sign and dss_sign types are used for that function; a separate signing type is not needed to sign Diffie-Hellman parameters. TLS does not include the Fortezza scheme.

Certificate_Verify and Finished Messages

In the TLS certificate_verify message, the MD5 and SHA-1 hashes are calculated only over handshake_messages. Recall that for SSLv3, the hash calculation also included the master secret and pads. These extra fields were felt to add no additional security. As with the finished message in SSLv3, the finished message in TLS is a hash based on the shared master_secret, the previous handshake messages, and a label that identifies client or server. The calculation is somewhat different. For TLS, we have PRF(master_secret, finished_label, MD5(handshake_messages)|| SHA-1(handshake_messages)) where finished_label is the string "client finished" for the client and "server finished" for the server.

Cryptographic Computations

The pre_master_secret for TLS is calculated in the same way as in SSLv3. As in SSLv3, the master_secret in TLS is calculated as a hash function of the pre_master_secret and the two hello random numbers.

Padding

In SSL, the padding added prior to encryption of user data is the minimum amount required so that the total size of the data to be encrypted is a multiple of the cipher's block length. In TLS, the padding can be any amount that results in a total that is a multiple of the cipher's block length, up to a maximum of 255 bytes. For example, if the plaintext (or compressed text if compression is used) plus MAC plus padding. length byte is 79 bytes long, then the padding length, in bytes, can be 1, 9, 17, and so on, up to 249. A variable padding length may be used to frustrate attacks based on an analysis of the lengths of exchanged messages.

8.3. Secure Electronic Transaction

SET is an open encryption and security specification designed to protect credit card transactions on the Internet. The current version, SETv1, emerged from a call for security standards by MasterCard and Visa in February 1996. A wide range of companies were involved in developing the initial specification, including IBM, Microsoft, Netscape, RSA, Terisa, and Verisign. Beginning in 1996.

SET is not itself a payment system. Rather it is a set of security protocols and formats that enables users to employ the existing credit card payment infrastructure on an open network, such as the Internet, in a secure fashion. In essence, SET provides three services:

1) Provides a secure communications channel among all parties involved in a transaction
2) Provides trust by the use of X.509v3 digital certificates
3) Ensures privacy because the information is only available to parties in a transaction when and where necessary.

SET Overview

A good way to begin our discussion of SET is to look at the business requirements for SET, its key features, and the participants in SET transactions.

Requirements

The SET specification lists the following business requirements for secure payment processing with credit cards over the Internet and other networks:

1) **Provide confidentiality of payment and ordering information:** It is necessary to assure cardholders that this information is safe and accessible only to the intended recipient. Confidentiality also reduces the risk of fraud by either party to the transaction or by malicious third parties. SET uses encryption to provide confidentiality.
2) **Ensure the integrity of all transmitted data:** That is, ensure that no changes in content occur during transmission of SET messages. Digital signatures are used to provide integrity.
    - **Provide authentication that a cardholder is a legitimate user of a credit card**

account: A mechanism that links a cardholder to a specific account number reduces the incidence of fraud and the overall cost of payment processing. Digital signatures and certificates are used to verify that a cardholder is a legitimate user of a valid account.

- **Provide authentication that a merchant can accept credit card transactions through its relationship with a financial institution:** This is the complement to the preceding requirement. Cardholders need to be able to identify merchants with whom they can conduct secure transactions. Again, digital signatures and certificates are used.
- **Ensure the use of the best security practices and system design techniques to protect all legitimate parties in an electronic commerce transaction:** SET is a well-tested specification based on highly secure cryptographic algorithms and protocols.
- **Create a protocol that neither depends on transport security mechanisms nor prevents their use:** SET can securely operate over a "raw" TCP/IP stack. However, SET does not interfere with the use of other security mechanisms, such as IPSec and SSL/TLS.
- **Facilitate and encourage interoperability among software and network providers:** The SET protocols and formats are independent of hardware platform, operating system, and Web software.

Key Features of SET

To meet the requirements just outlined, SET incorporates the following features:

1) **Confidentiality of information:** Cardholder account and payment information is secured as it travels across the network. An interesting and important feature of SET is that it prevents the merchant from learning the cardholder's credit card number; this is only provided to the issuing bank. Conventional encryption by DES is used to provide confidentiality.
2) **Integrity of data:** Payment information sent from cardholders to merchants includes order information, personal data, and payment instructions. SET guarantees that these message contents are not altered in transit. RSA digital signatures, using SHA-1 hash codes, provide message integrity. Certain messages are also protected by HMAC using SHA-1.
3) **Cardholder account authentication:** SET enables merchants to verify that a cardholder is a legitimate user of a valid card account number. SET uses X.509v3 digital

certificates with RSA signatures for this purpose.

4) **Merchant authentication:** SET enables cardholders to verify that a merchant has a relationship with a financial institution allowing it to accept payment cards. SET uses X.509v3 digital certificates with RSA signatures for this purpose.

Note that unlike IPSec and SSL/TLS, SET provides only one choice for each cryptographic algorithm. This makes sense, because SET is a single application with a single set of requirements, whereas IPSec and SSL/TLS are intended to support a range of applications.

SET Participants

Figure 1.8 indicates the participants in the SET system, which include the following:

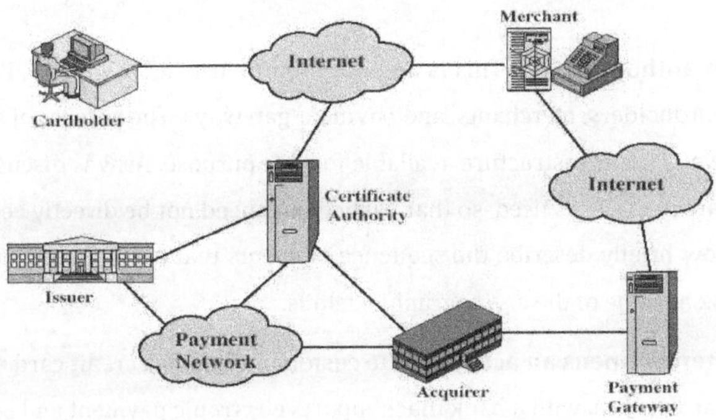

Figure 1.8: Secure Electronic Commerce Components

Cardholder: In the electronic environment, consumers and corporate purchasers interact with merchants from personal computers over the Internet. A cardholder is an authorized holder of a payment card (e.g., MasterCard, Visa) that has been issued by an issuer.

Merchant: A merchant is a person or organization that has goods or services to sell to the cardholder. Typically, these goods and services are offered via a Web site or by electronic mail. A merchant that accepts payment cards must have a relationship with an acquirer.

Issuer: This is a financial institution, such as a bank, that provides the cardholder with the payment card. Typically, accounts are applied for and opened by mail or in person. Ultimately, it is the issuer that is responsible for the payment of the debt of the cardholder.

Acquirer: This is a financial institution that establishes an account with a merchant and processes payment card authorizations and payments. Merchants will usually accept more than one credit card brand but do not want to deal with multiple bankcard associations or with multiple individual issuers. The acquirer provides authorization to the merchant that a given card account is active and that the proposed purchase does not exceed the credit limit. The acquirer also provides electronic transfer of payments to the merchant's account.

Subsequently, the acquirer is reimbursed by the issuer over some sort of payment network for electronic funds transfer.

Payment gateway: This is a function operated by the acquirer or a designated third party that processes merchant payment messages. The payment gateway interfaces between SET and the existing bankcard payment networks for authorization and payment functions. The merchant exchanges SET messages with the payment gateway over the Internet, while the payment gateway has some direct or network connection to the acquirer's financial processing system.

Certification authority (CA): This is an entity that is trusted to issue X.509v3 public-key certificates for cardholders, merchants, and payment gateways. The success of SET will depend on the existence of a CA infrastructure available for this purpose. As was discussed in previous chapters, a hierarchy of CAs is used, so that participants need not be directly certified by a root authority. We now briefly describe the sequence of events that are required for a transaction. We will then look at some of the cryptographic details.

1. **The customer opens an account.** The customer obtains a credit card account, such as MasterCard or Visa, with a bank that supports electronic payment and SET.
2. **The customer receives a certificate.** After suitable verification of identity, the customer receives an X.509v3 digital certificate, which is signed by the bank. The certificate verifies the customer's RSA public key and its expiration date. It also establishes a relationship, guaranteed by the bank, between the customer's key pair and his or her credit card.
3. **Merchants have their own certificates.** A merchant who accepts a certain brand of card must be in possession of two certificates for two public keys owned by the merchant: one for signing messages, and one for key exchange. The merchant also needs a copy of the payment gateway's public-key certificate.
4. **The customer places an order.** This is a process that may involve the customer first browsing through the merchant's Web site to select items and determine the price. The customer then sends a list of the items to be purchased to the merchant, who returns an order form containing the list of items, their price, a total price, and an order number.

5. **The merchant is verified.** In addition to the order form, the merchant sends a copy of its certificate, so that the customer can verify that he or she is dealing with a valid store.
6. **The order and payment are sent.** The customer sends both order and payment information to the merchant, along with the customer's certificate. The order confirms the purchase of the items in the order form. The payment contains credit card details. The payment information is encrypted in such a way that it cannot be read by the merchant. The customer's certificate enables the merchant to verify the customer.
7. **The merchant requests payment authorization.** The merchant sends the payment information to the payment gateway, requesting authorization that the customer's available credit is sufficient for this purchase.
8. **The merchant confirms the order.** The merchant sends confirmation of the order to the customer.
9. **The merchant provides the goods or service.** The merchant ships the goods or provides the service to the customer.
10. **The merchant requests payment.** This request is sent to the payment gateway, which handles all of the payment processing.

Dual Signature

Before looking at the details of the SET protocol, let us discuss an important innovation introduced in SET: the dual signature. The purpose of the dual signature is to link two messages that are intended for two different recipients. In this case, the customer wants to send the order information (OI) to the merchant and the payment information (PI) to the bank. The merchant does not need to know the customer's credit card number, and the bank does not need to know the details of the customer's order. The customer is afforded extra protection in terms of privacy by keeping these two items separate. However, the two items must be linked in a way that can be used to resolve disputes if necessary. The link is needed so that the customer can prove that this payment is intended for this order and not for some other goods or service.

To see the need for the link, suppose that the customers send the merchant two messages: a signed OI and a signed PI, and the merchant passes the PI on to the bank. If the merchant can capture another OI from this customer, the merchant could claim that this OI goes with the PI rather than the original OI. The linkage prevents this.

Figure 1.9 shows the use of a dual signature to meet the requirement of the preceding paragraph. The customer takes the hash (using SHA-1) of the PI and the hash of the OI. These two hashes are then concatenated and the hash of the result is taken. Finally, the customer encrypts the final hash with his or her private signature key, creating the dual signature. The operation can be summarized as

$$DS = E(PRc, [H(H(PI)||H(OI)])$$

where *PRc* is the customer's private signature key. Now suppose that the merchant is in possession of the dual signature (DS), the OI, and the message digest for the PI (PIMD). The merchant also has the public key of the customer, taken from the customer's certificate. Then the merchant can compute the quantities

$$H(PIMS||H[OI]); D(PUc, DS)$$

where *PUc* is the customer's public signature key. If these two quantities are equal, then the merchant has verified the signature. Similarly, if the bank is in possession of DS, PI, the message digest for OI (OIMD), and the customer's public key, then the bank can compute

$$H(H[OI]||OIMD); D(PUc, DS)$$

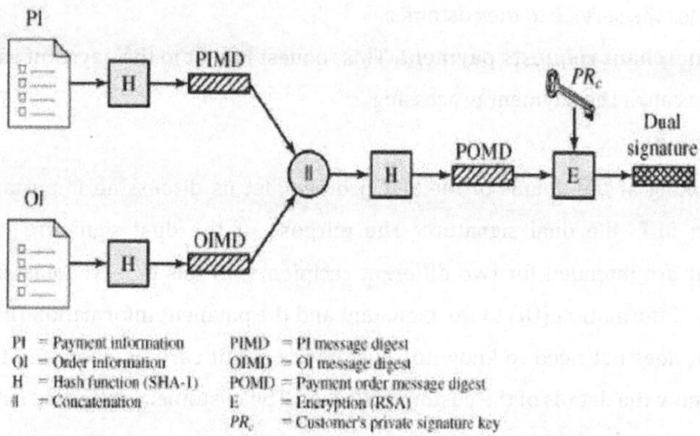

Figure 1.9: Construction of Dual Signature

Again, if these two quantities are equal, then the bank has verified the signature. In summary,

1. The merchant has received OI and verified the signature.
2. The bank has received PI and verified the signature.
3. The customer has linked the OI and PI and can prove the linkage.

For example, suppose the merchant wishes to substitute another OI in this transaction, to its advantage. It would then have to find another OI whose hash matches the existing OIMD. With SHA-1, this is deemed not to be feasible. Thus, the merchant cannot link another OI with this PI.

Payment Processing

Table 1.3 lists the transaction types supported by SET. In what follows we look in some detail at the following transactions:

1) Purchase request
2) Payment authorization
3) Payment capture

Table 1.3: SET Transaction Types

Cardholder registration	Cardholders must register with a CA before they can send SET messages to merchants.
Merchant registration	Merchants must register with a CA before they can exchange SET messages with customers and payment gateways.
Purchase request	Message from customer to merchant containing OI for merchant and PI for bank.
Payment authorization	Exchange between merchant and payment gateway to authorize a given amount for a purchase on a given credit card account.
Payment capture	Allows the merchant to request payment from the payment gateway.
Certificate inquiry and status	If the CA is unable to complete the processing of a certificate request quickly, it will send a reply to the cardholder or merchant indicating that the requester should check back later. The cardholder or merchant sends the Certificate Inquiry message to determine the status of the certificate request and to receive the certificate if the request has been approved.
Purchase inquiry	Allows the cardholder to check the status of the processing of an order after the purchase response has been received. Note that this message does not include information such as the status of back ordered goods,but does indicate the status of authorization, capture and credit processing.
Authorization reversal	Allows a merchant to correct previous authorization requests. If the order will not be completed, the merchant reverses the entire authorization. If part of the order will not be completed (such as when goods are back ordered), the merchant reverses part of the amount of the authorization.
Capture reversal	Allows a merchant to correct errors in capture requests such as transaction amounts that were entered incorrectly by a clerk.
Credit	Allows a merchant to issue a credit to a cardholder's account such as when goods are returned or were damaged during shipping. Note that the SET Credit message is always initiated by the merchant, not the cardholder. All communications between the cardholder and merchant that result in a credit being processed happen outside of SET.
Credit reversal	Allows a merchant to correct a previously request credit.
Payment gateway certificate request	Allows a merchant to query the payment gateway and receive a copy of the gateway's current key-exchange and signature certificates.
Batch administration	Allows a merchant to communicate information to the payment gateway regarding merchant batches.
Error message	Indicates that a responder rejects a message because it fails format or content verification tests.

Purchase Request

Before the Purchase Request exchange begins, the cardholder has completed browsing, selecting, and ordering. The end of this preliminary phase occurs when the merchant sends a completed order form to the customer. All of the preceding occurs without the use of SET. The purchase request exchange consists of four messages: Initiate Request, Initiate Response,

Purchase Request, and Purchase Response. In order to send SET messages to the merchant, the cardholder must have a copy of the certificates of the merchant and the payment gateway. The customer requests the certificates in the **Initiate Request** message, sent to the merchant. This message includes the brand of the credit card that the customer is using. The message also includes an ID assigned to this request/response pair by the customer and a nonce used to ensure timeliness.

The merchant generates a response and signs it with its private signature key. The response includes the nonce from the customer, another nonce for the customer to return in the next message, and a transaction ID for this purchase transaction. In addition to the signed response, the **Initiate Response** message includes the merchant's signature certificate and the payment gateway's key exchange certificate.

The cardholder verifies the merchant and gateway certificates by means of their respective CA signatures and then creates the OI and PI. The transaction ID assigned by the merchant is placed in both the OI and PI. The OI does not contain explicit order data such as the number and price of items. Rather, it contains an order reference generated in the exchange between merchant and customer during the shopping phase before the first SET message. Next, the cardholder prepares the **Purchase Request** message (Figure 1.10). For this purpose, the cardholder generates a one-time symmetric encryption key, *Ks*. The message includes the following:

1) Purchase-related information.
2) Order-related information.
3) Cardholder certificate.

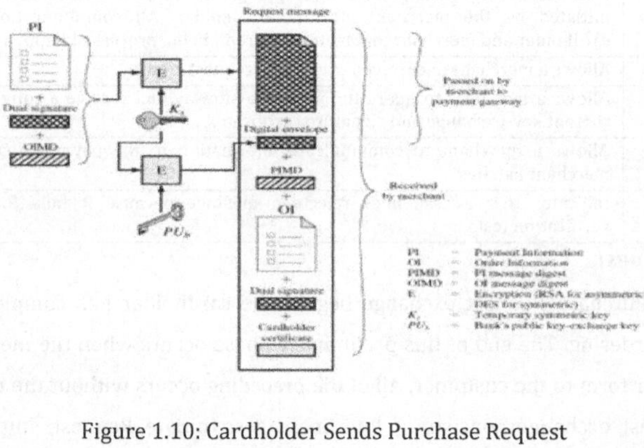

Figure 1.10: Cardholder Sends Purchase Request

When the merchant receives the Purchase Request message, it performs the following actions (Figure 1.11):

1) Verifies the cardholder certificates by means of its CA signatures.
2) Verifies the dual signature using the customer's public signature key. This ensures that the order has not been tampered with in transit and that it was signed using the cardholder's private signature key.
3) Processes the order and forwards the payment information to the payment gateway for authorization (described later).
4) Sends a purchase response to the cardholder.

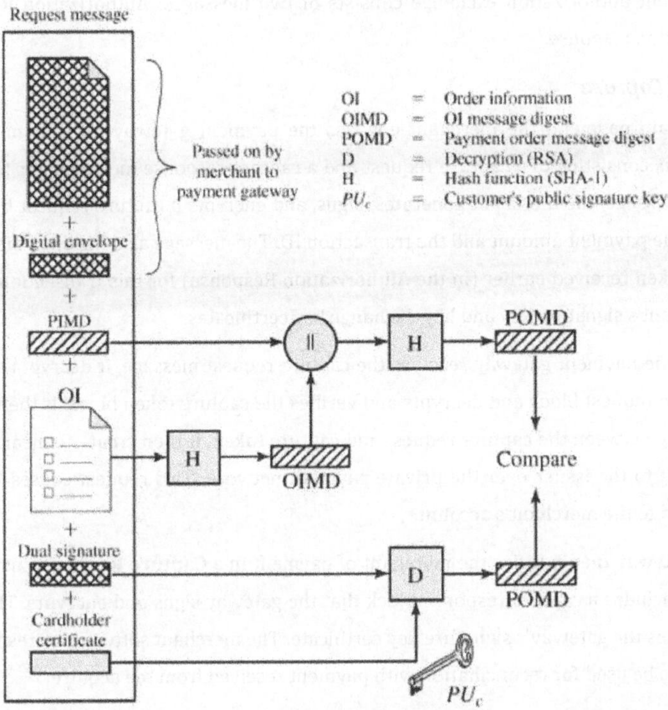

Figure 1.11: Merchant Verifies Customer Purchase Request

The **Purchase Response** message includes a response block that acknowledges the order and references the corresponding transaction number. This block is signed by the merchant using its private signature key. The block and its signature are sent to the customer, along with the merchant's signature certificate.

When the cardholder software receives the purchase response message, it verifies the merchant's certificate and then verifies the signature on the response block. Finally, it takes some action based on the response, such as displaying a message to the user or updating a database with the status of the order.

Payment Authorization

During the processing of an order from a cardholder, the merchant authorizes the transaction with the payment gateway. The payment authorization ensures that the transaction was approved by the issuer. This authorization guarantees that the merchant will receive payment; the merchant can therefore provide the services or goods to the customer. The payment authorization exchange consists of two messages: Authorization Request and Authorization response.

Payment Capture

To obtain payment, the merchant engages the payment gateway in a payment capture transaction, consisting of a capture request and a capture response message. For the **Capture** Request message, the merchant generates, signs, and encrypts a capture request block, which includes the payment amount and the transaction ID. The message also includes the encrypted capture token received earlier (in the Authorization Response) for this transaction, as well as the merchant's signature key and key-exchange key certificates.

When the payment gateway receives the capture request message, it decrypts and verifies the capture request block and decrypts and verifies the capture token block. It then checks for consistency between the capture request and capture token. It then creates a clearing request that is sent to the issuer over the private payment network. This request causes funds to be transferred to the merchant's account.

The gateway then notifies the merchant of payment in a **Capture Response** message. The message includes a capture response block that the gateway signs and encrypts. The message also includes the gateway's signature key certificate. The merchant software stores the capture response to be used for reconciliation with payment received from the acquirer.

References

1) Cryptography and Network Security, Principles and Practices, William Stallings, Eastern Economy Edition, Fourth edition.
2) Cryptography & Network Security, Behrouz A. forouzan, The McGraw-Hill Companies, Edition 2007.
3) http://williamstallings.com/Security2e.html

Questions

8a). What is SET? Discuss the requirements and key features of SET.

(December 2010)(10 marks)

8b). write short notes on SSL handshake protocol.

(December 2010) (10 marks)

8a). Explain the parameter that define the session state and connection state in SSL.

(June 2012)(10 marks)

8b). Describe the SET participants.

(June 2012) (5 marks)

8c).Explain the construction of Dual signature in SET with neat diagram. Also show its verification with merchant and the bank.

(June 2012) (5 marks)

8a). Explain the dual signature in SET protocol. What is its purpose?

(June2010) (10Marks)

8b). Explain the different alert codes of TLS protocols.

(June 2010) (10 Marks)

8a). Explain SSL handshake protocol with a neat diagram.

(June 2011) (10Marks)

8b). List out the key features of secure transaction and explain in detail.

(June 2011) (10 Marks)

8a). Discuss the SSL protocol stack.

(Dec 2011) (5 Marks)

8b).What are the service provided by SSL record protocol? Describe the operation of this protocol. (Dec 2011) (8 Marks)